All News Is Local

All News Is Local

The Failure of the Media to Reflect World Events in a Globalized Age

RICHARD C. STANTON

McFarland & Company, Inc., Publishers
Jefferson, North Carolina, and London

LIBRARY OF CONGRESS CATALOGUING-IN-PUBLICATION DATA

Stanton, Richard.
    All news is local: the failure of the media to reflect world
events in a globalized age / Richard C. Stanton.
      p.   cm.
    Includes bibliographical references and index.

    ISBN-13: 978-0-7864-3069-7
    softcover : 50# alkaline paper ∞

    1. Journalism. 2. Mass media. I. Title.
PN4731.S679   2007
070.4—dc22   2007009485

British Library cataloguing data are available

Cover photograph ©2007 PhotoSpin

Manufactured in the United States of America

McFarland & Company, Inc., Publishers
  Box 611, Jefferson, North Carolina 28640
   www.mcfarlandpub.com

To the memory of
J.K. Stanton, 1894–1933

Contents

Introduction

This book is an investigation into the three-hundred-year-old model of global journalism used by the Western news media. It argues that the model is fragile and unable to cope with the issues and events, the agents and institutions of globalization that exist, and that current methods, along with the model of news gathering and reporting, require rethinking and reimagining.

A few years before the September 11, 2001, terrorist attacks on the World Trade Center and the Pentagon, the Western news media had made considerable progress towards transforming themselves into competitive agents capable of interpreting complex issues and events for a variety of stakeholders. They had begun to differentiate themselves from mass infotainment media. September 11 created a crisis of confidence that pushed the transformative shift of the Western news media back to their outdated three-hundred-year-old model of reporting. Since that time they have been too busy attempting to understand the complexity of globalization to reach out for a new way of imagining. The magnitude and volume of global issues and events have contained the Western news media so that they have been unable to step back onto the path of change. They have continued to investigate and report global issues and events within an unacceptable frame of what I call localization.

In its investigation of the existing model, this book presents evidence that it is still possible for the Western news media to make a paradigm shift, a transformation that will allow them to sustain their existence among the highly complex institutions of globalization that they attempt to investigate and report. It provides an outline of a new model that can sustain the Western news media as competitive agents in global democracy.

The book argues that the Western news media present globalization and democracy as the most positive institutions available for the socioeconomic well-being of humanity, but in this it is not a defense of globalization or democracy. It analyzes coverage of specific issues

1

and events by élite Western news media to demonstrate the inadequacy of the journalism model that they employ. It shows that Western news media, far from understanding the complexity of globalization, are only able to imagine it clearly by grounding it in the local. It shows conclusively that localization of world issues and events does not assist the process of informed decision making necessary for the maintenance of a dynamic political public sphere, either locally or globally. In this it focuses on a number of Western news media but particularly the weekly newspaper, the *Economist*, as an agent supporting global trade and democracy. It presents an argument for a refashioned model of news reporting based upon the theories of the conversational and information models presented by German philosopher Jurgen Habermas.

The Western news media investigate, analyze and report to stakeholder publics on issues and events that occur around the globe on a 24-hour, 365-day news cycle. News is a highly valued commodity in the West, particularly for its capacity to assist the process of trade, and specifically for its ability to provide a reference point or a mirror for society to reflect its own actions, behaviors and attitudes. News has always been crucial to the balance of trade: early on as a localized commodity traveling between villages and towns in small geographical areas, then later developing a life of its own to become a highly valued element in the global trade between nations and other unified actors in the 21st century.

Unlike gold or other high-value commodities, the financial value of news has remained consistent and unchanged for the past three hundred years. Its ownership value, however, has changed markedly between the establishment of the two most important related inventions during that time: the printing press and the personal computer. Global use of technology and the practice of global trade in goods and services between countries and continents do not provide an overwhelming justification for rigid belief in the validation of globalization as a platform for good. Global news is a product of technology and trade, yet most global news is received by its stakeholder publics *after* it has been reimagined and localized. The fragmentation of the news media allows the representation of news to be imagined in too many unidentifiable frames. News is distilled so that it can be localized. It is, though, not a local commodity.

Terrorist acts in North America, Indonesia and Spain, earthquakes in Japan, and floods in South America become news in other parts of the world when the event or issue has been imagined in terms of its local actors. For CNN, a conflict in the Middle East between Israel and Lebanon can be imagined in its complexity not as a product of Iranian support for Lebanon's political terrorist group Hezbollah, but as a terrifying ordeal for American citizens caught in Lebanon. CNN coverage of the event is imagined in terms of the safe evacuation of those citizens.

This book describes news as it is imagined by Western news media through the various institutions and agencies that proscribe its existence, particularly the United Nations which, through its chief prolocutor, the secretary-general, identifies numerous global issues and events that fail to measure up to Western world social, political and economic standards. The problem for the Western news media is that their empirical (observable) ideology does not fit with the deductive nature of institutions. It does, however, fit with *agency* and the observations of agency policy around the globe. I will define and expand the notion of *agency* and *institution* in detail.

The book begins by arguing that there is no real global news media, therefore there can be no real reporting of global news. Western news media localize global news for the purpose of allowing citizens in developed and developing countries to perceive they are part of the action attached to global institutions and agencies. But this is not a realistic assessment of the situation. News is a commodity traded between élites.

The book argues that while all news in the West can be localized, global interests strive to establish a position for Western news media as a "sushi train" in which issues and events must be contextualized by reporters so that genuine unplanned news rises to the top of the value hierarchy.[1] The book argues that reporters imagine news by accepting professional norms of what is news rather than investigating issues and events outside a conventional framework. They have difficulty in seeking to investigate "ideal" policy when "acceptable" policy is close by. This is not an indictment of the individual as reporter or journalist, rather it is a critique of economic rationalism in developed countries, that which has come to dominate the news media. By examining how the news media imagine global issues and events, the book shows how global performers (news generators) attempt to influence and persuade critics (news media) so that stakeholder publics in both the developed and developing worlds will reflect attitudes and behavior desirous of the performer's goals.

3

Introduction

The book sets out to provide an understanding of how Western news media represent global issues and events. In doing so it maps the relative positions of a variety of actors and audiences (stakeholder publics), all of which are given equal political weight. In other words it is not an attempt to show that transnational corporations, as financial investors in the news process, are a negative force in the globalization debate. Nor is it to portray in any particular light the role of powerful regional and global agents such as the World Bank, the International Monetary Fund, or the World Trade Organization. If anything it is sympathetic to the intervention of such actors, arguing that the need to localize is in oppositional mode to the public pronouncements made about the merits of globalization. In this it is important to highlight the central role of the United Nations as an institution that is unclear and unsure about its overlapping roles as actor, critic and audience in the news.

The Western media localizes news so that it can be easily digested and rendered practical. News is a commodity traded between élites. The complexity of issues and events requires journalists to understand a huge range of material. They are meant to research widely and to then distill the complexity for the average citizen. But this is not what happens. The issues and events are too complex to distill into eight hundred words, so the journalists keep the level of discourse relatively élite. Complex global issues and events such as energy security and a G8 meeting, cannot be imagined within a local frame. Harmonization of tariffs or the issue of codification of standards remain theoretical until they are grounded in the "local." Codification of standards for the manufacture and distribution of a particular good—a computer component, for example—is a non-newsworthy issue until it is grounded in the local, for example, Hungarian manufacturing standards being maintained at a particular level if Hungary is to continue trading with its European Union (EU) partners.

This is not a book about globalization. It is a book about news media and its local grounding in an increasingly globalized world.

What is meant by imagination in this work? The Romantic era English poet Samuel Taylor Coleridge suggests that imagination is either primary or secondary. Primary, he argues, is the living power of all human perception. It is no coincidence that Coleridge, like many Western writers, moved freely between literary and journalistic pursuits and thus applied *imagination* equally to the literary task as to the journalistic. I will apply the term imagination to the idea of a new model of journalism. In this the work must traverse some unmapped territory. In defining *imagination* I will attempt to define news as it is shaped through the image of stakeholders, other agents working on behalf of actors, those with an interest in influencing the critics. Let me offer an example.

Reporters and journalists produce news on behalf of client stakeholders in the same way that coal is produced and generated as energy on behalf of clients. Coking coal is extracted from the Powder River Basin in the United States and generated as energy in steel mills in Japan and Korea. Steaming coal is extracted from the Hunter Valley in Australia and generated as energy in power stations to electrify the states of New South Wales (NSW) and Victoria. Clients of the commodity owners in the Powder River Basin are Japanese car manufacturers and Korean shipbuilders. There is no citizen involvement in the trade. Clients of the commodity owners in Australia are the governments of NSW and Victoria. Clients of commodity owners can be involved in private enterprise, state enterprise or be dual organizations with interests in both private and public sector activities. Clients of commodity owners of news are the same manufacturers, the same shipbuilders and the same traders, all of whom have an interest in the validity of the trade taking place in the competitive market in which they operate. Thus, journalists and reporters are producing news for the benefit of those with the capacity to act upon or to verify something in response. The citizen is not part of the action or verification in any important way. Citizens may act or verify in some marginal way—acquiring end products or services generated by the initial activity—but involvement is restricted to a peripheral role as observer of the main game. The mere act of consumption of news does not place a citizen in the main game because other than in a minor role, there is no avenue for that citizen to become an actor in either a political or economic sense. In this, business journalists and reporters are of special interest as they work in environments where the citizen is even more marginalized. The news gathering and producing activity revolves around generation of interest *by* commodity owners *for* commodity owners in much the same way as 19th-century economist David Ricardo outlined the operations of earlier mercantilists in a competitive market. Business journalists and reporters gather and produce news specifically for business clients. The citizen has little or no interest in it. Business news is thus imagined in such a way as to fit the frame of business activity. Whether it is global or local is irrelevant; it is the news of business that creates actions or verifications in the competitive market. This action has remained unchanged since the establishment in England in the early 18th century of weekly news journals that supported emerging global trade. We will discuss this at length.

In understanding how the news media imagines issues and events in political and economic terms, we can begin to understand how these imaginings are translated into a 21st-century society and how news might shape all types of communities in the Western world. To achieve a successful transformation, the Western news media require a new model of imagining. But a new model requires the Western news media to make a decision on whether they are agents of the democratic institutions they support, or whether they act for other purposes.

I suggest that the Western news media was never an *institution* in itself, as described by Macauley, Habermas and others, but an *agent* of institutions such as trade, the rule of law, national sovereignty, and democracy. In the following pages, I will attempt to make good my argument.

Chapters are linked to my argument so that the whole work is read as a single piece. This does not mean it must be read from front to back. Chapter 7 on the United Nations as a global news agent, for example, can easily be read before chapter 3 on journalists, editors and reporters. Doing so might provide an insight into the institution before arriving at a point of discussion about how it is reported. Chapter 3 on democracy and the obligations of the Western news media might be read before chapter 8 on trade and participation.

1

Imagining News

In early 2006, the highly respected newspaper the *Economist*, under a business story headlined "The Public Relations Industry," made a frank admission about members of the profession of journalism. The newspaper stated that "some branches of journalism have come to depend on a drip-feed of information and products from the PR industry. Journalists focusing on electronics, fashion, travel, beauty and food have a huge appetite for free samples" (*Economist* January 21, 2006, p. 59).[2] The admission was not revelatory—journalists have always accepted *samples* as part of the process of news gathering, even though it may not be known to the wider stakeholder public— but it was important for its focus on specific areas. A new beauty product, a rebadged computer chip and a competitive price for a holiday destination are stories worthy of publication in a variety of media. But are they newsworthy? Do they compete for space in news media with stories on the war in Iraq, poverty in the developing world, or the U.S. Supreme Court having for the first time a majority of Catholic judges? The *Economist* judiciously excluded areas it considers important; trade and commerce, agribusiness and energy, manufacturing and investment. The *Economist* does not report new beauty products or revamped holiday destinations. It represents itself as a medium that reports as news global issues and events of significance. In this it imagines news on behalf of stakeholders whom we can consider to be élite. But it does so by creating a local angle. It looks to *ground* its stories this way so they might resonate with citizens at a personal level. A story on polygamy in Turkey begins by describing an individual, the head of a village, as "a man with a mission." A story on Israel's prime minister's health begins by imagining how the surgeons who operated on him might feel. And a story on health care and litigation in the U.S. begins by asking readers to imagine how women in Maryland might feel when they are unable to find an obstetrician. The *Economist*, like all other news media that will be investigated in the following pages, represents itself as a global publication interested in global

7

issues. But as we will see, it must ground in the *local,* issues and events it imagines as news if they are to resonate or have significance for a wider stakeholder public who can then imagine them in individual terms related to how they themselves feel. This creates an interesting effect. Rather than thoroughly investigating the institutions and agencies of democracy as part of its journalistic mandate and its imaginative processes, the Western news media reinforce institutional and agency existence. By localizing global issues and events, the news media validate the institutions and agencies of democracy in the citizen's imagination, aligning them with important issues and events that frame the everyday existence of individuals. In localizing complex issues and events, the news media abrogate their duty of representation as truth.

Actors in the Local, Actors in the Global

This means there is no such thing as *global* news. News exists at *local* levels throughout the Western world to provide information and certainty to its stakeholders, the citizens of countries that see themselves as dominant in the global political economy. But at the same time, the Western news media imagine issues and events so that they appear to have global relevance. To achieve success, they must be grounded in the local imagination to be considered as news in the global imagination.

Western news media influence and persuade their various stakeholders, most importantly citizens and governments in the Western world, by imagining issues and events as reality, distilling words and pictures through a *reality funnel* so that viewers, listeners and readers are presented with fair and balanced reporting as if the issues and events have a direct link to individual citizen well-being and consciousness. This reality funnel is effective because it relies for its validity on the individual acting in self-interest rather than for the good of a community. The importance of the individuality focus of citizens in the public sphere is critical to my argument for two reasons: individuality requires citizens to be less communicative with each other and thus more reliant for information on other sources; and media technology development in the past thirty years has not been random.

The second point rests on the assumption that technology creates *individualness* and the desire for individual well-being to drive the possibility that information sources other than those supplied by news media will be unable to survive. World issues and events, for the élite Western media, are not global news, but local news imagined as world news. They may have economic and political significance beyond their local boundaries but they remain local. I am not referring here nor am I concerned to describe nonconstructed events: an avalanche that destroys a village, or an earthquake that destroys a city—natural events—do not fall within the frame of the argument. It is the constructed event, the issue intervention, or the public communication campaign that becomes news that is of most interest.

A counter-argument to the idea that news media can never be global might include the rationale that issues such as health and education are universal and thus require global solutions. At least this is the argument that occupies large global organizations such as the United Nations. And it is a valid argument in part. There are global issues such as health and education that have wider interest. But they are imagined at a local level by news media.

Why News Needs a New Focus

In the past thirty years (a generation) the power and influence of the industrial nation state has been overtaken by the power and influence of the industrial global corporation. Previously powerful and influential nation-states such as England, France, Germany, Spain and Russia, which for more than two hundred years built their existences around strong manufacturing and agricultural models, have been overtaken by the relocation of manufacturing and agriculture to parts of the world in which labor, energy and raw materials are comparatively cost-effective. Like many of the agents and institutions that formed the basis of the nation state, the Western news media has had difficulty adjusting to the change and to thinking about the required paradigm shift that might make the field of journalism more relevant to a globalized world of trade and business. The *local angle* model of news reporting is no longer an acceptable position in a world in which China makes most of the West's affordable clothing, and oil production from Russia and the Middle East fuels most of its motor vehicles. The Western news media are represented by an outdated model of reporting that had significance when they emerged as agents of the nation state. The model is now neither relevant nor appropriate for the media to report news as it was imagined in the past.

When we imagine, we locate our thoughts. Between the middle of the 20th century and the collapse of the USSR in the mid–1980s, the West imagined itself in terms of a confrontation of liberty and freedom associated with democratic institutions. In the relatively short space of time since the collapse of the USSR and China's more flexible approach to a global market economy, the Western world had no major conflict to imagine itself against. All this changed at the beginning of the 21st century when a previously little-known organization planned and conducted one of the greatest peacetime attacks against a Western country. The rise of the terrorist organization known as al-Qaeda provided the Western world with a threat to its imagined freedom and liberty that equaled World War II. The Western news media responded to the attacks on the World Trade Center and the Pentagon by reporting them in much the same way that they had reported for the duration of the second half of the 20th century. They used their existing structure and model to localize an issue of global significance. Consequently they framed the issue in a way that reflected certain values and ideals around the idea of freedom and liberty as they are attached to the notion of democracy. There is nothing inherently wrong with such a position. Citizens require contests at all levels so that they can measure their own worth against the worth of others. But it also had an additional effect. It forced Western news media to continue using outdated models of news gathering, investigation and reporting when they were beginning to think about new models and theories that might have assisted the paradigm shift that the field of news journalism requires if it is to sustain its existence in the 21st century.

It is my belief that the Western news media at the beginning of the 21st century were ready to shift their news reporting focus so that global issues and events could be imagined outside the frame of localization. Localization relies for its effect on fear, threat or punishment, or a combination of all three to sustain it. Western news media had almost exhausted this model; alternative sources such as the Internet have provided citizens with access to unprecedented levels of information—some good, some not so good—which they can imagine without engagement with orthodox news media. The Western news media is now unable to create the paradigm shift that they needed to sustain themselves because a global issue of significance has forced them to continue using an outdated method within a model that is well past its use-by date. In this they will continue to report global news issues of vast complexity by distilling them to become locally palatable, as they have for the past fifty years.[3]

Generational Change, Generational Familiarity

As we will see, the adoption of a new model will allow complex institutions and agencies such as the World Trade Organization and International Monetary Fund to be adequately imagined by stakeholders other than élites. The question is, is it in the interests of the Western news media to begin to reveal to non-élites the real nature of these complex institutions and agents of democracy?

In 1976 the Western news media were reporting on conflict in the Middle East, particularly between Israel and Lebanon and the closed economy of communist China. Thirty years later—a generation—the Western news media were still reporting on conflict in the Middle East: the political position of the militant Palestinian group Hamas and its opposition to the existence of Israel, Lebanon's Hezbollah and its opposition to the existence of Israel, democratic elections in Iraq, and the role of China in global politics and trade. They report on the closed economy of Korea. In 2036—another generation from now— the Western news media will still be reporting on political issues in the Middle East, possibly a direct conflict between Iran and Israel. They will also be reporting on the completed democratization of China and the emerging democratization of North Korea.[4]

Again in 1976 the user-friendly Macintosh computer was more than ten years from production. Genetically modified mass consumption food was in its initial research stages. Europe was emerging from a thirty-year reconstruction program after World War II. And Japan was poised to become the first Asian "tiger" economy, building cheaper and higher-quality electronics and motor vehicles. Western news reporting, however, differed only slightly from its present shape. It was grounded in a set of values that were clearly identifiable: *good* rather than *bad* (today, bad has become evil), *capitalism* rather than *socialism*, and *democracy* rather than *theocracy*. Today's Western news reporting remains grounded in good, capitalism and democracy. The structure of reporting remains constant and unchanged. It is this unchanging structure that reveals why the Western news media imagine news today much as they did three hundred years ago, and as it will in 2036.

Journalists imagine news as part of a formula for filling spaces in newspapers, radio and television broadcasts. On any given day or at any given hour, news is framed to fit spaces that surround other spaces that have been sold as advertising. News, imagined by journalists, is made up of issues and events that present themselves as being fit for the available frames, and that resonate with the sociopolitical position of the medium that is the focus for the journalist. In the Western world, news is framed by its association with the democratic agents and institutions of the West. In other parts of the world, news is framed by fiat against a backdrop of governing alliances. The democratic institutions and agents of the West allow news to be imagined in any conceivable way, yet it exists within a narrow frame circumscribed by advertising. For news to make sense, journalists must imagine it in a local context. Global issues and events make sense when they are grounded by a local angle that a citizen can relate to as an individual rather than some imagined global stakeholder. Under the present model, a global issue or event can only make sense when it is imagined as local.

Television news imagines issues and events outside the West as vast spaces—African deserts, Middle Eastern unpaved highways and the outside of buildings. Inside the West, its coverage is only minimally more imaginative. It provides views of the outside of corporate office buildings and corporate logos because it has no access to the private spaces that these images represent. It is the public space, or public sphere, that is the site of news gathering in the Western world as it is in the non–Western. Journalists have access only to those sources of information that are observable. To imagine a news story, they must imagine more than the outside of a building or an unpaved road. But access to the private sphere is limited, so there is an overbalance of images of the public sphere. Private spaces, when they are made accessible, become disproportionately important as sources.

As political scientist James Hamilton (2004) argues, news is a commodity but its value lies in its capacity to allow citizens to believe they are connected to the commodity, to each other, and to the world through its dissemination. When the *Washington Post* reports on its front page the news that the U.S. Supreme Court now has a majority of Catholic judges, with whom is it engaging? When the *Economist* represents a news story on Bolivia and its newly elected president, also the leader of that county's coca farmers, who are its stakeholders?

News has its basis in economic rationalism. What is good for a town is good for its citizens. Jobs, construction, and investment are all *good* news stories. But news filters downwards from global economics to local economics. By localizing issues and events, citizens are persuaded to believe localization is more important than global-ization. So when the UN argues for global trade to alleviate poverty in developing countries, it is weighed by citizens of developed countries against local issues that affect them directly, such as good roads, schools and health care.

News as a Local Commodity

Journalists are trained to imagine news as a local commodity. This creates the possibility of an enormous margin for error when they are investigating and reporting global issues and events because they cannot always be imagined as local. Most issues and events are too big to be distilled into sound bites, vision and fifteen-paragraph front page stories. But the Western news-gathering model and its associated techniques require distillation in the partial belief that citizens can only engage with issues and events that appear to effect or have an effect on their individual existences. This is a fallacy. It is the basis of my argument throughout this book that Western news media imagine news as an 18th-century commodity. Localization assumes a number of things, foremost that citizens are unable to differentiate between issues and events that are real and those that are fabricated. Sociologist Leon Mayhew defines this position by arguing that a "new public" has emerged in which citizens are subject to mass persuasion through systematic advertising, lobbying and other forms of media manipulation and that professional specialists using market research and promotional campaigns dominate public communication (Mayhew 1997). Mayhew's argument relies for its validity on the idea that a process worker in Peoria, Illinois, is unable to grasp complex issues such as Russia's presidency of the Group of Eight (G8) or insurgency in Iraq, unless they are localized, unless they have context so that the issues can be rationalized as if they might have a direct effect on her existence. Similarly a service industry worker in Belgrade, Serbia, cannot differentiate between issues of global industrial relations and the changing nature of the European Union unless they are described in simple terms relating to his take-home paycheck. Mayhew and others reinforce the notion of localization of news reporting by seeking to ground complex issues in the familiar.

News as Experience

Journalists control the imaginative process of news gathering, news framing, and news writing. Journalists imagine news very differently from citizens. News journalists learn to write in an entertaining style, some good, some bad. Before writing, journalists gather information, misinformation, facts and errors. The process of interpretation of an issue or event is tied to the journalist's image of the issue or event at both promotional and educational levels. Journalists have a worldview that consists of personal experiences and how they resonate with an issue or event. A journalist will observe, interview, and read background material, then search for an angle that lets a story relate to a stakeholder or groups of stakeholders. Citizens imagine news in two ways: as issues and events that affect other people, and as those that affect them personally. News is not always immediate or urgent. Political issues and events unfold so that they create a rolling news cycle, frequently leading to other linked issues. It is a rare issue or event that stands in isolation as a newsworthy story. Journalists imagine news within a very narrow frame circumscribed by those in seniority in a news room and by their own personal experiences. But journalists are not experts. They rely on the supply of information from sources. This helps them gain expertise. News must reflect exactly the issue or event it is reporting. The death of a nation's president can only be reported as the death of a nation's president. It cannot be imagined in any other way other than the death of the president. If it does, it ceases to be news and becomes instead analysis, opinion or speculation.

There is an additional aspect of news which reinforces the journalistic belief in its importance. It is that all citizens are interested in news and the news process. But only a small percentage of citizens consciously seek news outside their local community; a notion that helps reinforce the idea that global news must be distilled so that citizens will engage with it. I have argued elsewhere that citizens have no access to news as a commodity that can be of any real value to them. It is at this point that the importance of localization comes into play. Commodity owners act strategically, and in this news owners are not exceptional. Journalists are located strategically at sites where the commodification of news is greatest. The greater the availability of resources, the greater number of sites covered.

A growing number of journalists promote illegitimate causes

through their imagining of news. Minority issues are reflected in the angle of the news story because journalists have strong personal interests in how the news is framed. A Muslim journalist working for *Le Monde*, for example, is likely to frame the issue of France's national assimilation policy differently from the frame that might be constructed by a Christian journalist working for the same newspaper. A Brazilian journalist working for the *Baltimore Sun* might have a particular view of agricultural trade between the United States and Brazil. Like all citizens, journalists cannot avoid being emotionally involved in issues and events, so the image of an issue or event as news reflects to some degree the journalist's emotional position. Journalists claim objectivity when reporting news, but the claim is rarely borne out by the reality of what is published or broadcast.

News can be framed so that it alters perceptions of reality. Where once daytime temperatures were acceptable up to 104°F (40°C), now weather becomes a news issue globally when temperatures reach 95°F (35°C). A five-degree shift in imagining can become a catalyst for a variety of issues and events, most notably global warming.[5] It is no coincidence that weather as news on television and radio is frequently followed in the bulletin by news of global warming.

A Sense of Imagination

Imagination, image and *imagery* are words that define the act or process of shaping and forming impressions that we use to identify ourselves in terms of the presence of others. Werner's *New World Dictionary of Media and Communication* (1990) describes *image* in the media as a body of impressions, feelings or opinions regarding an organization or entity as held by its publics. The cynical view is that public imagining of private or corporate entities does not match reality. But such is the case with news and the organizations and entities which produce and disseminate it.

Journalists and reporters around the world investigate facts about issues and events, then write and file copy for print and broadcast. For copy to have value in editorial terms it must be relevant to its medium's consumers, fit the style of the medium and be written to a length that fills the available space. These criteria seem elementary, but when they are considered against the requirement to create a new *content* each day for the same *product*—imagine a breakfast food manufacturer is required to change the content of its cereal packets each morning—then the job of the journalist becomes more interesting. Added to this is the requirement of the journalist to act objectively when investigating issues and events. This involves journalists in stepping outside the frame so that they are no longer engaged citizens. They must become observers rather than participants. To avoid isolation when moving outside the citizen frame, journalists instinctively frame issues or events in a way which is familiar to them. They try to imagine an issue or event as it relates to their own position within a particular social, political and economic frame. The frame they choose, while it must be in alignment with that of the medium for which they are investigating, also carries the weight of their own opinion, as they investigate and as they write. This may sound contradictory to the notion of objectivity, but it is embedded in the investigation and writing processes rather than appearing as an outward motivator. Very few journalists are capable of avoiding this self-framing process. It is an instinctive mechanism that substitutes for the isolation of operating outside the frame of citizen. Modern investigation requires a style of reporting that is based less on the facts of issues and events than on the provision of information by a third person—an agent—that can be rewritten or reimagined as news. The tendency is for a single point of investigation to become diffuse; the subject of news, editorial, op ed opinion, talk-back radio and television debate.

Investigation fulfills a number of objectives. It raises questions about journalistic sources and source motivation, it provides evidence of accuracy, and it seeks to present news in balance. Despite the availability and value of technology, fewer resources are available for journalists to pursue investigative work given the constraints applied by the reduction in the number of journalists working in the West at the beginning of the 21st century compared with the numbers employed a generation ago. To be effective, journalists must do less investigative work, but it is their duty to maintain a high level of copy filing. In the Western world, for this process to succeed, there has been a shift in the way journalists treat investigation and, thus, the *framing* and writing of news. Where once a journalist may have worked across general news, evolving a specialization in some minor way over a period of time due mainly to an inherent interest in the area, 21st-century journalists without specialization are rare. This position is validated by the appearance of classified employment advertisements for journalists in which specialization is viewed positively in an applicant.

Special Issues Need Special Treatment

Specializations in journalism range around law, economics, politics and science with subgroupings such as finance, health, environment and education highly valued. Specialization, however, brings with it a set of problems that journalists must deal with if they are to maintain balance. One of the problems is the reliance on specialist sources. A specialist journalist gains knowledge of issues and events through the pursuit of individual research, but also from the supply of information by interested parties.[6] Information about health, for example, may be sourced from a disparate array of organizations or individuals from the largest, such as the World Health Organization, to the smallest, a journalist's local town community hospital. Similarly, information that can be recast as news about environmental issues and events can be obtained from activist groups, governments or academic sources, for example. In all cases, it is the job of the journalist to investigate the issue or event for news value and balance, but it is also to investigate the source.

Specialization in the West however, supports the notion of relationship building, a subset of public relations. Specialist journalists must, of necessity if they are to continue to report their specialization, build relationships with field experts. And this is where the dangers arise. Journalists keen to investigate issues and events that are already part of the mainstream Western imagination—education, health, finance and employment stand out as the four most important domestic issues—will do so regardless of source credibility given that they are constrained by time and resources. *New York Times* journalist Tom Friedman describes this processing of information in two ways: from the perspective of the journalist and from the perspective of the analyst, or the *broker*, the information provider that the journalist relies on so heavily to assist in the creation of issues that become news. From the analyst's viewpoint, the 21st century world is awash with deregulated markets and diversity requiring constant and complex investigation. Deregulated markets mean organizations are less accountable to governments and more accountable to other stakeholders such as investors. This in turn makes organizations less transparent and their governance less accountable to other stakeholders with no direct interest in the organization's issues and activities. The work of the analyst, on behalf of investor stakeholders, is more complex given the variety of possibilities that global market trading provides, and consequently the work of the journalist is equally complex, but with the ability to draw on fewer resources than the analyst. Friedman argues the financial markets act like an "electronic herd" with a herd mentality, looking to graze while grazing is good, but to move on swiftly to other, sweeter pastures when bare earth remains (Friedman 1999).[7]

The same can be applied to the news media in the way it seeks out stories, running as a pack or herd, feeding until bare earth remains. Rather than digging into the earth in an attempt to uncover more detailed material, the media herd runs off to look for the next surface growth. Australian journalist Derek Parker has described this as the consensus view that journalists seek, making them unable to investigate material outside the frame because they might miss something being pursued by the herd (Parker 1991). The idea, in this case, is to stay with the herd but to be faster, going in the same general direction, but getting there before the majority. Journalists employ this strategy at all levels from international television broadcasters to local weekly town newspapers. The difficulty lies in the need for journalists to stay one jump ahead of their competitors, so they are forever seeking to color or embellish their stories with something their competitors do not have.

This is how issues and events receive support from the news media, or become the subject of negative reporting. During the 1980s, the news media throughout the Western world generally supported the issue of deregulation of the banking and finance sector. Western governments and corporations framed the issue in positivist terms which the news media reflected in their coverage. Support from organizations other than government is crucial if an issue or event is to be framed in positivist terms. Additionally, an issue or event will be viewed and reported favorably by news media if it is framed in positive economic terms. To support a proposed policy to deregulate the banking sector, Western banking in the 1980s was framed as being rooted in 19th-century values. It was a small step to convince citizen stakeholders that a deregulated banking sector would allow them as individuals to make a far greater range of choices in products and services that would benefit them in more ways than their existing systems. Such a strategy, when viewed in retrospect, appears to have had some coordinated strategy throughout the West. Deregulation occurred at around the same time in most Western countries. But the coordinated strategy was more like the herd mentality of the media. If a couple of large Western countries were to create such a policy—the United States, Britain, France and Germany, for example—then it was imperative that economically less powerful Western nation states—Canada, Australia, Italy, Spain, Sweden and Norway—would need to follow to avoid being stuck with an outdated system. The role of the news media in each individual country was integral to the shift. In the Australian case, the federal government argued that its sound economic position would deteriorate globally if it did not deregulate. The Australian news media, following the lead of their British and U.S. counterparts, heralded the proposed legislative changes as sound economic management. There was no argument that can be put to counteract such a position because there was no long-term precedent available for analysis or examination. The citizens of Australia had to take on face value the proposed policy. Citizens were only able to imagine how the benefits of increased availability of banking products might benefit them at some point in the future. Journalists developed images based on information supplied by different sources: governments, corporations, the banks and financial institutions themselves, and consumer advocacy groups. There were enough sources for balance to be seen to be part of the reporting.

News and the Public Sphere

Habermas (1989) regards the press as the original preeminent *institution* of the public sphere, citing its foundations in craft-based business interests as overwhelmingly more focused on public good than the present commercial operators whose ideologies and viewpoints overshadow news gathering and news dissemination. I suggest that its institutional status has been eroded to the point where the Western news media now act as *agents* for other institutions such as democracy and the rule of law rather than acting themselves as institutions. Habermas defined and conceptualized the public sphere within a social science paradigm. In Western democracies the public sphere is viewed from a number of competing positions. Habermas's public sphere was defined as a meeting place or public forum—a mediating environment—between citizens and the state in which information about relevant issues and events was discussed openly and objectively. Thus, he considered it to be an information model which supplanted the earlier conversation model. For Mayhew (1997), professional communicators now dominate public communication, displacing Habermas's free public of the enlightenment—in which objective discussion formed public opinion—and setting up in its place a new public which is subject to systematic mass persuasion. Mayhew's new public sphere can be viewed as a refeudalized Habermasian public sphere in which the processes of rationalization of persuasion, developed in advertising and market research, dominate public communication. For Habermas, the notion of public discourse meant communicative action of discursive contests over public policy issues, functioning specifically to allow citizens the opportunity to understand and formulate opinion without perceived rhetorical influence. Mayhew, however, argues that a new public, being moulded and shaped during the second half of the 20th century, has little interest in such contests, valorizing them in terms of the rhetoric of persuasion and influence and believing them to be less forums for what he calls the redemption of tokens than forums in which persuasion and influence will overwhelm the underlying issues and events.

The existence of a public sphere is central to any global news argument. The suggestion that a public sphere in which discursive processes in public spaces embodies the *good* in a society resonates with us as citizens (see, for example, Schudson 1999). For us to be persuaded by Mayhew's outline of a new public sphere, we must acknowledge Habermas's argument that the field of journalism transformed the original public sphere from one in which actors oriented their own actions by their own interpretations of issues and events to one which Mayhew describes as an amorphous mass, subjected to persuasion through systematic processes. As we will see in later chapters, however, this is an oversimplification of the role of journalism in Western democracies.

Framing the News

News framing requires us to think about an issue or event in a particular way. It needs us to think about issues or events as part of a wider ideological position and to frame them within that ideology. It also requires us to have some understanding of the ideological position of the media so that our frame matches the *agenda* embedded within the media ideology. But this is not something that is available to the average citizen. News media ideologies come in all shapes and sizes but, most importantly, they are linked to a central position which is the ideological position of ownership. Opinion writers and reporters working for U.S.-based News Corporation, for example, may hold different views from News Corporation's majority stakeholders—Rupert Murdoch or Liberty Media's John Malone—and sometimes, their writing may reflect this position. But generally speaking, the ideological position of ownership or majority shareholding will be paramount.

News framing takes its lead from earlier work by Erving Goffman (1974) in which the idea of what an individual could actually be attuned to at any particular moment was defined by the *framework* that was built around a particular situation. Goffman began his investigation into framing and frame analysis by asking what it was that an individual did when confronted by any current situation: the 1970s version of *What's happenin' ma man?* or, *'s up dude?* For Goffman, the question itself required us to be alert to a number of possibilities, chief among them that the answer could be framed in any way that supported whatever needed supporting. Goffman argued that the width or narrowness of focus of an issue or event was determined by who answered the question *what is it that's going on?* (Goffman 1974).

Following Goffman, the news media answer the question by investigating the frame in which the issue or event has been presented and try to make sense out of it by matching it to already known frames of reference. These known frames of reference may have been established or entrenched in the mind of the individual journalist for some time, or they may be the product of some sharp occurrence that has had a profound effect on that individual's beliefs or codes of ethical and moral conduct. For example, the journalist may have had a profoundly moving experience in childhood—the death of a parent—which sets up a frame around the issue of parenting generally, and single-parent families specifically. In the social world (leaving aside for a moment the physical and biological worlds) the *organization* of issues and events governs the way in which we see them and the level of acceptance we apply to them. Principles of organization, Goffman suggests, and our subjective involvement in them cause them to be *framed* in a particular way. If, for example, we feel confident in the government and, by extension, the principles upon which it organizes the health system in our country, we are less likely to show panic in the face of the threat of an avian influenza outbreak than if we have less confidence in the government and the health system. We frame our personal response to the threat by remaining calm. If we have less confidence in the government and the health system, we may be more likely to panic. Both responses might be the result of how we frame the issue in our own minds.

But Goffman, whose work provided a basis for future scholars such as Robert Entman, among others, was concerned with an additional aspect of framing, one which provides an ethical dimension to the work of news journalists. Goffman was concerned that fabricated issues and events could be framed in a certain way or *embedded* in reality through the use of persuasion so that they took on the shape of reality. It became difficult to tell the fake from the real. And it is no coincidence that this process reached a particular level when the U.S. Defense Department began referring to news journalists working in war zones as being embedded with its troops. They are effectively, to highlight Goffman's point, taking up space in the *reality* of the war, rather than reporting it from an objective sideline.

Goffman suggests that whatever it is about the *real* that makes us believe in it, those in the business of producing the *fake* will use the same ingredients, making it difficult to know fake from real. Just ask any New York street vendor with a trolley load of Louis Vuitton handbags selling for $40 each. Or, as an award-winning Australian television reporter once told a group of undergraduate student journalists, the important thing to remember in television journalism was to "fake it till you make it."

In our private lives we spend a great deal of time classifying and arranging things within our range of experiences. We do this so that we can make sense of what it is we are engaged in. Without classification and control it all becomes pointless and confusing. In so doing we interpret issues and events in a certain way according to our life experiences. And when we do this, we put them into specific frames, just like when we stick a picture in a frame and hang it on a wall or take a photo of a musician and encase it in a plastic sleeve in front of a music CD. In this, framing requires us to interpret and find meaning, to imagine what it is we are looking at. But it also needs us to work through a theme for an issue or event. It is not enough that a mediated issue or event can find its place among a stakeholder public which understands what is being published or broadcast. It must have some degree of continuity so that meaning can be constructed in a particular way. The threat of an avian influenza pandemic, for example, can be constructed around a number of competing frames (government, health providers, pharmaceutical companies) but for it to have meaning for a particular audience or public, it must carry a theme throughout its mediated life. (Most news stories run in cycles from a day to a week.) So it is unlikely the news media will switch themes over the week of a story's life. CNN, for example, is unlikely to frame the issue around government inadequacy, then switch to pharmaceutical company competency, then switch again to World Health Organization support for the issue.

When organizations, governments and individuals frame an issue or event, they do so with different stakeholders in mind. Sometimes it is the news media, at other times it might be what we refer to as the general public, or it might be smaller stakeholders such as community groups or specialists that require a message to be framed so that meaning can be taken from it. Whatever the nature of the stakeholders being pitched to, we can add to the definition of *framing* by suggesting that it is the process of imagining, in words and pictures, something that is meaningful to its source, whose meaning can be transferred to others (agents and forces) through the construction of issues and events. And this is where the news media become important stakeholder agents in the dissemination of messages as issues and events for every conceivable reason. But there is another dimension to this. The media have a duty to investigate the political or nonpolitical context of an issue or event so that it can be reported in an equitable and meaningful fashion. A complex issue or event may have one or more frames. A simple event such as the launch of a new music CD may have one dominant frame (univalent) and a concert to raise money for Africa's poor may have two dominant frames (bivalent), namely the donation of their performance by highly paid musicians and the issue of poverty; whereas an issue with many significant frames (multivalent) such as avian influenza requires meaning to be applied across a number of levels to a number of stakeholders.

If, as political communication scholar Robert Entman (1993) suggests, frames focus our attention on some aspects of reality while blurring or avoiding others, they have the potential to provide different stakeholders with diffuse reactions. A passive action to the probability of an avian flu pandemic from normally healthy Westerners—a visit to a medical practitioner for a prescription medication—might translate into an aggressive action if thousands of Westerners reschedule vacations and travel to destinations other than Southeast Asia. One aspect of reality attached to avian flu and its pandemic frame is the increased possibility of death. But the focus on death blurs other frames such as cure or treatment, containment and limitation. When a controversial social issue or event arises, interested stakeholders frequently attempt to engage the news media to adopt a chosen frame to assist in persuading and influencing other, more diffuse stakeholders. Strong emotional rhetoric assists this process, but rhetoric alone is not sufficient. It must be bolted to a frame so that it stands out as being more important and more substantial than its competing frames.

Imagining Global Issues and Events

As individual citizens in the West we share a close interest in the income that will provide us with food, shelter, energy and transport. We create tribal communication allegiances with other individuals at a variety of locations: the supermarket, the local school, the cinema. We seek out relationships that provide us with a sense of our own worth and individuality. We seek information at a local level that informs our worth. We are less interested in the worth and individuality of those outside our immediate zone of influence unless it is a relationship that will increase our income, our worth, our sense of self, or all three. In China, this is known as *guanxi*, a form of mutual opportunity that is finding its way in the West. We are less interested in communicating with a call-center customer-service operator telephoning from India to talk to us about changing our mortgage or credit-card account, and more interested in what the local butcher's kids did on vacation. We know of the existence of the United Nations, the World Trade Organization, the World Health Organization and the International Monetary Fund, but we do not relate to their significance, their work and their power because they have no imagined impact on our lives. Like corporations and governments, they exist without emotion in a rational world removed from our own emotional daily lives.

For the journalist, the transfer of imagination from the rational to the emotional becomes part of the process of reporting globally significant issues and events and grounding them in the local. In the following chapters, we will investigate the relationships between news reporting and the institutions and agents that make up the democratic existence of the West, and how the journalistic imagination has the potential, through the application of a new model, to create and maintain the links that are necessary for these institutions and agents to be accepted as part of a tribal community.

2

Presentation of Global Image: Editors, Reporters and Journalists

The Journalistic Process

Journalists and reporters are sent into the field by editors and producers to investigate issues and events, gather information, and write crisp, clean copy that fits the available spaces and policies of the medium for which they work. They do this on a daily basis, every week of their working lives. For most of them, finding a story, investigating it and writing about it, is a process that U.S. scholar Gaye Tuchman has identified as "routinizing the unexpected" (1973). By this Tuchman means that journalists and reporters will find ways to distill outrageous or uncommon issues and events so that they can be interpreted rationally by news media stakeholders: their readers, viewers and listeners. The reality, though, is that this process is one of commodification.

While Tuchman has identified a factor that assists journalists and reporters to survive the most boring, mind-numbing assignments they can be sent on by editors, there are two other aspects to their work that require discussion so that we have an idea of why news becomes newsworthy and, more importantly, why global news is treated a certain way.

There are generally two ways journalists and reporters acquire news. At a daily news conference a reporter might be assigned to an issue or event that has arrived in the newsroom from an outside source or agency. Such stories can be generated from public relations agents, directly from governments and other institutions, or from other sources known to an editor. In this an editor assigns the story. Alternatively, a reporter or journalist might introduce a story to the news conference that has been picked up from his or her own source. If it is perceived by the editor to have news value, the reporter will continue the investigation.

In both cases, the reporter will be required to imagine a news angle and to develop the story along the line of the angle and the frame that fits policy. One of two things can occur here. The reporter will routinize the story: investigate and write it within the frame, to the required length, file the copy, and move on to the next story before deadline. This is normative in most newsrooms. Sometimes, however, a reporter moves outside this routine and reflects on the story before beginning an investigation. While deadlines and the imposition of limited resources rarely allow such reflection, on occasion a reporter gets the chance to imagine a story more completely than as a routine item.

Such reflection is what assists journalists and reporters to balance devastating news stories when they occur: the terrorist attacks on New York and Washington in September 2001 and the tsunami tidal wave in the Indian Ocean in 2004 that killed more than two hundred thousand people are two examples that provide evidence of how reporters, in almost indescribable circumstances, are able to describe the circumstances to wide-ranging stakeholders.

But because the routinizing of news is what reporters and journalists do most of the time, there is a tendency to commodify global issues and events the same way as they commodify local news. Global issues and events are imagined the same way whether they are significant or insignificant. This is partly to do with how a newspaper is structured. Global news will make the front page of the *Baltimore Sun*, for example, if it is considered significant. Otherwise, and it is the same for most Western newspapers, global news is relegated to a section somewhere after general news titled "world news."[1] As U.S. media expert Joshua Meyrowitz (2004) argues, even a globally élite newspaper such as the *New York Times* devotes more editorial resources to covering New York news than it does to covering the rest of the world.

Aspects of the reporter's work have been described as the interpretative moment, the interrogative moment and the adversarial moment (McNair 2003). A typology of reporting is therefore required to relate these three aspects to news generation, news gathering and news reporting. But it is the adversarial moment, the actual interview between a reporter (actor) and a performer, which is of most interest. An important aspect of the typology of the adversarial moment is the reporter interview in which information from the performer is accepted without qualification, transcribed as fact and published as news. A typology of reporter relationships highlights some of the problems confronting those gathering and interpreting news. Reporters can be either proactive or reactive in sourcing material and assessing its newsworthiness. Proactive reporters are those who develop and maintain a strong book of contacts regardless of political affiliation. In this group, contacts would be those not outwardly motivated by politically partisan or commercial gain—clergy, school principals, police commanding officers, senior government officials, business owners, senior health administrators—those with a high level of knowledge who are able and willing to provide background information on issues and events.

In the event that a reporter does not maintain a strong contact list, there must be a reliance on either the reporter's own knowledge or the veracity of the information supplied by the source. As the motivation for supply of information from a source is frequently self-interest, it must always be verified.

Reactive reporters rely on politically motivated sources for most if not all their information. This is a dangerous position to be in as reporters are already vulnerable to disinformation, the reporting of untruths and sophisticated information and propaganda machinery.

The reporting of global news is also the consequence of how Western media news workers—editors, producers, journalists and reporters—imagine "other" places and spaces in direct relationship to how they view their own environment and their personal values. Unless they have had direct experience of "otherness," for example, north Asian political economy and culture, they must frame news around the experiences of sources and other agents. Such a position can have interesting consequences which I will discuss below.[2] When confronted by an issue or event, journalists and reporters imagine an angle, then pursue the story to its conclusion. It is a quest in the tradition of the West to conquer, so the news story takes on a conquest role.[3]

Hollywood fires our imagination in the West so that we think about our self-importance and our selves as imagined heroes bound for glory. Journalists, by the nature of their creative writing work, imagine themselves in the heroic mold—breaking news that will lift them to glory. And in this there is no small coincidence that they resent the elevation of institutions to the postmodernist position of glory previously acknowledged as being reserved for deities. Nineteenth-century English politician and journalist Thomas Babington Macauley is partly responsible for imaging the news media as being linked to the high estates of lord spiritual, lords temporal and representative honors. Macauley coined the term "fourth estate" to include members of the news media as they sat in parliament reporting on proceedings (1910). To acknowledge them in such a form elevated them above the public with whom they supposedly shared allegiance and to whom they owed their livelihoods, but in reality demonstrated that they were, as they wished to be, acknowledged as being as important as elected and higher representatives. Commodification and homogenization of news grounds the imagination below the level required by Hollywood and draws it into the realm defined by Tuchman.

So on one hand we have journalists and reporters who imagine themselves as elevated above the common citizen, but on the other hand they imagine themselves as not as elevated as other actors on the high stage such as national and supranational institutions. The tensions played out between the actors require additional mediation.

The Decisions of the Editor

Editorial decisions on newsworthiness of material are grounded in the policy of the medium. The *Economist*, for example, clearly states its mission is "to take part in a severe contest between intelligence, which presses forward, and an unworthy, timid ignorance obstructing our progress" (*Economist*, all issues, p. 2).

Policy can be interpreted in many ways, but generally in Western media news policy has a direct link to advertising revenue, profitability and ownership. I will discuss in chapter 4 the issues of ownership and control of media interests and the idea that national politics are intertwined with a news medium's editorial policy. What we are interested in here is the relationship of the editor of a newspaper, a producer of a radio news program or a television news program and how the individual editor or producer makes decisions about the commission or omission of global news issues and events based on newsworthiness and news values.

The way an editor or producer imagines global issues and events as news begins the framing process for the reporter or journalist. Editors tend to imagine news as a sporting contest in which there must be winners and losers. Global institutions and agents such as the World Trade Organization, or the International Monetary Fund, due to their relative size and power, are perversely viewed as losers (the opponents of the institutions and agents are imagined as "the underdogs") while nations, especially emerging or developing nations, are imagined as winners (closer to the ideal of community). Countries can be either winners or losers, depending upon their position at any particular time, and individual citizens are imagined in their struggle to be the ultimate winners because they are imagined as neither institutions nor agents.

Western news editors imagine Asian countries as if they are football teams competing for position on the league table. Layers are built into the imagining so that some global issues such as trade are seen to be more important than others, while local issues such as health and education are benchmarks against which nations can measure their comparative success.

The *Economist*, for example, provides a weekly score sheet divided into economic and financial indicators for what it considers developed countries, while emerging market indicators are provided for all other countries, including, somewhat paradoxically, the powerhouse north Asian economies of the Republic of Korea and Taiwan Republic of China. As I will demonstrate in the following chapter, Korea and Taiwan field all the players that are needed to be considered part of the West.

Western news editors have a particular homogenized image of the world; it is one in which their own value system plays a decisive role in framing global issues and events as news and in which right and good are products of Western diligence. All other cultures, notably Middle Eastern and Asian, are imagined as alien. But in some Asian countries sheer weight of numbers of population reduces individual and national competition to an expression of survival, as in India and China. In large cities such as Beijing and Calcutta, where populations exceed the total of some advanced Western countries (such as Australia), the idea of the individual in competition is a ridiculous concept. For a daily routine of productivity to succeed, order must struggle to supplant competition in the individual. Western editors, journalists and reporters rarely interpret order as a different dynamic because it is not competitive. It is imagined as a cultural difference.

Localizing the Angle

Localization of a news angle such as a piece in the *Economist* in mid–2006 on property prices in Argentina reduces the news value of the story. The difficulty for the reader is in determining where the core of the story lies. When a news story is localized it begins with a human interest angle: in the case of the Argentine property market, it opened with an image of a New Yorker lamenting the fact he could not buy in to the New York market. The story described John Kahoun as being deterred by the cost of property in Manhattan, but wishing (with some level of desperation, the story implies) to invest in property, he buys an apartment in Buenos Aires.

While this is a short piece—ten paragraphs—it is created to fill space in the predetermined section of the newspaper titled "The Americas." And it is a newsworthy story. But there were a number of stronger news angles "buried" in the body of the story that outweighed the foreign investor angle, especially given the *Economist* strongly supports trade and investment liberalization. In this case a strong news angle rather than a warm fuzzy local angle for the consideration of Western readers might have been more appropriate.

In this the *Economist* is similar in its approach to all other Western news media. The common strategy behind the use of the local angle—the human face of the news—grounds issues and events so that they resonate with readers and viewers rather than with the institutions that the news reflects. This is a purposeful position. Grounding news in a local angle and reporting within a local frame creates cleavage between the image the citizen constructs of institutions. As citizens we work hard to become or remain connected to communities that we trust and with which we feel comfortable. When the news media report on an issue as large and complex as global property prices, by grounding it in the local they attempt to explain the issue in terms that will link to the knowledge or opinion an individual citizen might hold on the issue. But in fact what the media do is reinforce the image of a chasm between institutions that appear to manipulate such things as property prices and citizens who are powerless in their own localities. The example of the New York property buyer retreating to Buenos Aires suggests citizens are powerless against global property markets. The image we take from the story is two-pronged: we might despair because we cannot secure space that we would like in the place we want to live, but we can feel joy that there are still places in the world where we can afford to invest. The irony appears to be lost in the story.

A local human focus creates undue cleavage between the image citizens have of institutions and agents and how the issues and events that surround them filter downward to communities and individual citizens. Citizens will generally act negatively towards institutions—especially national governments—and voice opinions that suggest they are not working, a natural instinct at ground level. It is an instinct that supports the argument that institutions have replaced deities; supranational institutions in the West have become substitutes for religion. In their complexity they create and maintain a position that supports the idea of enormous space between them and their stakeholders (citizens and communities). News media support this position by localizing their story angles. They set up their stakeholder viewers, listeners, and readers to consider the gap between them and the institutions being reported. In this, élite media such as the *Economist* are adopting populist media techniques that fail to have the desired effect of drawing readers in to a more complex understanding of the issues and events being reported or a better understanding of the chosen position of the medium itself. When *USA Today* or the UK's *Daily Mail* report on global issues (which is rare, as they believe their readers are uninterested in such things), they do so by grounding them hard in the local—the loss of jobs in Oklahoma or Manchester—reflecting on the failure of global economics (and thus, by implication, local politicians) to look after the well-being of individuals who are powerless within the global market.

For an élite newspaper such as the *Economist* to take a similar position in its housing story reflects a misunderstanding of the requirements of its readers. But more importantly it reflects a news management issue: a strategy designed to balance how readers feel about the political position of the newspaper (liberal free market) with how they generally feel about their own powerlessness within early 21st-century globalization.

Reliance on Media

Citizens of Western countries, as they become ever more mobile through the increased use of private motor vehicle transport and a decrease in use of public transport and, thus, public spaces, consequently become more reliant on mediated information to fulfill their needs to know what is occurring around them. While cellular telephony and wireless computer technology allow individuals to access news and information anywhere they can find a satellite footprint in the world, there remains an innate need and desire for human contact and connectivity. Otherwise, universities around the world would need to occupy no physical spaces: students would work from wherever they were (most likely at home in front of the television) while faculty would run lectures and seminars via satellite from their houses on the Carolina coast or the shores of the Adriatic.

The human need for contact through verbal and interpersonal communication still exists in the West. U.S. navy personnel travel to the Republic of Korea for an information technology conference rather than viewing proceedings via a more cost-effective video link; academics from around the globe meet in Cairo to present research findings at a four-day gathering rather than disseminating the results of their investigation via the more cost-effective Internet; delegates from 191 United Nations member countries regularly travel to New York for sittings of the security council rather than using more cost-effective telecommunications resources. In fact, when we think about these examples, we might be forgiven for imagining that the need for personal communication is just as important and frequent now as it was before the invention of wireless information technology and telecommunications. But all these examples are differentiated from other levels of interpersonal communication by their élitism.

The majority of the world's human population does not travel widely nor have the capacity to share information for economic or political advantage. Indeed, fewer than twenty percent of United States citizens hold passports, which means that of the potential three hundred million population, fewer than sixty million are eligible at any given moment to travel outside the country. This is still a large number of people, but it reflects an important image of the majority of American citizens as being more interested and concerned with matters at home than with matters abroad.

Thus citizens have a strong reliance on mediated images of worlds outside their own. This is true not only of the United States, but of most of the Western world and, indeed, non–Western countries in which citizens have much lower wages. Ordinary citizens of countries such as India and Brazil are in no position to travel outside their countries as costs are prohibitive. News of European Union legislative amendments, United States defense policy or World Bank funding, for example, must be received through mediated channels.

Media, however, are less interested in the delivery of news of such institutional and agency issues and events imagined as global politics than in presenting them from a local perspective. The consequences are that a country's news media ignore global issue and events unless they have a local angle.[4]

Sources and Other Agents

The power of Western journalists lies in the decisions they make regarding what to report and what not to report, a process of informed decision making rather than luck (Seib 1994). While the journalist must make a decision about inclusion or exclusion as a primary motive, there are numerous other factors which assist in the decision process. Notable among them is the rise of public relations in the late 20th century and its marked impact on the profession of journalism.

Political journalists and reporters, by their nature, are partisan towards either social equity platforms or conservative business platforms, a position which has been examined in detail (see Nimmo 1978; Paletz 1987; Simms and Bolger 2000; Tiffen 2000). Most frequently though, there is a leftist leaning (Weaver 1998). A journalist makes daily decisions on the construction of political news based foremost on continuity of supply. It is in the journalist's best interests to suppress stories which could damage sources.

The distinction between "news reporting," which should be descriptive, accurate and explanatory (de Burgh 2000) and "political news reporting," which is frequently mediated, (McNair 2000), can be drawn in a number of ways. The difficulty for the journalist lies in the interpretation of the rhetoric. And it is the capacity to interpret or mediate the rhetoric that lies at the heart of Mayhew's fear that marketers and public relations counselors behave unethically when acting as sources (Mayhew 1997). One way to overcome this is to concentrate on relatively few issues and subjects, but this invariably leads to citizens' perception that they are therefore more important than other issues or subjects within the public sphere. There is a limited amount of space available on a daily basis for news coverage. In newspaper terms, the space available for news is in direct proportion to the amount of space sold for advertising. On any given day in a process of "mocking up the book," the advertising department has final control of space ratios. If, for example, London's *Daily Telegraph* is ready for "bed" at 6 p.m. and an advertising sales representative calls in a late advertisement, it will take precedence over news which may have already been set and waiting on the page to be printed. The page will be changed, the advertisement added, the news removed and the only people in the process who will be aware are the advertising manager, the compositor (typesetter), the "stone sub" and the editor. The journalist who wrote the removed piece will discover its removal when the paper is distributed the following day. The reader will never know.

As Mayhew argues, there has always been a rhetoric of presentation in which the display of symbols outweighs discursive argument. However, when he attempts to define this argument more specifically, stating that media specialists have produced antidiscursive models which present high levels of information as being dangerous, he appears to avoid the significant presence of journalism and its capacity to "filter" and "distil" the specialist rhetoric of presentation. Mayhew argues that it is standard practice in advertising or political persuasion to imply positive position but not specify exactly how promised benefits will materialize. The same argument can be applied to Western journalism, as we will see below.

Contractual Arrangements

Western news media establish implied agreements with sources and agencies. The nature of these agreements is private. The denial of public access means the transaction between the news media and the source or agent inflates the value of the transaction because it (the news that is produced from the transaction) becomes something that is eagerly sought from those within the public sphere. Other than those who may be eye- or ear-witnesses, citizens can only access news after it has been mediated. One of the most important features of the transactions between sources and news media is its dissemination, and the most widely employed vehicle in the West is the news media conference.

Media conferences are not accessible to citizens. United Nations, presidential and, indeed, corporate press briefings are all held in private. They are contractual arrangements between the members of the media and the news generator. At the UN, news media are issued with green-and-white identity cards which allow them to attend closed briefings with the secretary-general. UN delegates with full rights to all other spaces in UN headquarters, including the Security Council chamber, are not allowed in to the news media briefing room. The news media briefing reinforces the notion of exclusion by imagining the requirement of engagement to be between equals.

The Western news media imagine issues and events in parts of the world that are accessible, and they maintain contractual arrangements in those places. Closed economies such as North Korea and Cuba provide no engagement for imagining, so they are excluded from the news cycle. Media imagine events and issues on the margins of their own experience. They report when there is a direct connection from the issue or event to the West. All others are considered alien in terms of engagement.

South African scholar Eric Louw (2004) makes a strong case describing the hegemony of Western journalism and how its values are represented in news of the rest of the world. Louw says journalists in the West are not equipped to "read" foreign issues and events so that they resonate with home audiences. They are, therefore, most often imagined as conflict or as victim and villain situations. Louw suggests that Western journalists covering foreign issues and events misread and misunderstand the context in which they have been located because they have preconceived images that are grounded in their Western sociopolitical culture.

But Western news images of issues and events in some countries are not as binary as others. For Western news media, Africa and the Middle East fit a binary position described by Louw because they do not conform to Western sociopolitical values. They can be seen in terms of their opposition to Western sociopolitical and cultural positions. But some countries, especially those formerly imagined in binary terms, as I will show below in my Taxonomies of Inclusion, present difficulties for Western news reporters because they no longer conform to conventional images of opposition.

Two interesting examples in which there are regular globally newsworthy issues and events that could be imagined positively in terms of Western news values are Japan and Korea. Both countries have in the past been imagined in oppositional mode to Western sociopolitical values. Issues and events were consequently reported as if they were still grounded in events more than half a century old.

I am not advocating historical amnesia, nor am I ignoring the conflict between both countries that is still alive in the minds of some communities of citizens and élites. What I am suggesting is that Western news is unable to frame issues and events for both countries without some historical link that grounds both these countries as villains, despite my taxonomies demonstrating conclusively that both countries can be considered Western for the purposes of this work.[5]

Unification of the two Koreas and Japanese whaling are two issues that receive attention in the Western news media. Neither is imagined within a positive frame. A third important issue which has strong newsworthiness and value—sandstorms from Mongolia's Gobi Desert that blanket South Korea and Japan with thousands of tons of topsoil each year—is ignored by the West. Within the Republic of Korea, there is a strong wish for reunification with North Korea for economic, social and political reasons. At the border, in an area known as the Demilitarized Zone (DMZ) two important events have taken place in the past few years, one of which was reported in mildly negative terms by the *Economist* and the other ignored generally by the Western news media.

The *Economist* reported the development of a trade zone that has been set up by South Korea inside the DMZ. Known as Kaesong, it houses South Korean manufacturing plants in which labor is supplied by the North. South Korea, its government and its citizens see this as a positive move towards reunification with the North. The *Economist* led a twelve-paragraph story of May 27, 2006 (headlined "An Industrial Park Causes Tensions With America"), with "America's chief negotiator on North Korea, Christopher Hill, visited Seoul on May 25, part of an effort to restart talks over North Korea's illicit nuclear programs. Increasingly though America and its ally South Korea are at odds about the North" (*Economist*, May 27, 2006, p. 27).

The story represented American interests, noting that the government of the United States sees South Korea as being "soft" on its northern neighbor. The angle of the story supports my argument. The *Economist* was unable to frame the issue as it is seen in Asia at government and street level: as a North-South dialogue that had the potential to lead to a reduction in tensions between North Korea and the West. The issue could have been imagined by The *Economist* as a classic example of developing diplomacy, but it did not conform to Western news values of diplomacy and political communication because it did not include the United States. Additionally, the issue had the potential to redirect U.S. foreign policy on North Korea. In 2003, United States president George W. Bush used powerful rhetoric to describe North Korea as a third pillar in an "axis of evil" that included Iraq and Iran. After applying military force in Iraq and in 2005 turning attention to Iran's nuclear development program, the U.S. government would have been uninterested in having a friendly neighbor developing diplomacy when it had made clear and unambiguous statements about the confrontation it intended with North Korea.

The news report in the *Economist* implied support for the U.S. position by highlighting human rights issues of low wages and conditions in the Kaesong plants, and argued that while the factories might be seen by the South to encourage reform in the North, the development did not supply freedom of association for workers nor the ability to take industrial action or become involved in wage negotiation. In highlighting these particular factors, the *Economist* is imagining the issue of manufacturing in Asia as it would like to believe it exists in the West. While freedom of association, industrial action, and wage negotiations are enshrined in industrial mythology in most Western countries, the reality is that individual contracts and enterprise agreements have become normative when manufacturing is still located in Western countries. As U.S. economist Jagdish Bhagwati (2004) demonstrates, the real issue for Western labor unions is not the wages and conditions of Asian factory workers, but an unacceptable decline in Western labor standards when Asian workers accept relatively lower standards and conditions. This is the real issue behind the *Economist's* imaginative representation of dialogue and diplomacy between the two Koreas: human rights. U.S. foreign policy on North Korea is grounded and framed around that country's poor history of human rights, a position which Western news media such as the *Economist* adopt as it fits snugly into their image of Asian exploitation of citizens.[6]

A second example, reported widely in the Korean press at the time that supported the argument that South Korea was employing a diplomatic strategy in its aim of reunification, was the proposed train journey between the Korean capitals of Seoul and Pyongyang scheduled to take place on the reconnected inter–Korean railway line. For a variety of reasons, most notably the cancellation of the event by the North, which cited the absence of a military accord to guarantee safe passage, and unstable political conditions in the south (*Korea Times* May 27, 2006, p. 2), the event was reported widely in Asia. For the West, however, the idea of a test-run train journey between North and South adds tension to the issue of North Korea being imagined as a nuclear threat. Train journeys in the imagination of the West are gentle things taken by tourists and citizens traveling for pleasure and work. They cannot be reconciled with images of aberrant nations developing nuclear warfare programs. Train journeys do not fit the image of non–Western societal organization that has become what Louw (2004) describes as despicable and incomprehensible to the Western journalist. Additionally, Koreans traveling by train from Seoul to London via North Korea and Russia does not fit the nuclear war frame.

Japanese whaling, on the other hand, is an issue that can be reconciled as despicable and incomprehensible in the imagination of the Western media because it conjures every sense of the bad days of colonization and empire when the West itself was guilty of exactly the same "crimes."

For the Western news media, the issue of Japan reigniting its whaling industry is a euphemistic parallel to Japan reigniting its military expansion in the Asia-Pacific region. Commercial whaling has become unacceptable in public opinion in the West. Public opinion in the West imposes political pressure on elected representatives to take action on the issue of whaling, partly in response to globalization, but more deeply as an emotional response to its own legacy of destruction through overfishing of global fish stocks. Western politicians apply political pressure on Japan by threatening trade sanctions (which have less effect in a liberalized global trade environment) if commercial whaling is reignited. Western news media support the public opinion of their constituents (customers), and thus support the position of those Western governments who seek to stop Japan from whaling commercially.

The position adopted by the Western news media appears immutable, yet there is another frame in which the issue could be acceptably imagined. If we consider as acceptable the idea that Western citizens grow and slaughter three-day-old calves, call it veal and enjoy eating it, or forcefeed geese, then slaughter them to harvest their liver, call it fois gras and enjoy eating it, then it should be acceptable for the Japanese to slaughter whales and to enjoy eating them. This, however, is not the issue. All these actions are in reality unacceptable, but two of them are imagined in the West as being within the frame of acceptability. Western news media make occasional forays into the ethics of animal slaughter and consumption in the West, but it is generally undertaken by alternative media. Commercial news media, if they were investigated, would be found to have direct links to agribusiness on a very large scale so it might not be acceptable for an Australian television network, for example, to produce news on the ethics of slaughter when one of its sister companies might own some of the largest beef cattle holdings in the world. Similarly Brazilian television would not be interested in investigating poor abattoir and slaughter conditions when it is owned by the same organizations that own the beef production that sustains Brazil's strong global balance of trade.

On the issue of Japanese whaling, the Western news media could easily find similar outrages within their own boundaries, yet they pursue the whaling issue for a specific purpose: to demonstrate that it is in accord with the opinions (as short-lived as they are) of their Western constituents and the need to distill issues as complex as this into comprehensible sound bites and twenty-paragraph lead stories.[7]

For the Western news media then, the issue might have been better placed had they found an angle that attacked the Japanese government rather than Japan as a nation. But this is not the nature of conflict and cleavage that Western news media have come to enjoy. To attack the Japanese government is similar in intent to attacking the U.S. government or the French government. This is what the Western news media do all the time. In order to resonate with their constituency, the Western news media must look to attack larger interests so that the idea of globalism itself is seen to be responsible for such actions as the lowering of Western wages and the destruction of ocean wildlife.

As I have discussed elsewhere, this relates to the image of self that exists in the West, the image of a well-constructed conscious being with a moral and ethical responsibility to the planet. Its origins can be traced to guilt by association for previous Western crimes against humanity and the planet. Its importance lies in its contextualization of the us-them model and draws down in layers from global to local: even local government can be imagined as "bad" if it does not comply with individual expectations of policy in the delivery of services such as trash removal or road maintenance.

In the final example for this section—sandstorms that carry from the high plateaus of the Gobi Desert to the densely populated cities of South Korea and Japan—we can see the interest of the Western news media is marginal because it is an event that does not directly affect the West. It is most certainly a global issue and has the potential to affect economic growth in two of the world's most powerful economies but, until Western interests are affected, it remains marginal. Additionally, it is not imagined directly as an economic or political issue. The idea that the South Korean government is investing heavily in tree planting in the desert to arrest further degradation is an econopolitical event, but for the Western news media it might be imagined as a natural disaster similar in scale to an earthquake in Indonesia or a flood in India: it has human consequences but mainly for the poor, and as it does not affect Western interests directly, it is to be seen as victimizing, but otherwise of no continuing news value.

News Imagined as Local Commodity

Western news media report the crash of a British helicopter in Iraq with all hands killed. In Australia, the report of the crash provides no information about the hands, neither names nor number of deaths nor rank. When an Australian is killed, the Australian media frame the news of the death around first disbelief, then immense detail concerning the individual. In England, the Australian military death in Iraq does not make the news other than as a sidebar due to a mix-up between bodies; the wrong body has been shipped to Australia. When the mix-up is discovered, the body of the dead Australian soldier is shipped a few days later. This event makes news because it is unusual. In Australia, the detail of the dead soldier represents a local angle, as we might expect, but Australian citizens are equally unknown to the dead soldier as might be citizens in Britain, Canada, or Spain. It is a tragedy for his family, his friends and others close to him, but to Australian citizens he is no more known than the British soldiers who died in the helicopter crash and remain, to Australian citizens, unidentified.

Providing detail does not create for us a relationship with the dead Australian soldier, any more than we form a relationship with the unidentified British soldiers. What then does it do? When news media attempt to create relationships for us between the objects of news and its subjects, they are asking us to believe we are linked directly to the issues and events they report and that they consider newsworthy. If they can create a link and we believe there is a relationship, we will continue to buy news as a commodity in much the same way that we buy other goods and services that we have come to know and "trust." This idea of trust can then be linked directly to the idea of liberal democracy.

The localization of news means journalists and reporters do not have to look far beyond the ground in front of them for material. While there may be a long horizon out in front of them, they are content to search the immediate ground, going over it until it has been sterilized.

In Australia in early May 2006, a gold mine on the island state of Tasmania suffered from an earth tremor that blocked the escape of three workers. One was killed in the crush of rock that occurred, but the other two were saved by a metal cage they had been working in. Rocks lodged on top of the cage, preventing the two men from being crushed and killed. The two men were discovered to be alive a week after the event, and it took mine rescue workers a further week to free them. The story of the survival of the two men was indeed newsworthy. But for Australian television news, it became an event of unprecedented magnitude, culminating in the death of one of their own.[8]

The idea that the news media want us to imagine news as issues and events with immediacy, urgency, and threat comes undone when they are unable to achieve finality—a satisfactory newsworthy denouement—within a prescribed deadline. Witness the Tasmanian mining event. Each evening, for more than a week, television news channels attempted to beat up the rescue operation so that it would be completed when they wanted it to be completed. It took days longer, but if they had been able to orchestrate it they would have. The fact that two men's lives were in the balance was set aside in the competitive environment of news. It would come as no surprise to discover that news crews sought to have their cameras in the mine and in the small hole that had been augured as a conduit for food and water to be sent to the trapped miners. The urgency of the news deadline attempted to impose itself on the rescue.

An equally interesting example provided entertainment masquerading as news in June 2005. The revelation that 1970s news source "Deep Throat" was a former FBI agent with a penchant for posing as a Western movie gunslinger in his middle years, who was now in later life unable to properly tuck in his pajama top, came as no surprise to many. Indeed, there was always speculation that former FBI 2IC Mark Felt had provided *Washington Post* reporters Carl Bernstein and Bob Woodward with information about how far up the chain of command went knowledge of the Watergate burglary. Given the length of time since the events surrounding Richard Milhous Nixon's remarkable presidency (more than a generation), of greater interest was the motivation for publication of Felt's identity by *Vanity Fair*, a magazine that retained Bernstein as a correspondent, and, equally, the role of the *Washington Post* in chasing Nixon. For a few days in the June spring sunshine in 2005, media activity inside the Beltway was ratcheted up as speculation and counterspeculation com-

41

peted for air and print time. Amid all the debate, all the rancor, the best question came from a relatively obscure ABC reporter at the end of a soft interview with former *Post* managing editor Ben Bradlee. Bradlee, like all the remaining President's Men, came out of retirement to relive what most of them would consider the greatest moment in Washington reporting history. But Bradlee (a friend of President John Fitzgerald Kennedy) was not ready for the sharp hook at the end of the ABC line. The smiling interviewer asked him why, when the *Post* had gone in so hard at Richard Nixon's administration, it had failed to even begin to investigate some of the policies and actions of the George W. Bush regime. Bradlee appeared nonplussed by the question, and indeed he was, because it was one of the best questions ever asked. The answer to why the *Post* and other élite American news media, notably the *New York Times*, the *Baltimore Sun*, NBC, or CNN, were so long reticent in portraying the Bush administration other than in positive terms has been the subject of a lot of research.

Washington reporting, argues U.S. media expert Donald Ritchie (2005), shifted during the 20th century from centering on Capitol Hill to focusing unambiguously on the White House. Ritchie's portrait of early 20th-century syndicated reporters and columnists, notably Walter Lippmann, Joe Alsop, and Arthur Krock, provides enormous insight into the crossover between news reporting, public relations and government advising, crossover that we frown upon today. Lippmann's is an extraordinary case. As one who between World War I and World War II published a textbook on public opinion that remains current for university students, Lippmann was a columnist who never really enjoyed living in Washington when his heart lay in New York City. Like others before and after him, Lippmann cultivated personal relationships with senior government and bureaucratic types all the way up to presidents. Lyndon Johnson, while despising Washington columnists for making him the "ultimate victim of ... syndicated opinions" (Ritchie 2005, 149), nonetheless personally visited Lippmann at his Georgetown home.[9] This is unbelievable stuff. Or is it? Can we envisage Bob Woodward being visited in his Georgetown home by George W. Bush? (Does British prime minister Tony Blair have tea with journalist Martin Wolf at his home? Does Australian prime minister John Howard share a private cup of coffee with columnist Paul Sheehan?)

Élite relationships have existed across generations between reporters and highly placed government officials in the West. Reporters shift between news work and government advising, between toiling at public relations on behalf of clients, then shifting back into news reporting and opinion writing. Images of élite relationships and the generation of news are linked inexorably to the image the Western news media has of itself.

The News Media's Self-Image

The use of the local angle is not the only factor in global news investigation and production that has shifted since the beginning of the 21st century. The approach to the image the news media show of themselves has also altered. This is not necessarily a good thing. The continuing representation of Western news media's self-image has a lot to do with the casting of events of September 11, 2001.

Front covers and lead stories on front pages that parody high office have a long history in the West. As I will discuss below, the parody began in earnest in England in the 17th century with Addison and Steele's *Tatler*, *Guardian* and *Spectator* news sheets.

The *Economist*, for example, is less serious in its representation of itself and its image as an élite newspaper than it was at the end of the 20th century. The *Economist* has always positioned itself as a serious, conservative élite medium, unlike the *Spectator* or a more recent addition, the *Nation*, in which leftist libertarian humor is normative. In its existence the *Economist* is no different from other news media: it must compete hard for subscriptions and newsstand sales. In a market that is less advertising-driven, a weekly global newspaper competes poorly with the immediacy of the Internet and other electronic media. By popularizing its front cover and locally humanizing its story lead paragraphs, it is attempting to capture the imagination of a new generation of stakeholders, but in so doing it is homogenizing its product. The appalling consequence is the *Economist* reduces its voice as a supporter of economic globalization.

The particular image a global Western news medium has of its interpretation of news is tied tightly to its image of self. Investigation, interpretation and publication or broadcast of issues and events are framed by the values and traditions of the society within which the news medium operates. But, equally, the frame is circumscribed by how a particular news medium views its place in that society and what it is attempting to achieve.

When a medium can define its position relative to the society in which it is situated, it can define what it means by news. Others have attempted to define news by what it is that is being reported or investigated (see for example McNair 2000, Boyd-Barrett 2003; Tuchman 2006; 1973, 1978), but news must be defined by the factors that created the medium in the first place.

The *Economist* has always defined itself in a particular way—as a supporter of trade and trade liberalization. But since 9/11 it seems less sure of its position and more concerned with the parodying of issues and events and, indeed, the institutions that are seriously attempting to frame sociopolitical and economic globalization to create the greatest benefit for the greatest number. [This is partially its mission—to find a new model for reporting—but it is not well researched.]

The image of news and news media in the West has altered significantly since 9/11. Paradoxically for the *Economist*, most other global news producers—the *Financial Times*, the *International Herald Tribune*, the *New York Times*, the BBC and CNN have been treated with greater respect by citizens. Global media have strengthened their positions as they contrive to represent global news as an important persuasive and influential device. Towards the end of the 20th century news media had become less important. Citizens turned to alternative sources for the delivery of information. September 11, 2001, removed the confusion between news and information. Mature reporting of the catastrophic events, outside the frame defined by Tuchman as "routine," demonstrated that the boundaries between news and information had been breached. The requirement for accuracy and factual reporting that required balance and objectivity, even while being faced with an issue that was so close to Western emotions, meant large numbers of media that had attempted to position themselves as serious contenders were swept aside as citizens sought accuracy from those media they recognized as being capable of delivery. For a generation of Western news journalists and reporters, there was no routinizing the unexpected; this was not an earthquake in Indonesia that had killed six thousand. (Imagined news conference: where is Indonesia? Okay, it's in Southeast Asia. If they knew the volcano that caused the earthquake had been active for a few weeks beforehand, why didn't they do something about it?)

The image the Western global news media had of themselves during and immediately after the crisis of 9/11 has helped to sustain some and to reduce others to the infotainment media they really were, and, as I will demonstrate in the following chapter, has led conclusively to the need for adoption of a new model of reporting global news.

3

Democracy and Media: Obligations of International Participation

Defining Democracy

This chapter is interested in two important aspects of media globalization. The first is that Western news media have an obligation within the democratic frame that they operate to participate as global actors in the quest to spread the virtue of democracy. The second is that the homogenization and commodification of the Western news media prevent them from acting autonomously within the democratic system if they so desire.

Democracy is a loaded word that means different things to different stakeholders. In the West, it defines certain rights and obligations. Citizens generally understand it to mean freedom of expression. In the Middle East, it means subjugation by external powers. In Japan and other East Asian countries it has its beginnings in subjugation. So it could be thought of as a system that is not flawless and that might have been imposed on many countries and nations as an expression of the hegemony of one or two Western countries.

According to Tessler and Gao (2005) more than half the world's population at the beginning of the 21st century live within societies that might be labeled democratic. But democracy was not imposed on its originators as an econopolitical system. It began in the United States in the 18th century as a system of order and freedom that stood above those that existed in Europe—the power of the authoritarian state governed by monarchs and the landed. Democracy has existed in one form or another and has been adopted by countries with a variety of alternative systems since the 19th century. Hafez (2005) suggests democracy has occurred in history in three waves: the first in the 19th century in the United States, Canada, France, Britain and

Italy, the second in Germany (then West Germany) and Japan after World War II and the third, thirty years ago in Spain and Portugal. Hafez adds a number of other countries, but here we are interested in those countries which occupy our imagination as the *West*, another slippery term, which we will attempt to define shortly. While Argentina was among the first countries to adopt a democratic system, it does not occupy space in this narrative. Nor do India, Israel and those democratic countries of Eastern Europe—Romania, Hungary and Poland, for example—despite their recent accession into the European Union.

Our focus is on what I describe as Western news media, defined by the term *West* and how the news media act in a global sense. Despite the transition to democracy made by these countries, their media institutions do not yet fit the frame of Western news media that we are interested in here. We are however, very interested in how the Western news media report issues and events that have an impact on emerging democracies. How, for example, does the *Economist* frame the policy issue of Turkey becoming an EU member? How does it frame policy issues that relate to Japan's interest in sovereignty?

Here it becomes important to define what we mean by *West*. What factors are common to countries that mark them as Western? Language is not one because English, French, German, Italian, and Spanish are among the languages spoken in countries that we consider Western. Culture is not a common factor, nor is the economy of each country, as they vary considerably in gross domestic product and any other economic measuring device. Democracy itself is not a common factor, as many countries have a democratic system—Taiwan and South Korea for example—but they are not part of what we might consider the West in a traditional sense.

We might consider free news media to be one possibility. Free media are not necessarily part of some countries that consider themselves democratic, but it is part of those countries that call themselves Western. Historically, we might imagine the West to be Europe and to have its border at the Bosphorus. But then we have the problem of the possible accession of Turkey into the European Union, which negates the idea of a body of water forming an East-West boundary.

What then defines *Western*? Free news media seems to be the single factor. We cannot define it historically as Europe and America relative to Asia and China, nor can we define it as the non–Communist part of Europe. Free news media allow debate and opinion to exist within the public sphere. As Tepe (2005) remarks, such considerations are not part of the process in countries such as Turkey, where the government introduced a number of important reforms in 2005, but in which there was a complete lack of public debate or feedback. While the ideas of feedback and public debate have their basis in democracy, it cannot be fully appreciated unless it is combined with mediation. Tessler and Gao (2005), examining the possibility of democracy becoming part of the Middle East, question whether the theoretical support for a model of democracy in countries such as Algeria, Iraq, Jordan and Palestine include a shift towards embracing Western values as part of a democratic model.

Taxonomies of Inclusion

In an attempt to define *Western* and how it fits with media globalization and democracy, I have developed simple taxonomies that serve to illustrate the difficulty in representing *Western* in traditional forms.

Table 3.1 lists fifty countries described by the *Economist* as either capitalist or emerging markets. I have developed taxonomies for inclusion that show whether or not the countries might be considered Western. They are:

1. Allow the Operation of a Free Media
2. Operate Politically Within the Principles of Democracy
3. Operate as a Market (Capitalist) Economy
4. Use English as the Language of Business
5. Have United Nations Membership
6. Have World Trade Organization (WTO) Membership
7. Have Organization for Economic Co-operation and Development (OECD) Membership
8. Have North Atlantic Treaty Organization (NATO) membership
9. Grain Index: Wheat or Rice

Using this model, countries such as South Korea and Taiwan must be considered Western. The only distinction is in their net consumption of grain; traditional Western countries appear to be net consumers of wheat while South Korea and Taiwan are net consumers of rice. India also fits all categories, including a balance between rice and wheat consumption, whereas Singapore, long considered to be a strong economic entity, is excluded as it has no free media nor full democratic rights for citizens. Using this model, China and Russia are excluded entirely as they have none of the requirements for inclusion. South Africa would also be excluded on the basis of restricted media as would Brazil, the economy, along with China, most favored to do well in the next decade.

An interesting category is that of NATO membership. A specific requirement of the North Atlantic Treaty Organization is that countries seeking accession must demonstrate that they are democratic. Thus, we have the situation where former foes of NATO—former Russian states such as Georgia and Ukraine—have shown strong interest on joining the organization. But it also illuminates other countries which are not members—Austria, Sweden and Switzerland, particularly—as European nations and Western in all other categories (for more on NATO see chapter 6).

These taxonomies serve to identify countries in terms of their Western-ness. And for the purposes of this work the idea of Westernness also equates with democracy. But democracy is not the only option. The world remains divided about the value ascribed to democracy as an alternative to all other systems. Even within democratic countries, there are a number of conflicting views about its efficacy. At least three principles can be identified within the democratic state:

1. Liberal Democracy
2. Constitutional Democracy
3. Democratic Sovereignty

As political economist Francis Fukuyama (2006) suggests, the United States has an abiding belief in the legitimacy of constitutional democracy, yet, for Europeans, direct experience of constitutional democracy has been less than rewarding. In the United States, however, citizens apply stringent checks and balances on their internal institutions, but claim to have implicit trust in wider global affairs and in their overall democratic system, especially when the United States is involved in the dissemination of democracy in other countries.

Democracy and Its Relationship to Global News Media

Global news media have two roles to act out in the 21st century: to support global trade and to sustain democracy. Western global news

Countries	Free Market	Free Media	Demo-cratic	English (Business)	UN Member	WTO Member	OECD Member	NATO Member	Grain W/R
Australia	✓	✓	✓	✓	✓	✓	✓	x	W
Austria	✓	✓	✓	✓	✓	✓	✓	x	W
Belgium	✓	✓	✓	✓	✓	✓	✓	✓	W
Britain	✓	✓	✓	✓	✓	✓	✓	✓	W
Canada	✓	✓	✓	✓	✓	✓	✓	✓	W
Denmark	✓	✓	✓	✓	✓	✓	✓	✓	W
France	✓	✓	✓	✓	✓	✓	✓	✓	W
Germany	✓	✓	✓	✓	✓	✓	✓	✓	W
Italy	✓	✓	✓	✓	✓	✓	✓	✓	W
Japan	✓	✓	✓	✓	✓	✓	✓	x	R
Netherlands	✓	✓	✓	✓	✓	✓	✓	✓	W
Spain	✓	✓	✓	✓	✓	✓	✓	✓	W
Sweden	✓	✓	✓	✓	✓	✓	✓	x	W
Switzerland	✓	✓	✓	✓	✓	✓	✓	x	W
United States	✓	✓	✓	✓	✓	✓	✓	✓	W
China	x	x	x	x	✓	✓	x	x	R
Hong Kong	✓	x	✓	✓	x	✓	x	x	R
India	✓	✓	✓	✓	✓	✓	x	x	R
Indonesia	✓	x	✓	✓	✓	✓	x	x	R
Malaysia	✓	x	x	✓	✓	✓	x	x	R
Pakistan	x	x	x	x	✓	✓	x	x	R
Philippines	✓	x	✓	✓	✓	✓	x	x	R
Singapore	✓	x	x	✓	✓	✓	x	x	R
South Korea	✓	✓	✓	✓	✓	✓	✓	x	R
Taiwan	✓	✓	✓	✓	✓	✓	x	x	R
Thailand	✓	x	✓	✓	✓	✓	x	x	R
Argentina	✓	x	✓	x	✓	✓	x	x	W
Brazil	✓	x	✓	x	✓	✓	x	x	W
Chile	✓	x	x	x	✓	✓	x	x	W
Colombia	✓	x	x	x	✓	✓	x	x	W
Mexico	✓	x	✓	✓	✓	✓	x	x	W
Peru	✓	x	x	x	✓	✓	x	x	W
Venezuela	✓	x	x	x	✓	✓	x	x	W
Egypt	✓	x	x	x	✓	✓	x	x	W
Israel	✓	x	✓	✓	✓	✓	x	x	W
Saudi Arabia	✓	x	x	x	✓	✓	x	x	W
South Africa	✓	x	✓	✓	✓	✓	x	x	W
Czech Republic	✓	✓	✓	x	✓	✓	✓	✓	W
Hungary	✓	✓	✓	x	✓	✓	✓	✓	W
Poland	✓	x	✓	x	✓	✓	✓	✓	W
Russia	x	x	x	x	✓	x	x	x	W
Turkey	✓	x	✓	x	✓	✓	✓	✓	W

Table 3.1

media define their positions in much the same way as corporations, governments and consumer products; they devise a statement of intent which, in its brevity, is meant to encompass all the things they stand for. But only one—the *New York Times*—has really come close to the world-famous slogans of such products as Coke (*Coke Is It*) or McDonalds (*I'm Lovin It*). The *New York Times* slogan or mission statement, *All The News That's Fit to Print*, is as erudite in its intent as it is clever.

For global newspapers such as the *Economist*, the statement of intent is clear, yet at the same time provides evidence that the newspaper has a mission that must, by its statement, support the institutions that it sets out to investigate. In 2006 the statement was brought into the 21st century by outgoing editor Bill Emmott, who remarked, "the *Economist* was launched [in 1843] to campaign for free trade and all forms of liberty, what proponents and detractors alike today call globalization" (Emmott, April 1, 2006, p. 14). The *Financial Times* and the *Wall Street Journal* (along with its sister publication, the *Asian Wall Street Journal*) also have unambiguous statements of intent attached to their mastheads. For CNN, the BBC and other global broadcasters, similar statements attach to their existence and provide them and their stakeholders with a strong sense of place.

Another way of looking at the Western news media and their relationship to democracy is through the lens of time. News media, and the transnational corporations that own them, operate on the basis of profit and short-term reporting periods to investors and other stakeholders. Profit reporting, once an annualized affair, is now something that occurs in most corporations on a quarterly basis. Every four months, business units report on their profitability and, if they are below budget, strategies are altered to increase profits. The focus of the corporation is on the short-term nature of such goals and the ability of its component parts to continue to increase profits for all types of stakeholders.

Democracy and its pursuits is not like the pursuit of corporate profit. For democracy to be profitable it must go through a transformative process that refashions existing institutions, displaces old ideas and presents communities under the proposed democratic umbrella with social, cultural and political alternatives that take time to assess and agree to. It is a slow process and not in accord with the short-term profit reporting of transnationals.

The pursuit of democratic systems beyond those existing around the world is linked directly to the three-cornered relationship between the transnational corporation, hegemonic states such as the United States and China, and the idea that solutions to all problems are easily and quickly found as they must be for the survival of large transnationals and states.

In this the Western news media play a significant role. As the editor of the *Economist* states above, the very existence of that newspaper is the pursuit of free trade and all forms of liberty. It would not be unreasonable to suggest that the *Economist* has a great number of fellow travelers among what might be considered global news media, most notably the *New York Times*, the *International Herald Tribune* (owned by the *New York Times* Company), the *Times*, CNN, the BBC, and the *Wall Street Journal*. But such a statement requires some investigation into why these news media have little differentiation; why in fact they are becoming more homogenized, even to the extent that a perceived public broadcaster such as the BBC can be considered a medium that pursues free trade and liberty. In other words, the proposition that the world's leading public broadcaster, invented to pursue checks and balances on government and the management of the welfare state in the constitutional democracy of the United Kingdom, has come to be considered a supporter of globalization. This is not a difficult concept to grasp if we investigate the idea that the Western news media shifted towards homogenization during the latter part of the 20th century. The shift has its basis in the liberalization of trade, and news is a competitive commodity.

If You're Not with Us, You're against Us

President George W. Bush's response to the September 11, 2001, attacks on the World Trade Center and the Pentagon invoked a vast number of media words and images of good and evil. The problem for the Western news media lay in how to identify their reporting of such a binary opposition without appearing themselves to support the opposing position. While supporting the principle of democracy in which the Western news media operates, they were also required to question the legitimacy of the binary split and its consequences. Its consequences, of course, were the declaration of war against Iraq, a declaration which was not supported by the world's most important democratic institution, the United Nations, nor other important global organizations such as the OECD, NATO or Association of South East Asian Nations. At one end of the binary lie media organizations such as Fox News which, like the *Economist*, supports free trade and the virtue of liberal democracy. But opponents of Fox News, leftist academics specifically, argue that evangelical pursuit of one position without question is as dangerous as the imagined response from the other end, state-sponsored news media such as exists in China or Russia, to name two.

Origins of Partisan Media and Their Link to Democracy

Today's Western news media were shaped by events and issues that began in England three hundred years ago. I have invoked the three-hundred-year time frame specifically as it has broad ramifications for this work in both its presentation of globalization, presentation of the news media as one of the driving agents that assisted in framing globalization, and for the significance of what Australian economic historicist Graeme Snooks (1998) calls "longrun dynamics."

Within the three-hundred-year frame, I have already discussed in chapter 1 the idea that generational change—thirty-year narratives—can be conceived and imagined for all types of issues and events. Specifically I have discussed what took place in the mid–1970s and how changes in news media processes have occurred since then. I have also imagined additional changes within the next thirty years—up until 2036—a period that closes off Snooks' three hundred years as a "long run" and that also draws in the possibility of the period required for the Western news media to alter their direction if they are to refashion themselves before they become historical artifacts. But more of that later.

Before embarking upon an explanation of why the idea of long-run dynamics is crucial to an understanding of Western news media and their relationship to globalization, we need to come to terms with another important idea: the relationship of time to historical issues and events and the nature of news reporting as a natural diurnal process that has shifted in emphasis to issues and events without a definitive starting point and stopping point, the image of issues and events in continuity 24/7.

The historical position of the consciousness of the diurnal form can be traced to 17th-century Europe. In terms of the life span of modernity this is close to the period when imagination began to reveal itself as part of the shift away from the obvious. Imagination had existed, but not until the expansion of empires and vast ocean crossings did it embrace the parallel expanses of the mind.

There is a huge difficulty for us as human beings living at the beginning of the 21st century in which we have compressed time and space and taken advantage of technology. We can log on to the Net and imagine ourselves as part of any global issue or event, and in fact we are persuaded by the media that we are obligated to participate in global and local issues and events by registering our vote (as public opinion) on a variety of news media Web sites embracing everything from whether we like the color of UN secretary-general Ban Ki-moon's suit and tie to whether we agree or disagree with the incarceration of political prisoners at Guantanamo Bay.[1]

Such immediacy means we in the 21st century have either a limited grasp or no grasp of the image of the carriage of news as it was before the invention of the telegraph, the invention of the telephone, and the invention of the Internet. Imagine for a moment the idea that we are in Raleigh, North Carolina, in the early 18th century. We are going about our business—which might be any type of activity that generates income, manufacturing small arms, for example—the production of which requires us to think about our competitive position in the local market. Within the next few weeks a ship is due to arrive in Baltimore. On it, we are yet to know, is a comparable product to ours that is being manufactured in England. It is cheaper and easier to use. We want to know more about this product so we can compete effectively. On the next ship, we dispatch our trusted marketing manager. He will remain at sea for six weeks. He will then take three weeks to travel by horse and carriage to the place in the north of England where the rival product is manufactured. On arrival, he will be given a tour of the factory. He will make notes, especially about the use of labor, and a short time later begin his journey home. On the journey he will be confronted by hostile highwaymen in England and pirates in the Atlantic. The Atlantic crossing will be forced to detour and lay up for three weeks in Canada due to poor weather. Our marketing manager attempts to make his way home overland. He will eventually arrive home and we will begin to put in place the changes we require to remain competitive with the same product made in England and shipped to America. Sound familiar? Of course not. Today, marketing managers reverse engineer competitive products whose designs have been downloaded from the Internet. It takes a matter of hours. Our 18th-century manager took months to gather the information.

But the most interesting thing about this imagined anecdote is that one thing has changed very little in the past three hundred years and that is the dissemination of information as news. While our market-ing manager may not have picked up a copy of a trade magazine while in England, a trade magazine that might have supplied him with addi-tional information about his competitors, he may have been quick to spend a night or two in London and to sniff out one of the newly cre-ated and vital coffeehouses, possibly Button's, where he would have made conversation and read the latest issue of the *Tatler*. Our man-ager, being absorbed in business, may have been less interested or informed about politics and thus would have read the *Tatler* not as a Whiggishly focused news sheet but as an accurate record of the polit-ical state in England at the time. The *Tatler* was, though, a political publication produced by Richard Steele. It was the forerunner of other Steele publications, some in collaboration with Joseph Addison, most notably the *Spectator* and the *Guardian* mentioned earlier.[2] In the long space of time since Steele wrote and published, very little has changed in the way news is reported as commentary on issues and events. The daily newspaper adopted commentary before Steele had published the last edition of the *Guardian* in 1713.

If we combine the idea of diurnal form—the daily reporting of issues and events as news—with the idea of long-run dynamics, we come to a point where we can understand how Western news report-ing has been locked in place for such a long period of time without any need to alter its reporting practices.

The Inductive of Western Global News

The news media journalism model we have in the West at the beginning of the 21st century began in the early to mid–18th century. By 2036, it will have been in existence for more than three hundred years. While the idea that any type of model—a business model, a political model or a societal model—can sustain an existence for three centuries appears at first glance to be a ridiculous proposition, this is what the Western news media has succeeded in doing, with minor adjustments.

Part of the answer to the continuity of the Western news media informational model lies in its adoption of the principles of deductive reasoning, a paradoxical position, given journalism is, by its nature, inductive. Snooks (1998), drawing on Mill and others, argues that the problem for induction and why deduction has maintained its hege-monic position for so long (coincidentally, around three hundred years) is that induction, or empirical observations, are difficult to attach to a theoretical position. Thus, deductivism, or logic, is more easily argued because of the importance of technical skills such as deductive logic, mathematics and statistics. While technical skills, Snooks argues, can be quickly acquired, realist imagination emerges only slowly. This argument provides strong evidence to support the notion that the model of Western news reporting has survived for three hundred years because it is underpinned by a deductivist informational model. It has supported and paralleled its history with scientific deduction manifesting as comment and opinion. However, while it has a number of side attachments that are logical—reporting economic news—news as observable truths is inherently inductive, and relies on the emergence throughout historical time of issues and events that can be reported as news, as they are imagined directly by the observer journalist. The problem for the Western news media and the crucial events of 9/11, lies in their absolute inductiveness. The informational model of interpretation was as inadequate for reporting the tragic events just as it is inadequate for reporting other global issues or events of such magnitude. This provides part of the answer to the question of why news media report democracy in such a way and why they are obligated to do so: democracy is also an inductive or empirical model. It must by its nature be imagined historically through the long-run establishment of its institutions. It cannot be grounded in anything other than history.

If, however, as Snooks suggests, an antihistoricist campaign was undertaken in the 1950s by Karl Popper, Ludwig Von Mises and others to present inductive reasoning or empiricism as a tool of totalitarianism, then how can we argue today that empiricism is aligned with democracy, when democracy is the binary opposite of totalitarianism? Does this mean that democracy has shifted to a position that is similar to totalitarianism or does it mean, if we work from a circular argument, that the tools of democracy and totalitarianism are similar? Does this mean that institutions are either inductive or deductive? Are all institutions the same? Are transnationals inductive or deductive or do they borrow elements of both to support a third position?

If we consider democracy to exist when certain things are in place —government by the people, government in which the power resides in the people and is exercised by them either directly or through elected representatives, a form of society in which exist equal rights, tolerance of minority views and no hereditary or class distinctions—then we can safely argue that these things come about through observations, or induction, rather than deduction. But this places the idea of democracy at odds with the present deductive model of journalism and news gathering.

Let's look at democracy in a different way. Maybe it has all those things mentioned, but like communism and fascism—democracy's authoritarian and binary opposites—it rests on historical principles. If induction can be described as a process of inferring something through the process of observation of particular instances, then democracy emerged as a process of observing alternative models.

Modern democracy was invented in the late 16th century in opposition to societal models that were running out of time. But they were running out of time because they were being observed from positions that were not part of the hegemony of the institutions that sustained the alternative models. Inductive processes allowed democracy to manifest itself—revolutions in France, America and Britain among them. Democracy was borne from induction. Supporters of the alternative systems of authority used deduction, or logic, to evaluate the possibility that their models would be sustained. To their eventual surprise, it was not to be.

Citizens who live in social systems that are democratic, like journalists, need to observe and investigate—to empirically determine—what it is that is going on around them and what it is that makes their society function properly. If they can see that the roads on which they drive every day are deteriorating, then they will focus on the cause of the irritation, which is most likely to be the local government that is obligated to maintain the roads. If their public transport does not work as well as they expect, or their public hospital system is incapable of meeting demand, then again they will focus on the cause of the problems, namely government.

We can see then that democracy is a historical sequence of observations and that its empirical nature should provide Western news media with a symbiotic function within democracy that requires them to report global issues and events as they are observed. We can take the metaphor a step further and see that the Western news media has in fact sustained democracy through its empirical observations and reporting of democracy's successes during the past three hundred years. But it has done so obliquely. It is unable to engage directly because of its oppositional mode. If this argument appears reasonable we should look to the observations and reporting of a particular example to sustain it. Let's look at the case of Iran and its coverage by the *Economist* to see how it might have tracked that country's relationship with the West.

In its May 6, 2006, edition, the *Economist* attempted to balance its coverage of Iran's potential for developing nuclear weapons as both deductive and inductive. In the opening few pages, the newspaper provided editorial critiques of issues and events under the banner of leader. The leader on Iran, headlined euphemistically, "Unstoppable? Be tough now to prevent military conflict later" (*Economist* May 6, 2006, p. 11), presented a deductive argument based on logic: if Iran was going to continue to gather nuclear components and fuel, and defy International Atomic Energy Agency (IAEA) and UN directives, then it was making nuclear weapons. The natural position for any Western news media is adopted in this leader. It is the position of fear.

In an accompanying three-page essay titled "Special Report: Iran and the Bomb," the *Economist* acted inductively. It provided investigative reporting of facts and historical images of the relationship between Iran and its Middle Eastern neighbors. Its coverage of the issue and the potentially catastrophic event allowed its stakeholders to make deliberative assessments based on both inductive and deductive reasoning.

This is not an unusual approach to how a news medium takes a sociopolitical position. It may advocate using both historical evidence to ground its position and logical argument to show what it thinks should happen in the future. In the Iran example, the *Economist* suggested that diplomacy remained the most important tactic to avert the potential crisis but that the rhetoric of both the Iranian "outpost of tyranny" and the U.S. "great Satan" may limit diplomatic potential (*Economist* May 6, 2006, p. 23).

The problem for news reportage is its limited ability to act presciently in its deductiveness. News material may be framed in a similar way from week to week, but the direction it attempts to take with its editorial policy may not always be accurate.

According to Ladan Abdorrahman, director and co-founder of the Moroumand Foundation for the Promotion of Human Rights and Democracy in Iran, the Western news media have been duped by the communication tactics and the political and social rhetoric of the Iranian authorities.

Even in small localized issues and events such as the gold mine cave-in in Tasmania, mentioned in the previous chapter, news media must frequently speculate—and thus deduce—what might happen rather than investigating and reporting what is evolving.

Of course, there is an argument that reporting what is evolving is simply reporting history and that history is immediately not new, but old. But it is new at some precise point in time and, like our intrepid marketing manager, despite some long time delays, the delivery of what is available at the time is news. For the television reporters covering the gold mine cave-in and the long process of drilling though hard rock to rescue the trapped miners, immediacy and urgency that are the hallmarks of television news were unavailable because it took days for the rescuers to drill through the rock. This meant the news media had to deduce what might happen using logic rather than empirical evidence to deliver material to camera. When you have a lot of people and a lot of technology tied up at one site in a remote location at the end of the earth, you need to produce something more than the image of being patient. Fortunately for the news media at the mine site, one of their own decided it was the right time to suffer a heart attack and die, giving the gathered reporters and journalists, something immediately, if not disturbingly, close.

The News Media and Democracy

The Economist newspaper has a particular view of democracy and the democratic process. As its retiring editor remarked in April 2006, the newspaper is a vehicle for the campaign of free trade and liberty in all its forms and, thus, its policy of reporting is to devote two-thirds of its space to factual description and a third to opinion and critical analysis. While the *Economist* does not provide an outline of its policy on democracy, the foregoing on liberty and free trade can be conflated with any number of articles and opinions it produces each week to determine its position. And, like most other Western global news media, it is an interesting position with its basis in economics, politics and overt support of globalization. If we examine its reporting of the resignation of the Thai prime minister Thaksin Shinawatra in early April 2006, we get a strong feel for the position of the newspaper and its interpretation of democracy, which appears to be more ambiguous than first imagined.

In its self-described leader, the newspaper argued that the Thai élites who appeared to have run the campaign of street protests that had become the catalyst for Mr. Thaksin's resignation had been undemocratic in exercising their strategy. It stated the "spectacle of an urban élite overthrowing an elected leader, one who enjoyed great popularity among the rural poor whom he genuinely helped, is not only distasteful but potentially dangerous" (April 8, 2006, p. 13). It continued the fear metaphor by invoking other East Asian democracies which had, and could again with the provocation of minorities, drive elected representatives from office, namely the Philippines and Indonesia.

But the "undemocratic" strategy of a minority opposition had its basis in the democratic process. All those opposed to a regime can, as part of the process, apply strategies and tactics within the rule of law (rule of law being the first principle of sovereign democracy) that are aimed at the goal of overthrowing the regime. The *Economist* was unhappy that a minority of élites had been able to successfully apply a campaign to the process. It suggested the correct way to get rid of Mr. Thaksin—if that was what was wanted—was to do so at the ballot box, the most important single political element in democracy. But the campaign undertaken by the opposition, and the tactics used by the main parties to boycott the early April poll, and to use street rallies to disrupt business and traffic in the country's capital, Bangkok, were legitimate tactics that have been used successfully in the world's greatest democracies.[3]

The difficulty for a newspaper lies in how much support it can offer to some democracies and how little to others; how much it can be seen to be supporting the Western institutions of globalization while imploring emerging democracies to embrace trade liberalization as the answer to their struggle against poverty and poor human rights. In most of the world's oldest democracies, élites and the news media work together to support the democratic process. Elections are considered fair and equitable, news media report the candidates and parties before the poll, make predictions on who will lose, then provide comment and opinion after the event. Street rallies, street theater, media advertising, direct publicity to voters are all part of the legitimacy of the democratic process. There is rarely a suggestion that élites, even when they are in a minority, would be unscrupulous enough to shut down business or disrupt economic events.

Towards emerging democracies, Western news media represent a paternalistically benign view that is in keeping with how they see their own entrenched democracies. They expect the emerging democracies to play strictly by the rules. This view represents the unambiguous position argued by the *Economist* as its reason for existence; free trade and liberty are the grounding principles of its existence, and for it to be maintained it must assist the process of democracy throughout the countries in which globalized trade will continue to seek its manufacturing base. It supports this argument in its story on the problems in the Thai case by highlighting certain global issues that the prime minister's resignation has stalled: a proposed free trade agreement with the United States, a court rejection of the proposed privatization of an electricity generator, and government plans for increased spending on infrastructure projects such as transport. The reporting is thus a rebuke. It is aimed at the Thai élites and the opposition parties which it claims have a "duty" to rejoin the democratic process and to allow Thailand to take its place among world democracies. It is a persuasive argument in support of democracy, and it supports the newspaper's preferred position. It is an enormously generous position in terms of its obligation to participation—the title of this chapter.

A news medium demonstrates its obligation to participate in the democratic process by publishing in a certain way. It acts, as Macauley (1910) suggests, as a fourth estate, providing checks and balances against the insouciant comings and goings of elected parliaments and governments. In this the *Economist* attempts to place itself at the forefront, but, as we will see, despite Emmett's argument that "scepticism about government drips from every issue" (*Economist* April 1, 2006, p. 14). The *Economist* was always a journal of globalization rather than one of record or member of a fourth estate.

Obligations to Participation

Just as the *Economist* argues the opposition parties in Thailand must rejoin the democratic process out of a sense of obligation, so the wider news media in the Western world present an image of obligation to democracy by reporting certain issues and events. But this does not mean that they are discharging their obligations successfully. Indeed, the homogenization of the Western news media precludes them from discharging their obligation effectively. The *Economist* is the first to admit that, by supporting the U.S. case for war against Iraq in 2003, it failed to discharge its obligation. In the following discussion we will investigate how the *Economist* abrogated its responsibility and why it is impossible in a globalized world for media to even consider such an obligation, despite their statements of intent.

Like *Tatler*, today's media are more interested in igniting conflict in issues than in acting as observer and reporter. Witness the case of the Western news media frenzy when attempting to ignite conflict around U.S. secretary of defense Donald Rumsfeld in early 2006. The issue of a handful of dispirited former generals opposed to Rumsfeld's policies was quickly killed off when there appeared to be no real interest from the activists' intended stakeholder publics. It was kept alive for longer than it deserved in particular parts of the world: those countries where the news media disagreed with the policy of the governments who joined the "Coalition of the Willing" and declared war on Iraq in 2003. News media in these countries, particularly Australia and the United Kingdom, unlike the *Economist* (which we are considering to be a global medium) were opposed to their country's active involvement in the conflict. To be on the wrong side of a policy decision, as we will see below, creates a bitter struggle within the leading news media for a rebalancing of the ledger. When an issue can be reignited by an activist group such as the former generals, then the news media will allow it to become its leading news despite its imbalance and lack of newsworthiness as a leading story.

Within a democracy, the idea of news media acting as a balance between opposing powers is a nonsense. There are too many conflicting stakeholder interests imposing their persuasive and influential issues and events for the news media to be capable of observing and reporting in a balanced fashion. What becomes important is the news media's ability to self-fashion issues and events so they fit the agenda being presented as news.

In a democracy, news is something that affects every citizen in one way or another. But an average citizen in Germany or New Zealand, for example, is uninterested in the political and economic problems of an emerging democracy such as Thailand. If an average German or New Zealand citizen knows anything at all about Thailand, it is related to their proposed vacation, Bangkok's relatively cheap duty-free consumer goods and the belief that all Thais are friendly. They will become interested in the politics of Thailand only when it affects them directly. If there is a likelihood that during their vacation they will be subject to violence in the streets of Bangkok, they may consider changing their travel plans.[4]

Contrary to what is believed in most Western democracies, democracy itself is not the main requirement of a strong country or nation for it to engage with globalization. China provides the most striking example of a country that has become powerful, indeed almost too powerful, in the global, without engaging in the idea of democracy as some in the West understand it to be. China's news media is neither free, democratic nor appearing to embrace democratic principles, yet it is a vital component in the campaign by the Chinese government to inform its citizens of its participation and drive for leadership in a globalized economic market. So we cannot argue that democracy and a strong independent media are important elements of globalization. What we can argue is that news media in nondemocracies will operate within a globalized economic system the same way as news media operate within democracies: to ensure the well-being of the country or nation in which they are located. This is the biggest issue for news media in their obligation to participate in global economics and politics. They must weigh how much global news they present to their local citizens as being relevant to their everyday existence against the news they present to them as local. In this they fail to deliver global news.

Does this mean then that, in a democracy, the obligation of the news media to participate by observing and reporting socioeconomic and sociopolitical issues and events of a global nature is for the benefit of that country's citizens? I suggest that citizens within democracies, average citizens, are of no more interest to the news media of that country than are the average citizens of those countries claiming to be emerging democracies that news media in entrenched democracies claim to defend. In Western democracies, the news media imagine themselves as acting in the interests of the majority, but in so doing they are self-deluded, as they act continuously in the interests of the élites, in the same way that the news media in emerging democracies such as Thailand act to support those they consider hegemonic.

So if democracy is not the single most important requirement of engagement in a globalized system, what is?

For the Western news media to fullfil their obligations to international participation they must abandon their parochial and patriarchal image of the rest of the world. But this is not something that they have been willing to embark upon since the success of the establishment of Richard Steele's *Tatler* three hundred years ago. What Steele and his publishing partner Joseph Addison struck upon was a method of information dissemination as opinion—a tactic that resonated strongly with their chosen stakeholder publics; the élites, the merchant classes and the literate. Today's news media use the same method of delivery of information as news, employing the informational model as opinion and interpretation. Globalized trade and politics require knowledge and information that may previously have been of little interest to those with no direct financial involvement. For Steele and other élites of the 18th century, there were no "mom and dad" stockholders, no 97 percent literacy rate and no full employment as we know them today. There was, therefore, no requirement to pitch their publications anywhere but at those stakeholders with whom they were most familiar.

For the Western news media of the early 21st century the overarching image is of a citizenry that exists pretty much as it did three hundred years ago. They see citizens as unable to grasp the big picture of globalization. So they provide images of it in much the same way that *Tatler*, *Guardian* and *Spectator* would have provided images of international trade as impenetrable to Irish farmers, Scottish fishermen or West Virginia coal miners as $E = MC^2$. Part of the reason the Western news media imagine citizens in this way lies in its own desire for professionalization and acceptance within the élite sphere occupied by lawyers and medical practitioners, among others. But as Hallin and Mancini (2004) argue, the issue for journalism is one of the level of professionalization that occurs within different media systems. Thus, journalism is locked into a constant struggle with itself to provide an image of self that is above those it professes to serve.

A New Model for Global News

When the *Economist* reports from various places in the world, it does so using two possible sources: a paid reporter attached to the newspaper as a full-time staff member, or a "stringer," a journalist who may work for other organizations but has also a strong knowledge of the local issues and events and is retained by the *Economist*. The stringer is an interesting character in both the journalistic sense and the democratic sense. A stringer is not the same as a freelance reporter because the stringer has the luxury of reporting on a regular basis for various media, but lives with the assurance of a regular payment. This provides some degree of consistency, but it also allows the individual to present news in a different way from the freelancer.

Stringers are usually retained because they have the same political ideology as the medium for which they are writing. So a stringer in Thailand, for example, may be a Thai national also working full-

time for the *Bangkok Post*. A stringer in Australia may work full-time
for a British newspaper, such as the *Independent*, while a stringer in
India works part-time for the *Times* of India. By their nature the journalist working as a stringer understands the editorial policy of the
Economist in the same way that the full-time staff writer in the United
States, Britain, Canada or Hong Kong understands the policy and ideology; filed copy will reflect a local angle while being framed within
the policy supporting free trade and liberal democracy.

The convergence of different states into trade-oriented instruments has created a convergence in media systems, particularly news
and how it is gathered, interpreted and disseminated. The drive is
towards the liberal democratic model. Thus, convergence in news
media in the West has caused other media systems, particularly in
East Asia and the Middle East, to look elsewhere for the adoption of
professional ideologies and practice. Instead of adopting U.S. and
British models, looking elsewhere will eventually result in the West
also looking elsewhere, possibly to the East to rethink their models.
This has already begun with the television model practiced by Al
Jazeera.

It is quite conceivable that Western news media convergence can
lead to the development of an alternative model. Convergence and its
attached homogeneity might fit the requirement of globalization but
they do not fit the constant of localization of news. Liberal democracy is the model that most Western news media support and it is the
model that they expect developing countries to adopt if they are to
become members and beneficiaries in the globalized world trade market. In this there are external influences on homogenization and internal influences in the struggle for individuality. But the reality is that
global media disengage with citizens and engage with institutions,
which in itself supports the media position on global democracy. But
as Fukuyama (2006a) and French scholar Olivier Roy (2004) point
out, democracy is not necessarily the most appropriate model for all
countries. This is, however, the message conveyed by the Western news
media because they have converged and refashioned themselves as
part of global democratization. They see themselves as part of the
global push for liberal democracy as the best system because all Western news media is now, in some ways, part of the liberal democratic
model.

4

The Power Triangle: Media, Corporations and Governments

The Tau of Globalization

Globalization rests on a three-pillared platform. The pillars are each as strong as one another and represent corporations, governments and the news media. Without the recognition of the importance of all three pillars, the platform would list dangerously. On the platform sit the institutions of globalization: the United Nations, the World Trade Organization, the World Bank, the International Monetary Fund and others. Chapters 6, 7 and 8 discuss in detail the role of these institutions. For now it is important to understand why the three pillars exist and why they are mutually supportive, despite the occasional image presented by the news media that the pillars are in danger of collapse.[1]

In the ancient world the idea of three columns as a strong support structure had its basis in the reality and the myth that three elements provided security against attack or danger. A "three-pronged attack," a phrase used widely in Western military strategy, is not coincidental.

While the diurnal has played a vital role in the conceptualization and manufacture of time and space, a third dimension is required for perspective and depth of field. As a physical principle, when the temperature and pressure at which the solid, liquid, and vapor phases of a pure substance can coexist in equilibrium, it is known as a triple point. In Roman history the original meaning of *tribe* was ascribed to the three political divisions of people, and in Christian (read Western) theology, the Trinity is the most important aspect of its existence. Nations use three colors on flags to define their existence (the French tricolor, for example).

An understanding of how the three pillars lock together to support the institutions of globalization lies in their shape. For this I have invoked the idea of the Tau, or T-shape, where two pillars at each end of the top of the T represent national government and national and transnational corporations, and the pillar at the base of the T represents global news media. The closeness of the two pillars at the top of the T will become evident shortly. The elevation of the T, where all three pillars are at the same height is also important, as sheltering underneath the platform are all other sociopolitical and socioeconomic entities: citizens, domestic non governmental organizations, provincial governments, developing countries, and religious orders, to name only a few.

The Reality of Corporations

Since its birth, the Western news media have been sustained by the actions of corporations. In early 18th-century England the existence of the East India Company provided sustenance for all types of news media. Some news media (Daniel Defoe's *Review*, Jonathan Swift's *Examiner*, the *London Gazette*, and the *British Merchant*, as examples) applauded imperialism and the expansion of trade while others (the *Craftsman*, *Gentleman's Magazine*) came into being towards the middle of the century opposed to both.

Corporations, by their very existence and the actions that play out through them, create news. A corporation is a legal entity made up of the individuals it is composed of who have no legal corporate status as individuals. The dominance of the corporation in Western liberal democracies lies in its pursuit of profit and the ideology of conservatism. At times, the Western news media present images of corporations as trendy and leftist (usually information technology corporations) but, in reality, the nature of the corporation is conservative. It exists to make profits for narrow groups of stakeholders rather than the provision of wealth or socialization of profits to a wider constituency.

A transnational corporation is one which has adopted the Latin preposition *trans*, meaning "across" or "over." Thus, a transnational corporation moves across national borders or over oceans to "transact" business.[2]

Corporations are tied inexorably to national governments and to the news media. As German philosopher Jurgen Habermas points out, in the early part of the 18th century the public sphere was alive with issues and events imagined by the newly created news media supporting corporate and government activity. Indeed, the news media was most often established by the government of the day to support its legislative activity, which itself endorsed and funded corporate imperialism as expeditions in search of ever more important resources being discovered in "the new world."

While small and medium enterprises (SMEs) in the West provide goods and services to a wide range of customers, nothing compares with the volume and economies of scale that can be applied to a market economy by a corporation. SMEs operate from factories and offices often only located as strategically as limited financial and other resources allow, but corporations transcend all boundaries, establishing manufacturing plants in developing countries where labor costs are realistic, and setting up service industries in countries were technology is cheap and plentiful.

This is an issue that is taken on by globalization protesters and which receives inordinate coverage in Western news media. But the reason for such broad coverage lies in the position of the news media as one of the Tau pillars: it cannot directly be seen to undermine the other two pillars, yet its sociopolitical responsibility to report objectively means it must find a third person to enact its instinctive protests. Hence the exorbitant coverage provided for the antiglobalizers.

But the real reason why corporations receive so much attention from antiglobalizers and nonplussed citizens, and why they in turn receive so much negative coverage from the news media, lies in the fact that corporations, unlike SMEs, live in large buildings in which there is tight security protecting the human resources of the corporation, the financial and economic resources and the core competencies that provide comparative advantage. A bank, for example, cannot leave pallet-loads of cash lying around as inventory in its yard or warehouse, as can a SME leave sheets of metal, plastic or other components waiting to be fabricated into consumer products. And while citizens have access to retail stores, street vendors, or SMEs such as motor mechanics, the same is not true of corporations, which are most often housed in skyscrapers with one well-guarded entrance. Citizens, along with news media, do not have free access to corporations. News media have restricted access when the corporation is intent on disseminating information to become news, but otherwise access is either denied or restricted for them too.

Corporations, as I have already mentioned, are comprised of individuals who combine to create a legal entity, thus the individuals within a corporation bring to it individual skills and knowledge that allow it to succeed. In this a corporation is no different from any other organization: a university, a government department, or a defense force. The single most important difference—and one that is overplayed by the news media—is the corporate pursuit of profit over all other goals and objectives.

But persuasion and influence—both external and internal—are now playing a major role in the way corporations act, domestically and globally. Influence from internal and external stakeholders—employees, shareholders, suppliers, and customers—has created for the corporation the need to view profit as part of a wider obligation to the future of the planet. Thus, the terms *corporate social responsibility* and *environmental awareness* have come into play and to sit beside fiscal responsibility as important functions of the corporation.

Corporate social responsibility is relatively new in rhetorical terms, but it has been in existence in the Western world since the 19th century. It grew in the late 20th century out of the idea that corporations ought to be interested in more than the single-entry bottom line of profit. If they were to actively pursue a balanced existence, so the line of reasoning suggested, then profit must live side by side with social equity and a concern for the physical environment in which the corporation existed. This thinking shaped "triple bottom line" reporting: the idea that a corporation must place equal value on its social and environmental position as it does on profit, and that it must "report" all three as results to stakeholders (citizens as well as shareholders). While there is a strong rhetorical sense of triple bottom line reporting being communicated to stakeholders by corporations at the beginning of the 21st century, the idea of corporate social responsibility has its genesis in the tabling of legislation in England in the early 19th century. The *Health and Morals of Apprentices Act*, tabled in the British Parliament by Robert Peel in 1802, followed concern that children living in poverty in London were being forced to travel to the north of England to work in new cotton and wool processing factories and to work at all hours of the day and night where no parent or other relative might be interested in their well-being. The idea that legislation was required to persuade those early corporations to undertake socially responsible measures to secure the well-being of their employees assumes corporations were interested in nothing other than profit. Similarly, legislation was required across the Western world in the 20th century to secure corporate responsibility in order to secure the well-being of the physical environment of the planet. Again, the corporation appears to have been motivated first by profit.

Corporate social responsibility is a catchy rhetorical device that embraces all the social elements of triple bottom line accountability. It is the subject of international conferences and discussions in which corporate communicators present their credentials for sustainable business activity that is conscious of, and engaged with, the widest possible stakeholder interests imaginable. Thus, it has tactical relationship building and framing objectives. But corporate social responsibility is equally a natural position for the large transnational company and the small domestic business. The idea that a corporation requires legislative proscription to act responsibly is no different from individuals being proscribed by law so that they will drive their cars responsibly: it has relevance to a minority. Like individuals, most corporations and businesses will exercise judgment in any given situation and act responsibly.[3]

Corporate social responsibility rests on the notion of value. It makes assumptions about equating corporate values with societal and community values. But the idea that corporations will think seriously about long-term sustainable relationships avoids the reality of the short-term profit goal. Where once corporate profit reporting periods were as long as twelve months, in the late 20th century the shorter reporting period—quarterly—became widespread. Corporations, like all competitive environments, live by their ability to sustain a comparative advantage and in this the shorter the reporting period, the happier the shareholders. Motor vehicle sales, for example, are reported against monthly budgets and in the retail sector, sales budgets and forecasts are reported weekly. The question that this raises relates to the sustainability of long-term environmental and social goals when short-term profits are a substantial requirement of corporate shareholders.

Corporations and National Politics

While corporations are at liberty to transcend national borders and boundaries, they must at the same time live within the proscriptive legislation of those nations in which they take up residence. In this there are a number of flexibilities that become the focus for global Western news reporting.

National governments, as we will see in more detail in a moment, are responsible for social, political and economic stability within their democratic sovereignty. To act economically responsible, a national government must consider offering incentives to corporations so that they will set up shop in their country rather than their neighbor's. Naturally enough, corporations play on such strategies to gain the greatest advantage for themselves and their shareholders. This is a simple and obvious position. If the first principle of the corporation is to make a profit for shareholders, it will locate its activity where it can gain a competitive advantage from relatively cheap resources such as labor, energy and raw materials. If raw materials such as textiles can be shipped conveniently and cheaply from Europe to China, then an Australian clothing manufacturer is likely to take advantage of cheap labor costs in China rather than ponder the social responsibility of locating the clothing factory in Australia, unless the national government of Australia provides some flexibility or incentive for the clothing manufacturer that offsets the high costs of labor in Australia, against some other resources, such as energy.

And this is the point of a lot of the protests against the transnational corporation and its location of its production of goods and services. The same argument is made by American news media and citizens against the United States locating its telecommunications services in countries such as India. But this is the reality of globalization.

For corporations, the issue is one of national governments being interested in attracting corporate activity by offering incentives. For national governments the issue is the reality that corporations are transnational—they own and operate goods and services in any number of countries—and they are flexible enough to cross any boundary in pursuit of their goals and objectives. But corporations are not so dopey that they will cross borders where there is the likelihood of political instability. They are less likely to set up shop in North Korea or Russia, and are even hesitant about setting up in China, despite that country's small shift towards a market economy. Thus, a stable liberal democracy or the potential to move towards such a thing becomes the driving criterion of developing nations as they seek to secure a share of the corporate world's economic production. For established democracies, where inputs such as labor, energy and raw materials are more expensive, there must be alternative incentives if they are to attract the economic benefits of corporate goods and services production processes. Stable democracy is the most transparent.

But it is not enough. National governments create political positions that are opaque in their attractiveness to corporations. So it is here that the role of the Western global news media becomes important in investigating and reporting the links that develop between national governments and corporations, but reside outside the rhetoric of both and their generally positive rhetoric on globalization.

Kraus and Davis (1976) argue that political theorists historically considered news media to be part of the political process, a condition which allowed them to simply appear to reinforce élite leadership and to disseminate policy decisions as a one-way process intent on legitimizing political institutions and the actions of leaders.

Imagining the Corporate World

The difficulty for the global Western news media is in how to report the issues and events that transnational corporations act out—specifically those that appear to reduce domestic fortunes such as labor, which in turn affect domestic issues such as health and education. The resiting of a manufacturing plant from Peoria, Illinois, to Shanghai, China, has ramifications that are more complex than a Western news medium can report in a few pages or sound bites. The issue for the news media—their editors, producers, and journalists—is one of support for the global actions of the corporation, while maintaining a sympathetic position for the plight of the domestic town or city that has lost its economic sustainability.

The paradox lies in the Western news media—the agents through which global issues and events are reported as news—being mostly owned by corporations. It is easy for local newspapers and radio stations in Canada, for example, to work up a negative frame for news of a factory closure in a small town in western Ontario, the closure of which was brought about by the corporate owner's decision to relocate in China. It might even be acceptable for a network television station to report using the same frame, or for a national newspaper to do the same, but it is less likely if the national government of Canada has a policy of multiculturalism which is predominantly skewed towards Asia and is proposing a free trade economic agreement with China. National news media are more likely to investigate and report the issue in terms of its need to shift locations as supporting multiculturalism, further economic ties between both countries, and a need for Canadians to work "smarter" rather than "harder," leaving the ranting and wailing about the evils of globalization to the disaffected in the town that lost the factory.

Global news media have a special way of imagining that they reserve for national and transnational corporations and big business that differs from how they imagine national governments. Democracy imposes an obligation on national governments to provide information to stakeholders and for news media to have access to government issues and events as part of its process of evaluation and opinion forming. For corporations, there is a much less transparent obligation. Public corporations—those organizations that operate for profit and are responsible to shareholders—have a legal requirement (democracy exists when the rule of law is upheld by a national government) to reveal their financial market position but nothing more. There is no requirement for a corporation to reveal its sociopolitical intentions nor its sociocultural intentions. So the Western news media, while it is an equal pillar in the Tau of support for global institutions, must either investigate at an aggressive level or be reduced to reporting information that is supplied by the public relations agencies of the corporation. Part of the reason why the press and television in the West devote large spaces to business news is to ameliorate their relationship with corporations, whom they must regularly be seen to be investigating outside the supply of corporate business press releases. But news media can only investigate and report corporate activity from outside the organization. And they must be cognizant of cross-shareholdings. There is an added difficulty for a Western media news reporter that lies in how to investigate and report a corporation that is a shareholder in their own media corporation. The ownership of America's National Broadcasting Corporation (NBC) by General Electric (GE) was a classic case of corporate ownership, investigation and reporting. Ownership of NBC provided not only strong leverage for GE in advertising, it removed any potential for GE to be reported as news by that television network. A worse case existed in Italy with the ownership of Italian television network, radio and press by Italian President Silvio Berlusconi. The idea that citizens and other stakeholders in the sociopolitical process would view this objectively and form opinions of the government that were free of any persuasive images is ludicrous.

For news media such as the *Economist*, the corporation is generally imagined as an important element in the pursuit of free trade and liberal democracy. It is therefore difficult for it to frame its investigations in a negative way. In a story on Ireland's political divisions, for example it reflects on the idea that business between Northern Ireland and Ireland might be the catalyst for political reform. To frame its angle, the *Economist* provided a lead paragraph to the story that invoked an image of the era of mighty shipbuilding as "a cold wind drives over the Titanic's abandoned slipway, and nothing stirs where over thirty five thousand men hammered and cut in what was once the world's greatest shipyard" (*Economist* June 3, 2006, p. 59). But the image is also one that invokes disaster and chaos, for as history tells us, on its maiden voyage from the United Kingdom to America, the Titanic sank after colliding with an iceberg. It is possible that the *Economist* is attempting to temper its story about business collaboration between the two Irelands with a dose of reality: what has looked great in the past has also come to grief. But in this it would be better off to do what it normally does, to editorialize about the issue. In the issue that included the Irish business story, it chose instead to focus its leader on business in India, among other things.

The frame for its Ireland business story was very different from a similar business story about the two Koreas a week earlier on May 27 (see chapter 2 for details). While the Korea story was shorter in length and framed the issue of unification around negative labor supply and the interests of the United States, the Ireland story framed the issue of unification around positive labor supply and the interests of the two Irelands. The newspaper editorialized its denouement in both stories, yet its Korean story was its own opinion, while the Irish story it left to a third person to supply the opinion.

The difference in the stories, despite their parallel economic and political issues, is one of democracy and the image the *Economist* has of the future for both the Koreas and the Irelands. It clearly sees some bright light shining for the Irelands, less so for the Koreas. But in sum, the issues and events that led to separation of both countries are not dissimilar. What is important for the *Economist* in its imagining of economic and political unification is that Ireland is much closer to the model of Western liberal democracy than South Korea. And it is Western in every sense of the traditional meaning of *West*. The *Economist* newspaper has no choice other than to view them as distinctly different because it is part of the Tau of globalization. North Korea, in the image it presents to the West and to the *Economist*, is not.

The Reality of
National Governments

National governments throughout the world can be categorized and defined in a number of ways. For our purposes we will examine the role of national governments within globalization as they are reported by the global news media.

National governments come in for some bad publicity even when they are doing nothing wrong. Within the Western news media there is a belief that governments exist to be investigated and attacked because they are always in economic difficulty, using politics to persuade and influence, and never achieving enough social equity. When a journalist begins work he or she is told by an editor that there will always be a bad news story that can be found by investigating government. A weekly newspaper in the most out-of-the-way place will look to fill a couple of columns with something that a local government body has done badly. It might be the collection of rubbish or the filling of potholes; whatever the issue or event, there is always someone willing to comment. This type of attitudinal behavior towards governments is not limited to local or provincial governments. The larger a government, the more opprobrium is heaped upon it by Western news media.

There are a number of ways we can examine the reality of national governments. The following section will concentrate on their economic obligations—how to attract foreign and domestic investment into their countries against stiff competition—so here we are interested in the political reality. For the purposes of defining the political reality of democratic national governments, we might separate them into convenient categories, pretty much as they are separating themselves into global categories that are defined by globalization. Thus, we have North America (defined by NAFTA), the European Union and Asia-Pacific (defined partly by ASEAN but also including the Republic of Korea, Taiwan, Republic of China, Japan, Australia and New Zealand) and South America. These categories fit reasonably well with the departments presented by the *Economist*, with the exception of Britain as a separate entity and the exclusion of Africa and the Middle East from our list. As I mentioned earlier, we are interested in Western news media and democracy therefore Africa and the Middle East do not fall within our present frame of reference.

Important early work on the reality of national government and its grounding in democracy was undertaken by sociologist Martin Lipset. Following Weber and Schumpeter, Lipset argued that democracy was the underpinning of the political reality of the existence of national governments but that it had the potential to decrease or increase in legitimacy depending upon the social support of the institutions that underpinned it (Lipset 1960). Aside from being important for its conservative perspective on liberal democracy and its emergence, Lipset's work influenced contemporary thinkers such as Francis Fukuyama and Jagdish Bhagwati.

Lipset made a comparative study of complex social systems, concluding that democracy is a political system that must offer regular constitutional opportunities for changing government officials and a social mechanism that allows a majority of citizens to influence the outcome by having the choice of legitimate political candidates (Lipset 1960: 45). In applying this definition to national democracies Lipset concluded thirteen of the world's countries fitted his taxonomies. They were Australia, Belgium, Canada, Denmark, Ireland, Luxembourg, Netherlands, New Zealand, Norway, Sweden, Switzerland, the United Kingdom and the United States. Unstable democracies and dictatorships, he concluded, existed in Finland, France, Germany, Greece, Italy, Spain, and Portugal, among others. Brazil, Argentina, Mexico and Colombia were among countries he considered to have democracies and unstable dictatorships while Cuba, Peru, Venezuela, Bolivia and Panama were among those with no democracy, but stable dictatorships. Much has changed within the unstable democracies and the stable dictatorships defined by Lipset, notably the further in time from the events of the middle of the 20th century—World War II—that some countries have experienced a marked shift towards stable democracy at the expense of dictatorship (Spain and Portugal, Germany and France) while some South American countries have moved from stable dictatorships to unstable democracies.

Of most interest to us is the number of countries still on the original stable democracy list. If we apply my taxonomies from the previous chapter we will find that from the list of fifteen countries whose economic and financial indicators the *Economist* chooses to highlight each week, nine—Australia, Belgium, Britain (UK), Canada, Denmark, Netherlands, Sweden, Switzerland and the United States—were in Lipset's original taxonomy of stable democracies and have, thus, provided legitimate national government for more than fifty years. Some countries that were at the center of the conflict of World War II have joined the list: France, Germany, Austria, Spain, Italy and Japan, while Denmark, Luxembourg, New Zealand, Ireland, and Norway are not included in the *Economist*'s list. I suspect these countries were considered by the *Economist* to be too small for comparative purposes; nonetheless, they all remain stable legitimate democracies.

National governments that are popularly elected through a democratic process differ in their political capacity to achieve sociopolitical goals and objectives from authoritarian national governments. For an authoritarian national government, the issue of immigration is one which can be easily identified through legislation. As in the case of Cuba, or North Korea, legislative restrictions will be imposed automatically. For liberal democracies such as Canada and Australia, which must debate issues of immigration within the public sphere and which have policies of multiculturalism, the issue of immigration is more complex. Similarly the political reality for a country such as France, whose national government is struggling with the issues of multiculturalism and European constitutionalism, is such that debate on important complex issues is distilled by the news media into simple images of conflict and cleavage. Thus the French, when they read their newspapers or watch television, are confronted by the prospect of tradesmen immigrants from Poland taking all the jobs from French citizens.[4]

For British scholar and journalist Ian Hargreaves, the French revolution went some way to constructing an image of news for French journalists that appears to still have resonance. He argues the revolution provided a moment of national crisis in which journalists found themselves torn between their "professional role as detached observers" of the unfolding events and as actively engaged citizens (Hargreaves 2003). Hargreaves' dictum applies to news media in other countries as well, but it is its application to French national government that interests us most here. Hargreaves points to the "excessive control" of the French press—an issue pondered by James Mill (father of John Stuart Mill)—as contributing to the continuing turmoil in French journalism, whereas the freedom of the press in the Netherlands, Switzerland, Britain and the United States provided relative stability for national governments (Hargreaves 2003: 43).

National Governments and Economics

While politics plays a decisive role in framing the goals and objectives of national governments,[5] economic issues and events compete for space as news and shape the policies of national governments as they are directed by the will of the electorate.

National governments are not corporations; they are not competing for finite resources from which to make profit for shareholders. They are, however, competing for economic reputation, a situation in which their ability to demonstrate democratic stability and a high level of financial management that can be applied to the revenue they generate is of vital national importance. Attached to this is the issue of reputation and stability, that generates additional economic prosperity. A country that can demonstrate its economic and political stability and which has some attractions that might interest citizens of other countries, will benefit financially from the resultant tourism. Mountaineers and other tourists spend large sums traveling to Nepal in central Asia to enjoy the breathtaking heights and scenes of the world's highest mountains. Yet Nepal has no stable national government nor a stable economy—two of the underpinnings of democracy— so the economic value of tourism is a situational variable.

Within national governments that comprise the European Union (EU), the issue of constitutional as well as economic union is not an issue that deters large numbers of American and Asian tourists. Yet it has the potential to cause economic instability in any number of countries if it is imagined and reported in a particular way. If constitutional crisis within the EU is imagined and reported as an issue that provokes terrorism, riots and instability in France, for example, or the Netherlands,[6] then there is potential for the reporting to affect tourism and, thus, economic growth. Tourism is one of the driving economic forces for most liberal democracies. The movement of citizens across borders in pursuit of pleasure and leisure is unprecedented in history. News reporting of issues and events has the potential to alter the economic benefits that accrue to national governments from tourism.

Within most stable democracies, national governments during the past generation have been comprised of conservative and less conservative opposition parties. Where there is a two-party preferred system, the part of opposition is no longer seen by an electorate to be diametrically opposed to the party in government. The difficulty for these parties, their political and their economic ideologies and policies, lies in the fact that differentiation within electorates at the beginning of the 21st century is perceived to be economically less valuable for many of the domestic communities that make up a nation. With the reduction in the threat from communism and socialism, parties within these democracies, in opposition to capitalism and its parallel conservatism, have been reduced and redirected so that former socialist parties now have policies and ideologies that match the traditional conservative agenda. Examples are Tony Blair and the Labor Party in the UK, and Bill Clinton and the Democratic Party in the United States. The difficulty for a party in opposition advocating the same or similar policy platforms as an alternative government is that the news media becomes confused about the shift, as they have traditionally expected to witness conflict and cleavage in economic policies of parties seeking power as national governments.

National governments no longer have the luxury of focusing on national socioeconomic issues such as education, health and transport. National governments must now focus in two very different directions, downwards into domestic issues and upwards into global issues as they affect the national economic well-being of each country. As Bhagwati (2004) points out, the idea of the dual focus must be guided by good management and good governance so that the forces of globalization, if they are to continue their spread, will bring economic growth to developing nations as they move closer to the ideal of liberal democracy. For Bhagwati, managing short-term capital flows is far more complex and difficult than managing trade.

If we accept this argument, we can see why news media are softer on developing countries in reporting their approach to globalization and why Western journalists are harder on mature economies. If a mature economy has difficulty with the concept of short-term capital flow, then how is a struggling emerging market such as Chile, with foreign currency reserves of around US$18 billion (compared to China's US$875 billion) to compete? Capital flow was cited as the cause of the Asian financial crisis in the late 1990s and, as Bhagwati demonstrates, may have stopped the Malaysian financial market from spiraling out of as much control as did its neighbors, South Korea, Thailand, Indonesia and the Philippines. The Asian financial crisis, Bhagwati argues, "precipitated by panic fuelled outflows of capital, a product of hasty and imprudent financial liberalization" (Bhagwati 2004: 199), with the responsibility lying at the door of the powerful financial markets of the United States. The reporting of the crisis, at the time, by the Western news media, however, laid less blame at Wall Street and U.S. Treasury doors, and more at the feet of the Asian economies themselves, suggesting that they had burned too brightly too quickly and had not allowed for a major slump in their productive growth and investment. By 2003 the *Economist*, for its part, and quoted by Bhagwati, argued that restricted capital controls in certain cases have a role to play in a liberal global market grounded in free trade. Thus, economic prosperity and free trade are arguably the most important elements for continued peaceful existence between nations.

Imagining National Governments as Global News

As I have mentioned above, news media consider governments to be fair game when investigating and reporting, as they believe governments of all types to be unethical, both politically and morally. For every news medium that supports the British government of Tony Blair, there will be another opposed to it. For every medium that supports the federal U.S. government of George W. Bush, there might be two that are opposed to it. But not all of these media will report global issues and events as news either supporting or opposing the national government of the country in which their medium is located. In democracies where there are free news media, journalists and reporters will sometimes gravitate to a medium which has an ideology that fits with their own personal philosophy. In Australia, for example, journalism graduates seek to become employed by the leading élite broadsheet, the *Sydney Morning Herald* (*SMH*; John Fairfax Pty Ltd). They have no interest in working for the rival newspaper, the tabloid *Daily Telegraph* (News Corporation), believing that the *SMH* is more aligned with their leftist views than the right-leaning, Murdoch-owned *Telegraph*. But the reality is that the *SMH*, while it gave the appearance of providing less editorial support for the conservative federal government—a coalition of the Australia Liberal Party and the National Party, elected in 1996—in reality it provided strong support by not supporting the policies of the opposition Australia Labor Party. The *SMH* provided column space for opinion writers who supported the opposition but, in effect, journalism students who were raised on a narrow diet of one newspaper, and who were opposed in principle to the conservative policies of the national government, were in reality seeking to work for a conservative newspaper that provided tacit support for a conservative government.

For the global news media, national governments provide news when they do something wrong. The *Economist* will report on trade talks in Southeast Asia (*Economist* June 2, 2006) in positive terms, but include an editorial line that argues all could be done quicker and more easily if regional trade deals were set aside in favor of global institutional discourse (the Doha Round) because regionalism is seen by *The Economist* as a less than satisfactory approach to the goal of global free trade. By implication, national governments are imagined to be supporting free trade while maintaining special barriers for their own economic and political gain. If they won't come to the Doha table, the *Economist* line suggests, they must be interested in protection by other means, a point worth investigating journalistically.

There is an implied assumption in Western democracies that the role of the news media is to disseminate objective information and to have a deep background understanding of the issues and processes so that objectivity can flourish. Audience perceptions are that it is also to rebut the practice of public relations which, according to McNair (2000), is designed to subvert the normative integrity of the public sphere by transforming it into a vehicle for the pursuit of vested interests and the subordination of the public interest. For the Western news media to investigate and imagine national governments as news, they must first be able to differentiate what it is that is being supplied. Governments adopt a one-way process of information dissemination which they term public information (Grunig & Hunt 1984); the information that assists citizens to make choices and to develop opinions about all types of things that affect them, including health and well-being, education, social security and financial investments.

European scholar Barbara Baerns (1987) suggests there is a simple question which can be asked in analyzing patterns of news media influence, that is: whether that which purports to be journalistic news is in fact public relations. Baerns suggests such a question indicates an approach to the determination of latent interaction through analysis of patterns of influence as transcending news media content. Baerns is attempting to investigate the relationship between events as they are presented by the news media and what may have happened "in fact" or in "reality" (Baerns 1987: 88). Her argument has been developed from the premise set out by journalist and scholar Walter Lippmann (1922) that news media content can be described as results of a whole series of selections. Lippmann suggests the function of becoming the "printed diary of the home town" is what a newspaper must aspire to fulfill if it is to be a newspaper (Lippmann 1922: 210), but it is also a vehicle with which, in Mayhewian terms, to communicate the means of social influence. Lippmann asserts that a "stereotyped shape [is] assumed by an event at an obvious place that uncovers the run of the news, [and that] the most obvious place is where people's affairs touch public authority" (Lippmann 1922: 215).

Weaver (1987) suggests the news media specifically shapes and filters reality rather than acting as a transmission belt or a mirror of society, and concentration on relatively few issues and subjects invariably leads to a public perception that they are, therefore, more important than other issues or subjects. Weaver adds an important point to his argument. He says it is crucial to differentiate between agenda-setting by the news media and the passing on of priorities set by other actors and institutions within the public sphere.

Journalists frame global news in economic and political terms because the alternatives are less obvious or because they clash with dominant values. The dominant values of the capitalist market are politics and economics. Clashes occur when organizations attempt to frame issues and events in cultural or social terms. Attempts to frame health issues, for example, around cultural or social objectives usually meet with disapproval by the news media. Health for some is a social issue while for other stakeholders it is economic. For private health care providers—corporations—the issue of health-care investment is one of profit. Western governments, which sometimes act as providers of public health care, increasingly see the issue in economic terms and, thus, shift the burden of responsibility, within the political economy framework of rationalization, to the private sector. Claims made against the policy by other stakeholders, notably welfare advocacy groups (acting as NGOs), are treated less seriously by the news media because the issue is framed in social or cultural terms.

In methodological terms, the conservatism of the Western news media presents itself as a structural configuration of political concepts similar to other politically ideological concepts (see Freeden 1996). Leach (1993) identifies the conservative as one who continually searches for "the security of habit," reinforcing it as traditional and ultimately proscriptive. Thus, we have the generally conservative argument within the traditional family along the lines that "this is how it has always been done so this is the way it will always be done." There is little room for examination of the process and, indeed, in the vast majority of cases, there is no need of examination of the process, nor for continual decoding, because the process provides the required results. Within the family unit this application of time-honored processes allows the handing down of precious information and skills, but when it is transferred to the public sphere, it breaks down as an ideology. Conservative principles tend to exist where continuous development exists. At a national level, democratic countries which have evaded or overcome colonialism and social revolution, and adopted continuous infrastructure development at the expense of social equity, are most likely to be dominated by conservatism. These include the United States, the United Kingdom, and, to a lesser extent Canada, New Zealand and Australia (see Leach 1993). Continuous development also drives conservatism at a local level, presenting itself less as a cohesive definable structure and more as an economic imperative. It is this indefinability which allows conservatism the luxury of transferring what are normally termed "family values" to the public sphere. Conservatism, however, should not be confused in this context with right-wing. The emergence of ultra-right-wing religious/political organizations with family and religion-based ideologies does not equate with conservatism.

There is a conservative argument which says news media can only present news as fact and that the interpretation of facts resides with the audience. The corollary is that audiences have come to rely on message dissemination being factual. This is a situation which allows the news producer or editor to make decisions based on the likely outcome having the potential to alter the balance rather than on the presentation of facts. Such is the nature of the human element in the process that the balance more frequently is presented to an individual journalist or reporter than the source of the information may wish the recipient to enjoy.[7]

The News Media as Corporation

Global news media in the West act independently of government—unlike news media in authoritarian regimes, they are not accountable to government for what they publish or broadcast—but in this they can only achieve their goals and objectives as global news media *because* they have the financial support of corporations and, in the case of public broadcasters such as the BBC, the financial support of governments. So global news media are corporate in the sense that they are part of a legally constructed entity, but they act independently of that entity in sourcing and producing news. In ethical terms this is not much better than media in authoritarian regimes. News

82

media in the West are unlikely to investigate the policies of their major shareholders; it is unimaginable that the *Times*, for example, would investigate the actions of News Corporation with the objective of publishing some unethical business practices. Nor is it conceivable that the *International Herald Tribune* would investigate its parent, the New York Times Company if it had information that that organization or one of its subsidiaries had been involved in poor business practices. It might, of course, run a few pars in the business section so that it appeared to be objective in its reporting, but there would never be a full-scale investigation.

News media in non–Western countries point to the issue of ownership to question the differences between where they report from and where Western news media sit.

The other important part of the equation for the Western news media is that they must maintain their positions at the end of the Tau so that it stays in balance. Since Macauley named the action of the news media in Britain as the fourth estate, with responsibility to oversee the workings of parliament (and thus government), the Western news media has been unable to throw off the cloak of importance and to see themselves as something other than a parallel government. They do not, of course, want to see themselves any other way, given the importance of the task with which they have been charged. And Macauley was very clever to lock them into the task, as at the time they were beginning to slip away from the original position allotted them by Addison, Steele and others who aligned and practiced journalism as a high calling, along with the higher vocation of politics.

The News Media as Government

In this, the contemporary Western news media, while they are the financial offspring of the corporation, more importantly have the perception that they are the equal of government in the power and influence they exercise in the decisions they make about what constitutes global news.

Competition for news media space in the Western world involves complex layers of influence and persuasion, differing motivations and the capacity of the bearer of an issue or event to frame it in such a way that it resonates with what is already on—or about to be on—the news media agenda. Journalists have thus become narrowly focused in accordance with the main driver of economic rationalism: cost cutting. They have difficulty in seeking to investigate ideal policy when acceptable policy is close by. They readily accept professional norms of what is news rather than investigating issues and events outside a conventional framework. They focus on the success of an issue or event rather than the veracity of the information being presented.

Despite binary claims of subjectivity from within the public sphere, news media provide a nexus between a majority of the population and information interpretation, manifesting as daily news. Citizens take in information and ways of thinking about it from a variety of news media outlets including newspapers, radio, television, the Internet, magazines, newsletters, and billboard advertising. Access to most outlets, including the Internet, is diffuse. Radio occupies an important position as the main source of information for motoring commuters while television is the preferred medium for obtaining news as entertainment in the majority of households from mid-evening onwards. Newspapers account for a large percentage of political news and analysis actively sought by consumers. Magazines supply lengthier analyses of issues and events, and newsletters and journals fulfill the remaining requirements of a public actively seeking rigorous analysis and comment. McNair (2000) has described this process as mediated news. Mediated news is that which requires some level of interpretation before it can be absorbed meaningfully by citizens.

The role of the journalist is to provide a balance between the politicians (government) and the news media owners, and the journalists' citizen stakeholders as members of the public sphere. It is an easy argument to suggest politicians, especially prime ministers or presidents, are close enough to media owners to seek favorable coverage of policy or party issues. This is a standard argument of the left in Western democracies. Less illustrative is the journalist as individual, as expert, and as one, unlike the average constituent, more than vaguely interested in issues. According to most Western journalism codes of ethics, a journalist is obliged to provide a high level of veracity in reporting an issue, which is what the majority of journalists appear to achieve. Increasingly, however, journalists with specific party political affiliations reach positions of authority within media organizations. They reach these positions specifically because of their political associations or because of their relationships with political people. Journalistic veracity, however, can be measured not by how close an employee or staffer is to the political process, but by the direct relationship or sympathies the person has for particular political parties and policies. To be a journalist does not remove one from his or her personal preferences and beliefs.

Journalism is a vicarious profession but it draws emotional rather than rational people.

5

The Continuing Transformation of the Public Sphere: From Jürgen Habermas to Osama bin Laden

This chapter argues that globalization and its potential benefits for the world's five billion inhabitants is unraveling due to a number of concerted antiglobalization forces, most notably the terrorist group known as al-Qaeda, and that acts of global terrorism are forcing supranational and national institutions to seek comfort and security in regional relationships rather than continuing on the road to globalization. It examines the way the Western news media interpret terrorist acts and how the interpretation reinforces a withdrawal from the expansion of the global.

The space known as the public sphere, which I will attempt to define shortly, was transformed from its position in the medieval West by the act of consciousness-raising that occurred between the middle of the 17th century and the early 18th century. It was transformed from a space in which European royalty and aristocracy held court in palaces to one in which salons and coffeehouses became important places for the exchange of information about trade and commerce. The early 18th-century birth of the coffeehouse and parallel emergence of news journals created a space in which aristocracy and utilitarians could meet for purposes of mutually beneficial communication exchanges. The enormous expansion of trade linked to the journeys of imperial national discovery by powerful rulers in Britain, France, Holland and Spain, required the newly formed relationships between aristocracy and utilitarians to access wider information sources in order to keep up with the action. The birth of news media in the forms of weekly journals in Britain and France were soon emulated in other countries in Europe, thanks to the earlier invention of movable type by the German printer Johann Gutenberg and English typographer William Caxton.

But the early 18th-century transformation of the public sphere, from one in which royalty and aristocracy controlled trade, commerce, literature and art to one in which a more diffuse group of citizens controlled the means of production and distribution, has remained largely composed of news media and other actors that remained unchanged in its shape for three hundred years.

The public sphere was then transformed again, with similar results, at the beginning of the 21st century by acts imposed on the West by Saudi Arabian and other Middle Eastern terrorist groups. No other single act has transformed the shape of the public sphere in the West between the early 18th century and the early 21st century to the extent of the terrorist attacks on the World Trade Center and Pentagon in September 11, 2001. My argument here is that trade has been the hallmark of the global public sphere during the past three hundred years and in this, the upheaval of terrorism since September 11 has altered the shape of trade so that it has forced countries into what the *Economist* and other news media see as backup positions—narrowly focused free trade agreements between countries within regions that give the appearance of private agreements. Part of the reason for the establishment of these private agreements lies in their attempt to avoid becoming the focus of terrorist action.

But, for the moment, we need to return to the 18th century to see how the transformation of the public sphere at that time, three hundred years ago, created the circumstances that led to the terrorist attacks on the World Trade Center at the beginning of the 21st century.

The Habermasian Public Sphere of the Enlightenment

For Jürgen Habermas, the salons and coffeehouses established by the bourgeois and middle classes in the early 18th century took over the public sphere, the court of royalty. Within these newly constructed spaces, literary and political discourse took place that shaped public issues and events, but within this new sphere there was another level— a level that allowed the suspension of legal, economic and market activity (Habermas 1989: 36). The idea of groups being outside the frame of law and society is still extant. Some of these groups confound the issue by acting in the guise of NGOs (nongovernmental organizations). Education and literacy increased from levels of almost nothing in the late 17th century in Europe to 80 percent in Western democracies by the early 21st century. But *literacy* does not equate with *literate* in the sense that the global explosion of information does not inform citizens to a much greater extent that it did in the 18th century.

Habermas's concept of a public sphere derived from the 17th- and 18th-century development of the relationship between capital and the state. The sociability that grew as part of the transformation from feudalism, in which kings and lords opined, "L'état, c'est moi," to a balance between capitalist endeavor and state control, created the circumstances in which the aristocrats, merchants and businessmen communicated between themselves a desire to influence the state in matters of capitalist endeavor.

The role of information in this influencing process—news that could affect commodity and manufacture prices—was vital to the growth of the capitalist system; thus, those with the time and the need gathered in public places to receive and dispense. Due to the earlier discovery of mass printing, this news retrieval and dissemination became more widespread, but it remained part of the public place culture because not all news of value could be transformed reliably and validly into the written word, very much as it remains today in the West, where the most important information is reserved for the masculine business spheres of the golf course, the football club and the racetrack. Habermas argues the link that developed between news as trade information received and disseminated in coffee shops and other public spaces, lead to a culture of opinion that became more diffuse as printing became more popular. The popularity of published opinion in a literary sense led inexorably to the publication of political opinion as merchants and businessmen discovered the need to influence and have a say in the affairs of state.

Although Habermas was writing in German for a German audience, England was his model because it provided early evidence of a shift from violence as a measure of political success to a conflict-consensus model between government and opposition. With the notion of democracy and its institutional relationships in mind he was able to map the evolution of the transformation of the public sphere. The

German model, in contrast, lagged behind the English in development, and the French as well, where the ruling élite relied on the courts for authority, and, thus, as Calhoun suggests, "failed to develop strong enough lines of communication with bourgeois intellectuals to participate in creating a strong civil society separate from the state" (Calhoun 1992: 15).

For Habermas, the structural transformation occurred precisely because the foundation, the balance of civil society between the public realm and the private realm, was overcome by an interweaving of the private medium of money with the public medium of power. The transformation was complete when these previously distinct boundaries became so blurred as to be indivisible. And the catalyst for this gigantic blur was the shift from narrow literary communication within the liberal public sphere to populist persuasive mass communication, directed by advertising, that overpowered rational critical debate. In this, the communication of politics was also responsible for the breakdown. As with the bureaucratic apparatus that is the modern political party, so too early political advertising and campaigning was, according to Habermas, aimed squarely at "attracting the votes of those not yet committed" (Habermas 1989: 203). Thus, as Calhoun points out, "as parties dominate politics, and as state and society are generally intertwined, the material conditions for the old sort of public sphere disappear" (Calhoun 1992: 27). The rise of the "representative public" paralleled the development of the commodification of nature, the search for ever increasing profits within the private sphere of business and the devaluation of the news media from positions of serious actors to showtime warm-up clowns.

Why Three Hundred Years Is Important

For the Western news media, and the model of journalism established at the beginning of the 18th century that remains extant, the objectives were to report global news of economics and politics for the advantage of a home market. The focus of imagining global political and economic news was reduced to how much comparative advantage the ownership of news might accrue to a particular individual or group.

Despite the intervention of a few revolutions, notably in France, England and America, and the upheaval of two world wars and a number of other regional wars, the Western news media has not substantially altered the way it imagines issues and events in the past three hundred years.

As I have argued above, there is a specific reason for this. According to Snooks, history is replete with great waves of economic activity that last for around three hundred years. If this is an accurate reflection of economic history, Snooks suggests each wave has been driven by a different dynamic strategy, leading to his thesis of long-run dynamics playing a major role in economic growth. Snooks suggests the first wave—from 1000 to 1300—consisted of a conquest strategy, the second—1490 to 1650—consisted of a commerce strategy, while the third great wave—1780s to the present—consisted of a technological strategy. Snooks says the second wave was curtailed by the arrival of plague in Europe.

If plague cut short the second long wave of global economic development, and the third wave began in the late 18th century, then I would argue that the intervention of terrorism at the beginning of the 21st century has cut short the potential for the third wave to fulfill its destiny and to run until the end of the 21st century.

This is the point where the global news media have come unstuck. While they continue to report using the model adopted during the 18th century, issues and events have occurred at the beginning of the 21st century that should have had the same transformative impact on the model as the transfer of power from the aristocracy to the utilitarians had at the beginning of the 18th century.[1] It appears, however, that if what Snooks argues is correct, the transformation from one dynamic strategy to another is a process of evolution rather than revolution, as Western global news media do not appear to be searching for a new model to report the issues and events of the 21st century post–September 11.

Immediately after the events of September 11, media scholars questioned the role of journalism (see, for example, Zelizer & Allan 2002, Schudson 2002, and Cottle 2002) and how it was played out during and immediately after the crisis, but none questioned the legitimacy of the model of news reporting that had been employed for the past three hundred years. Some of them questioned whether journalism had the capacity to continue to work effectively through its existing instruments. Publisher of the *Nation,* Victor Navasky, came closest to questioning the future validity of the model in a foreword to the edited collection, *Journalism After September 11*

(Zelizer & Allan 2002). In this he said that journalism provided us with all sorts of information in the immediate aftermath of the act—terrorism and terrorists, Islamic fundamentalism, intelligence agencies, airport security and the architecture of the World Trade Center—but nothing about journalism itself and its relationship to the crisis.

I agree with Navasky, and more so with academic Ingrid Volkmer when she suggests there is a need to understand journalism as an integral element of the emergent global public sphere (Volkmer 2002). Volkmer argues that the events of 9/11 created new international political alliances that had the potential to reshape global news media reporting. Since 9/11, Volkmer says, Western news media particularly, have focused downward on the events, localizing them so that they resonate with their domestic audiences and become real for citizens of other countries, for example, Spain, England, and Indonesia, where linked terrorist events occurred after 9/11.

More importantly, and with direct relevance to my argument, Volkmer says that the events of 9/11 caused the global public sphere that had been developing and sustaining a long wave (defined by Snooks as around forty years) to collapse, so that regional and national issues and events took on greater significance, forcing the horizontally shaped global public sphere into smaller vertical layers based on traditional regional and national frames.

This argument supports the increased interest in regional trade that occurred in Asia in the first five years of the 21st century. For north Asian nations such as South Korea, Taiwan and Japan, which were not direct targets of terrorism, the idea of continued expansion of a globalized world economy—especially after the catastrophic financial market events of the late 1990s—allowed these countries to think more deliberately about setting up stronger regional trade agreements rather than expanding global agreements. In this, the acts of terrorism imposed on the West went a long way towards shaping how national politics and, therefore, global news might exist in the future.

Imagining an Alternative Public Sphere

Volkmer argues that the future for global news media might rest on the idea of microspheres appearing in "an extra-societal global public space" (Volkmer 2002: 243) in which global news "counter flows" balance out the reporting of Western news media.

But earlier work by U.S. political expert Michael Schudson (1992) questioned the idea of the existence of a public sphere, as shaped by Habermas, and asked whether or not such a thing could actually exist.

In highlighting the question of whether there was ever a public sphere, and if so when, Schudson grounds his argument and conclusions in the American model by comparing citizen participation in politics, suggesting that the more people participate, the closer we come to the ideal of a public sphere (Schudson 1992: 147). The elements around which Schudson's inquiry pivot are the Habermasian requirements of widespread rational critical participation. In other words the quality of discursive communication is as important to the concept of the liberal public sphere as is diffuse involvement. Schudson's inquiry into the existence of the liberal public sphere in America neither contradicts nor categorizes the Habermasian one; simply, it provides an inquiry into a societal position which possibly could have been substituted by Habermas for his English frame of reference. I think this is what Schudson is attempting to present as an alternative. Schudson invokes the work of Jane Mansbridge and her study of a town meeting in New England in the 1970s which 35 percent of eligible voters attended. Mansbridge compared this with attendance at town meetings in the 17th and 18th centuries, to which 20 to 60 percent attended and went as high as 75 percent, Schudson recounts, "during times of intense conflict" (Schudson 1992: 148). In the town under investigation, Mansbridge found that in the 19th century the average was similar, increasing to 75 percent during times of duress. Today, the same town registers 25 percent average attendance and 66 percent when threatened.

The introduction of mass-based party politics markedly changed voting patterns in the Jacksonian era. Again, in New England, where, Schudson argues, resides the most democratic culture in the United States, in 1820 the potential electorate that voted was 8 percent. By 1924 this figure had risen to 15 percent, by 1932 to 46 percent, and by 1944 to 80 percent. This presents for Schudson a "golden age" of American political culture between 1840 and 1900. While this is a somewhat later period than that presented by Habermas as his English model, it is useful as a comparison given America's present unabiding belief in its institutional and democratic principles as they form a contemporary liberal public sphere in the structural society model.

Schudson's inquiry seeks to answer the question of whether the discourse that occurred at the time was rational, critical, or "gossipy, incidental background to sociability rather than its centre" (Schudson 1992: 150), and whether citizens felt thus attached to politics. Like the English élite of the Habermasian model in which communication was framed around publication of literary discourse and important trade news, Schudson suggests that political pamphlet literature in the American colony was similarly pitched at the educated élite, "written in a florid style full of classical references that had meaning to only a few" (Schudson 1992: 151).

Tom Paine's *Common Sense* appears to be the first to break with this tradition, being written in what Paine himself describes as a style as plain as the alphabet. Its simplicity, combined with its timeliness, accounted for its popularity above all other political pamphlets of the era. Schudson points to the transformation of the news media, specifically the press, from a "conversational" model to an "informational" model as being critical to the existence of the liberal public sphere, but preventing citizens from political involvement by reporting events after they occur rather than providing mobilizing information before the event. Enabling information is provided when an event or issue coincides with media interest such as sporting events (Olympics sponsorship, football team ownership) or a popular health or environmental issue such as blood donation or a cleanup campaign. The shift to the present, in which journalism seeks proximity to validate its choice of news is very different from that experienced by citizens in 18th-century North America when, as Schudson argues, "news was self-consciously regarded as a safe alternative to political debate and polemic. The more remote the news the better. News of other colonies was more useful because it was regarded with greater indifference than news of one's own colony; news of European affairs was better still, because they had even less connection to local affairs" (Schudson 1992: 152).

Not so today, as the *New York Times* reporting staff numbers indicate, where a shift to an inward focus has occurred; of one thousand *New York Times* reporters, nine hundred are allocated to local New York news, sixty-five to other United States news, with the remaining thirty-five devoted to world or global news coverage (Meyrowitz 2004).

Schudson's point is that the press in America was not part of the liberal public sphere as Habermas describes it in the British model. For Habermas, the role of the pamphlet, the newsletter and, later, the news broadsheet, was to provide a vehicle that encouraged rational critical debate. Schudson suggests such a vehicle did not exist in North America and that, indeed, any rational critical debate that occurred was frequently *in camera*. He cites the example of the Massachusetts House of Assembly, which published its proceedings annually in 1715. Two years later, for an undisclosed reason, the House was publishing its journal weekly, but still not disclosing who voted for what policy. "Any newspaper or other commentator who revealed business of the House not printed in the journal was subject to a fine" (Schudson 1992: 154). As democracies go, this was far removed from the ideal of that based on rational critical discourse. In the event, Schudson appears to suggest the idea of a public sphere is necessary, indeed indispensable "as a model of what a good society should achieve" but he hedges his bets by suggesting he is acting as provocateur rather than advocate, which tends to leave dangling his question of whether there was ever a public sphere as it has been defined by Habermas.

Terrorism and Trade: An Arab Public Sphere

A clue to the continuing presence of the terrorist organization al-Qaeda in north Asia and the Middle East can be found if we conclude that there is an extant Western democratic public sphere and that we regard its democratic transformation as being capable of "internally democratizing a number of institutions whose activities impinge on the formal political process of decision-making" (Fraser 1992: 134). In this feminist scholar Nancy Fraser questions Habermas about his argument for the necessity of markets and state bureaucracies as a feature of complex societies and about his belief that "only relatively uninstitutionalized social movements can exercise the function of a critical rational opinion formation" that acts as a check and balance mechanism. If we take this line of reasoning further we can argue that Middle Eastern and north Asian action against the terrorism invoked by al-Qaeda has been restricted because collectively it sees the organization as having a legitimate place in the Arab public sphere—as an uninstitutionalized social movement—where it acts as a watchdog to curb American imperialism. Its extreme level of violence is justified—and legitimized by the Arab public sphere—because of what it considers extreme levels of economic and political violence being perpetrated against the Arab life world.

As a prolocutor, Osama bin Laden has created catastrophic convergence in attempting to reduce, through acts of terrorism, the capitalist state; the large-scale societal integration of the West in which the Habermasian "life world" and "systems world" are meant to join together to create a dynamic, populist public sphere. The life world cannot exist without the systems world and, as Habermas argues, reducing large-scale societal integration would have dangerous and catastrophic consequences.

It is to this position that Osama bin Laden has been drawn and enabled his followers through a public denunciation of the systems world of market capitalism. Thus, bin Laden has "refeudalized" the Arab public sphere exactly as Habermas determined the bourgeois public sphere of the 17th and 18th century West was refeudalized to become the populist, news media-driven public sphere that we now occupy.

The discursive public sphere of the West, however, despite its populist position, is not the same as the public sphere defined by the Arab terrorist life world of Osama bin Laden, in which discursive processes are dominated by antisystems world rhetoric. A critical rational discursive public sphere, as conceptualized by Habermas, is neither a reality in the market-driven capitalist West nor in the fundamentalist Middle East. Discursive practices in Western capitalism are dominated by news media. In the fundamentalist Middle East a similar two-way asymmetrical sphere exists, but it is dominated equally by news media and by the medium of fundamentalism.

The rise and sustained popularity of Al Jazeera News Television did not occur as a reaction to fundamentalism. It occurred as a reaction to the rise and sustained popularity of its Western counterpart, Fox News Television and as such it plays a critical role in supporting the life world of fundamentalism against the insurgency of the systems world of market capitalism.

Habermas acknowledges that religion declines as enlightenment expands; thus, the enlightenment of the West, with its overlaying systems world of power and money, provided a serious platform for oppositions to engage in passive or violent reaction.

Reporting Terrorism and Globalization

According to the *Economist* newspaper, terrorist group al-Qaeda, under its leader Osama bin Laden, is an organization of Islamic extremists and an ideology of Islamic extremism. Its fame, the newspaper said in 2003, has spread throughout the Muslim world because there was already embitterment over the imperialism and power of a dominant Western coalition meddling in Middle-Eastern economic and political affairs. By providing an ideological position that resonated with "a generation of militant Muslim youth," the *Economist* claimed al-Qaeda was scoring a "nightmarish success" despite its fragmentation globally, its leaders "lurking in the wilder parts of south Asia" and a "shriveled organization function." The importance of this observation lies in its description of those who are seeking to actively engage in the fundamentalist Arab public sphere created by the birth of al-Qaeda and of the description of al-Qaeda as an organization.

The point of departure in determining whether the Habermasian public sphere is a model for contemplation in either Western capitalism or Eastern fundamentalism lies in the observation by political scientist Martin Lipset that "the stability of any given democracy depends not only on economic development but also upon the effectiveness and the legitimacy of its political system" (Lipset 1959: 77). In Western terms this legitimacy is evident but in Eastern fundamental terms the clarity is less evident. While the *Economist* attempts to legitimate al-Qaeda by terming it an "organization," it shows no outward signs or organizational infrastructure as we understand Western institutions and organizations require to validate and ground them in relation to the public sphere. Evaluatively, al-Qaeda as an organization, in Western terms, does not exist, but if we refeudalize the idea of the organization or institution as something which requires scrutiny and is the object of critical rational discourse, then it fits well into the frame.

If we follow Lipset's argument further and agree that "legitimacy involves the capacity of the system to engender and maintain the belief that the existing political institutions are the most appropriate ones for the society" (Lipset 1959: 77), we can see how an organization such as al-Qaeda obtains legitimacy in a vertically stratified society like the Arab and Muslim Middle East.

The effectiveness of al-Qaeda as an organization was extreme for a brief moment, and, as the *Economist* argues, is more likely to become established as a group which undertakes more small-scale random acts of terrorism than any further large-scale attacks. So while al-Qaeda's effectiveness was primarily "instrumental," its legitimacy was "evaluative," resonating strongly with the anticapitalist, anti–

American sentiments that imbue the values of Middle Eastern youth and other disenfranchised groups.

Terrorism and Its Effect on Trade

Terrorism has changed the dynamic of globalization and created a reversion to safer regional trading blocs. It has had an effect on how the Western news media report global issues and events. In a number of important world regions, most notably the EU and North Asia, the concept of globalization seems less and less attractive with every terrorist attack, whether perpetrated by al-Qaeda or other terrorist groups attached to al-Qaeda or acting alone.

In France, the Netherlands and Spain, the impact of terrorist attacks has had direct political and economic consequences for the national governments of those countries. In 2005 France and Holland voted against the drafting of a European constitution, interpreted by the Western news media as a direct result of terrorist acts in those countries. In the same year Spain changed its political direction, interpreted by the Western news media as a direct result of a terrorist bombing of a train in the Spanish capital Madrid, killing hundreds, responsibility for which was claimed by al-Qaeda.

In India in July 2006, a terrorist attack claimed the lives of two hundred people after explosions occurred on a number of peak-hour trains in the heavily populated city of Mumbai. The synchronized attacks were interpreted by the Western news media as being the work of a Pakistani terrorist group with indirect links to al-Qaeda.

The effects of these attacks, like the effect of the unannounced North Korean missile launch, also in July 2006, were at the least unnerving for citizens and authorities of the countries in which they occurred. But at most they had the effect of chaotically undermining the path on which these and other Western countries had been traveling towards globalized trade and the wider embrace of democracy.

The effect of terrorism on world trade and particularly on globalization since September 11, 2001, has been enormous. It may not have played out transparently in the imagination of the Western news media nor in the minds of citizens, but its impact has been to cause those nations directly affected by it to rethink their commitment to globalization, particularly to the opening of their borders to trade, which, they rightly perceive, will lead to an opening of borders to

immigration and to the increased danger of further attacks. The alternative, as we have seen in Spain, is to elect a government that will
look to national security and the well-being of its own citizens before
all else. And when countries directly affected by terrorism begin to
shut down their borders, to change their thinking about tariff reduction, global trade and wider immigration, it causes a "domino effect,"
particularly among those countries that have direct trading relationships. Thus, we have the reversion to regional trading blocs in which
countries can feel the safety and security of familiarity.

While the terrorist attacks in Mumbai were generally attributed
to a Pakistani group linked to al-Qaeda, and seeking revenge for the
2002 demolition of a mosque in Ayodhya, the *Economist*, among others (the *Asahi Shimbun*, for example), interpreted the attacks as being
"too meticulously planned and too efficiently executed to be dismissed
as spontaneous retaliation in a campaign of tit-for-tat communal violence" (*Economist* July 15, 2006, p. 25). A deeper investigation lead
to the conclusion that they were choreographed to speed up the peace
process between Pakistan and India over the disputed territory of
Kashmir, but that in itself is not the full story. It must be seen as an
extension of the al-Qaeda campaign to disrupt the advancement of
globalization in trade, which in itself is designed to lead to increased
well-being and, thus, more peaceful existence for the world's five billion people.

The *Times of India* called on the government of Prime Minister
Manmohan Singh to take a harder line with Pakistan and predicted
that, in the event that terrorist attacks continue, the peace process
between the two countries would be severely strained, while the *International Herald Tribune*[2] interpreted the event as clear evidence that
al-Qaeda was still a serious threat to the global peace process (*International Herald Tribune* July 14, 2006, p. 14). The newspaper interpreted the event as having wider consequences than the peace process
between India and Pakistan. At around the same time as the Mumbai attacks, a number of other important events with the potential to
destabilize the global peace process and the pursuit of global trade
negotiations were occurring around the world. Two are more important for their impact on global trade and for how they were interpreted
in the Western news media. While others, most notably the failure of
the final negotiations in the Doha Round, will be discussed elsewhere
(see specifically my conclusions in chapter 10).

The Instability of North Asia

While the terrorist attacks were occurring in Mumbai, the Israeli government began blockades and air strikes against Lebanon, arguing it was intent on freeing Israeli soldiers captured by Lebanese terrorist group Hezbollah. Two weeks earlier, on July 5, the North Korean government set off a number of missiles, the worst of which spiraled out of control, landing in the Sea of Japan between South Korea and the Japanese mainland island of Honshu. The relative importance of the North Korean missile launch, while it did not have the devastating destruction of life of the Israeli attack, lies in the event's complete lack of announcement. It was more shocking, in other words, for its element of surprise than for its devastation. In launching its rockets and missiles without first announcing to the world its intentions to do so, the North Korean government acted in exactly the same way as all other terrorist organizations: it created an event that was designed to cause chaos among its enemies and among those countries close to it who are intent on pursuing a global trade network to the detriment of North Korea and other excluded nations.[3] The Western news media, and particularly the *Economist*, as agents of globalization, did nothing to assist the process of diplomacy that might have been required after the event. In fact, if one were to judge the media position from the cover of the *Economist* a few days after the missile firing, it might be assumed it was intent upon inflaming the crisis. For the *Economist*, the best way to demonstrate its cynicism towards North Korea was to imagine the North Korean leader Kim Il Jong as "rocketman," a reference to a 1970s Elton John song. The cover of the newspaper showed Kim Il Jong in trademark casual clothes and jacket propelled upwards by what appears to be an atomic mushroom cloud above the words "Rocket man" in white relief against a dark blue ground.

In North Asia, particularly in Japan, the news media interpreted the July 5 event in a number of ways. The *Daily Yomiuri*, a national daily English-language broadsheet published by the Yomiuri Shimbun, created almost continuous coverage of the event and its ramifications for Japan for two weeks, culminating in wide reportage of a UN resolution of July 15, voting unanimously to impose limited sanctions on North Korea (July 17), and the condemnation of the missile launches by the G8 summit in St. Petersburg (July 18). Most interestingly, on July 17, the *Daily Yomiuri* published the full text of the

UN resolution below a full-page report and analysis of the missile launches and their impact on Japan's political economy. Immediately after the missile launches, Japan imposed a trade sanction on North Korea, that, for the rest of the world, may seem insignificant, but for the diplomatic and political positioning of Japan was vitally important. The sanction was imposed as a six-month ban on a passenger cargo ferry—the only one of its kind—between Japan and North Korea. The ferry is used to carry supplies and funds to North Korea. The *Economist* interpreted the event as a North Korean push to engage directly with America over nuclear and trade issues, relegating Japan to one of North Korea's neighbors including South Korea and China. It did not mention the Japanese interest in greater power within the UN Security Council, choosing instead to imagine the missile launches as forcing Japan to consider a missile defense system (*Economist* July 8, 2006, p. 28).

In all the interpretation and imagining by the Western news media, the North Korean ballistic missile launches must be considered first and foremost a failed terrorist attack. For all the diplomatic discourse about North Korea feeling lonely,[4] the notion that it launched missiles in 1998 for the same reason—to get the world to take note of its humanitarian plight—it was a terrorist act designed to invoke terror. And in that it was successful. The same day that the *Yomiuri Shimbun* reported on the Japanese success in making its presence felt at the UN Security Council, it also reported the expansion of strategic relations between Japan and the UK (*Yomiuri Shimbun* July 18, 2006, p. 3). In this it was reporting on the disengagement of Japanese troops on the ground in Iraq; troops who had been working with UK troops in southern Iraq since the onset of war in that country in 2003. Its report was based on a joint security cooperation conference between Japan and the UK (cosponsored by the *Yomiuri Shimbun*) in which a declaration was made to continue and to expand the security and strategic relationships between the two countries. But as we have seen from the argument above, this is clearly a response to the threat of terrorism and its undermining of the process of globalization that countries such as the UK have heralded as the answer to humanitarian and other sociopolitical problems around the globe. It is a response that is not being reported widely, even by those Western media who support and defend the idea of globalization. Is it though, in its narrower reporting, an issue which fires the imagination of citizens, even in the countries that are under terrorist attack.

Two weeks after the North Korean missile launch I had dinner in Hiroshima with a Japanese businessman, Ken Tanaka, and his family. We discussed, in English, a number of Japanese cultural issues, but the event of July 5 did not enter the discussion. There may have been a number of reasons for this. The Japanese are less inclined to talk politics within a family-oriented gathering; there is little real interest in Korean politics at street level, especially in a place like Hiroshima, where the Koreans have only recently been recognized; or, given the nature of other terrorist attacks around the world, North Korea is not imagined as a terrorist regime. The Japanese, like all other developed nations, are more interested in the al-Qaeda-style attacks that occurred in Europe and the United States.

Terrorism and Its Impact on the European Union

While terrorist acts have had an enormous impact on most developed countries since the devastation wrought on New York and Washington in 2001, outside the Middle East they appear to have created the most shock and awe in Europe. Despite millennia of war and conflict, western Europe considers itself to be the most civilized and cosmopolitan region in the world. And this is a reasonable claim given the global reputational capital of such icons as the Louvre, the British Museum, the Palace of Versailles, and the streets of Venice, to name only a few. When we imagine ourselves to be something particular, and someone comes along and tells us we are something else, we respond in a number of ways.

For western Europeans, the shock of being terrorized by their ancient enemy, the barbarian from the Middle East, has been almost too much to bear. It has, in fact, caused political and economic instability, and not because the enemy is imagined as entering the cities to rape and pillage; it is because the enemy is "homegrown." In France, Spain and the Netherlands, the United Kingdom and Belgium, since 2001 citizens have been confronted by the specter of homegrown terrorist "cells" in which second- and third-generation Middle Easterners, predominantly Muslim, have been attracted to the call of al-Qaeda and to the destruction of the capitalist state in Europe. As Roy (2004) argues, there is no strategy in the true sense of the word attached to Osama bin Laden and al-Qaeda, so it is difficult to frame the terrorist actions of his followers in Europe in terms of orthodox thinking.

Thus, it is difficult for French or Spanish citizens to find meaning in the terrorist acts being undertaken in their countries, as it was difficult for English citizens to find meaning in British action against Northern Irish terrorism of the 1970s and 1980s. Or, of course, more recently for American and other Western citizens to find meaning in Israeli action against Hezbollah terrorism emanating from Lebanon.

For Western news media such as the *Economist*, terrorist acts in Europe are imagined as local news stories against a backdrop of global terrorism perpetrated against the West by a fragmented al-Qaeda and other loosely aligned groups and individuals. Individual feeling among European and America citizens is exemplified in the words of a song by Bruce Springsteen titled "Devils and Dust." Springsteen was writing about the war in Iraq, but the sentiment can be expanded to take in a general feeling of distrust that is being imbued in citizens of the Western world. Springsteen argues that even if you have your finger on the trigger and you do not know who to trust, if you look into the eyes of your opponent you will see only devils and dust. The song also embraces the idea that fear is a dangerous and powerful thing, that it has the capacity to turn black a heart that had been god-fearing and filled with love, and to fill a soul with devils and dust. The image of mistrust began in earnest in September 2005 when a Danish newspaper, *Jylland-Posten*, published cartoon versions of Muhammad the Prophet. Immediately Danish embassies in Syria, Lebanon, Iran and Indonesia were attacked by outraged Muslims. Ironically, Denmark is imagined to be the most contented of all Western countries.

The European Union and the United States are the two most important and powerful regions in the geopolitical landscape. But for citizens of the EU, the threat of terrorist attacks has caused them to reconsider their place in a globalized world. It has assisted the powerful industrial countries in the EU, most notably France, Germany, the UK and Italy, to consider the political stability of their countries as being more important than the development of globalized trade that has the potential to aid the developing countries that seek to open their markets. In this they are not alone. The global threat and reality of terrorism has done more to harm the continuing process of globalization than all the Western antiglobal protests combined. Governments within supranational institutions such as the EU have a responsibility to the well-being of their citizens, so it is no surprise that the French are more interested in supporting their farmers through the powerful lobby groups working on behalf of French farmers than in projecting a dominant position that might have supported and extended the Doha Round of trade talks. French public opinion, like the public opinion of all nations, is not necessarily in agreement with the reduction of tariffs and other trade barriers that might see the demise of the reputation of French cheese, or other agricultural products that are distinctly French. The difficulty for the elected French government is in maintaining some balance between the opening of its markets to developing countries' agricultural products, and the sustaining of its existing agriculture.

Public opinion is a powerful thing. It has the capacity to alter or shift the balance of argument and to transform an objective so that it fails or succeeds in opposition to its original goal. But public opinion in Europe, like public opinion in all other parts of the world is not always right nor is it always accurate. It can be easily influenced by all types of issues and events, most notably as I have argued above, by the threat of global terrorism. For the Spanish, such a threat transformed Spain's political landscape immediately after the terrorist attacks in Madrid in 2005. Public opinion, if it exists at all as an expression of the will of the people, is not something that is easily defined and it has the capacity, in democratic countries, to alter the shape of policy. This is the case with the EU and its appearance of being interested in the future of the Doha Round. Citizens of countries in the EU are more likely to want their governments to look to their well-being over the well-being of those in developing countries when their own lives are threatened by terrorism. In this they are no different than citizens anywhere in the world. The problem for the developing countries and their interest in increasing their well-being is that the EU holds the key to global trade because it is the region that has refused to lower its tariffs and other barriers, particularly on agricultural products. And it is agricultural products that have the most impact on the growth of developing countries.

The Transformation of the Public Sphere

Despite the argument that the world is a global village and that information technology allows immediate access to each other for the world's community, the public sphere as it was best described by Habermas has altered little in shape since the 18th century. It is, I would argue, less public and open today than it was before the invention of the Internet and other global information technology such as telecommunications satellites. While citizens in liberal and other democracies have rights that include access to debate on public issues and events, access to diffuse information about issues and events, and the freedom to vote in all types of electoral contests—rights that should create a liberal public sphere capable of resolving all human rights and poverty issues—citizens of Western developed nations are less inclined to embrace the idea of a public sphere than at any time in the past three hundred years.

For Habermas, the prospect of a public sphere in which citizens exchanged information and ideas and in which the well-being of the majority was placed above the self-interest of the individual began with the Enlightenment. At this time, the public sphere was transformed from one in which citizens were oppressed by the authority of the monarchy into one in which they could freely and actively form individual opinions, turn them into collective opinions, and thus shape their own sociopolitical world. They did this, Habermas suggests, with the assistance of the free and objective institution of journalism, an institution that provided empirical reporting of issues and events so that citizens could develop an informed opinion.

Where it not for the emergence of the global terrorism of al-Qaeda and its leader Osama bin Laden, the mythical idea of a global village and a global public sphere may have been kept alive by those organizations and individuals for whom it played a profitable role. In reality, the death of Doha and the retreat into regionalism heralded by the EU would have been much more difficult to achieve had not bin Laden appeared on the scene. Terrorism, in other words, is directly responsible for the failure of powerful national governments to continue to embrace globalization.

In his more recent work, Habermas (2006) has acknowledged the reshaping of the public sphere and in particular the impact of citizen opinion, as "shaped by the confused din of voices rising from both everyday talk and mediated communication" (Habermas 2006: 14). He argues that public opinion in a weak democracy will not have the desired effect of shaping policy because of the reflexive character of the public sphere and the inability of filtering mechanisms to allow only considered public opinions to pass through. Can we therefore argue that the democracies of the powerful developed countries are weak because they have allowed the threat of terrorist acts to shape public opinion and, thus, public policy on issues such as tariff reductions and free globalized trade? I believe so. The concept of weak democracy allows externalities such as terrorist threats to frame and influence domestic policy agendas. The general election in Spain following the Madrid terrorist attacks is a strong example.

For citizens, the threat of terrorism is enough to influence collective opinion. For governments and other authoritative institutions, the threat of the loss of political power if they pursue an alternative course to that reflected in the collective opinion of their citizens is equally startling. Shock and horror equate with pragmatism and decision-making that reflects crisis and confusion. Such action has caused the crisis in global trade that precipitated the demise of the Doha Round in Geneva in July 2006. The problem for EU members of the World Trade Organization and their deliberative approach to the political pursuit of the freeing of global trade was they did not deliberate for long enough.

Deliberative Politics as a Counter to Terrorism

One measure available to the Western world as a counter against terrorism lies in the practice of deliberative democracy. For Habermas, the idea of a modern democracy includes three elements: private citizens and their autonomy, citizenship in which citizens are free and equal as a political community, and an independent public sphere that provides a balance between society and the state (Habermas 2006: 2). This definition of a public sphere has shifted some distance from his original concept, which presented the public sphere as one in which the quality of the argument and the number of participants underpinned political democracy. In the public sphere that operates as an intermediary between society and state, as we have seen in the example of Spain above, and in any number of South American "democracies," the opportunity for the state to act as a powerful arbiter, rather than as an equal partner with informed collective citizen opinion, occurs when the public sphere is the intermediary actor.

In a deliberative democracy, the opportunities for citizens to be involved in the political process is outweighed by their perception that they can enjoy rights and liberties that allow governments to make representations on their behalf. Liberal democracies work on behalf of citizens, a majority of whom pursue individual liberties and rights while leaving the running of policy to their elected governments.

In France, the idea that agricultural subsidies and trade barriers can play a role in the demise of globalization can be imagined because citizens place emphasis on liberal democracies, leaving policy decisions to government rather than seeking inclusion and equal opportunity for participation that is required of deliberative democracy. We can make this assumption if we bring to the issue the argument that a reduction in subsidies and trade barriers has the potential to immediately reduce poverty in developing countries, as those countries seek to compete in the global agricultural marketplace. It is difficult to conceive that French citizens, provided with sufficient information, could collectively have an informed opinion that rejected a proposal seeking to reduce poverty.

We must therefore conclude that publicity and transparency, inclusion and equal opportunity, are not part of the public sphere in France and that the public sphere itself has failed to act as a independent intermediary between society and the state. This does not mean that the public sphere and its place in deliberative democracy has failed completely to maintain a globalized trading environment. What it means is that both the public sphere and the institution of deliberative democracy have the capacity to overcome terrorism and other opponents of globalization, but that they must be represented adequately to achieve success.

6

Global Institutions of Persuasion and Influence: Issues and Events Imagined as News

This chapter examines the shift in reporting since 9/11 from global institutions to regional institutions, issues and events, and the role of global institutions in attempting to sustain globalization. It presents an image of a world that is shifting from its globalization path to one of regional identity and security, partly as a response to external factors such as terrorism, but equally to the narrowing of reporting of issues and events that reflect regional identity as a more defining frame for developed countries.

The Western news media are not historically well-informed about institutions that they investigate and report. Part of the reason lies in their constant struggle to localize issues and events, to attempt to ground complex issues so that they resonate with local stakeholders. Gleissner and de Vreese go as far as to say that in specific regions such as the European Union (EU), journalists who report the EU[1] have not been provided with an adequate orientation training that takes in the complexity of the institution (Gleissner & de Vreese 2005: 222). The other part is the news media's historical acceptance of institutions as organizations that provide factual information that fits the media's required reporting frames, historically speaking. News media half knew, so they half reported. They relied heavily on specialists for information and comment, particularly from within the institutions on which they were reporting.

In the past few years most of the leading global institutions have enhanced their communications departments by appointing high-level specialists. This increase in the level of sophisticated communication coming from these institutions is due to the increased investigation being undertaken by the news media. And the news media are investigating more deeply because they are no longer satisfied with the level of information being supplied by the institutions. The ramping up of the sophistication of their persuasive and influential communications and the deeper investigation by the news media can be seen as equally costly and equally cynical.

Let's look briefly at the role of the communications specialists within these global institutions to see why things have changed. In the past, the communications director for an organization such as the World Bank was known as a "publicist." Today, the same person is a strategist. The publicist, in Habermasian terms, was one who was in the business of reporting. The transformation of the publicist into the strategist paralleled the transformation of the journalist from being in the "business of news reporting to one involving ideologies and viewpoints" (Habermas 1989: 182). While the journalist was becoming politicized, so was the publicist.

While the news media has been described as one of the preeminent institutions of the public sphere, as an institution it grapples poorly with the idea that it must investigate and report other, equally eminent institutions, distilling their policies so they make sense to diffuse stakeholders. Thus, we have the situation in which fewer élite news media spend time attempting to understand global institutions because they do not devote too much space to them on a regular news cycle. The institutions of the Western public sphere only become news when they are part of, or generate, crises.

For the news media, issues and events attached to global institutions are imagined as if they are, in Tuchman's words, mirrors of society. This is a difficult thing for the global news media. To imagine a global institutional event such as the biannual Food and Agricultural Organization conference in local terms is to narrow the focus of the event to the point where it becomes "routine" and thus loses all its impact as a forum for reducing poverty and world hunger. As I have mentioned elsewhere, the news media, to continue Habermas's metaphor, originally were in the business of reporting news, so what they did was inductive or empirical; they investigated the evidence and reported it factually in a standard way, with present tense and active voice. The transformation of the news media from one which reported public opinion to one which shaped public opinion shifted the empirical investigation to a deductive position, one that was shaped by the closing off of sources, as large organizations became institutionalized and professionalized.

108

The idea that everyone was strategic meant journalists' sources became less enthusiastic about sharing information, so journalists had to become deductive in their reasoning. After all, if you cannot go into and wander around NATO headquarters asking and observing, you have no capacity to write about what you saw. You must begin a process of deduction about what might be going on in there. And when the F18s take off from a German airbase, then you were either right or you were wrong. But at least by then you have something empirical to report.

The issue for the news media, as for the average citizen, is the amount and quality of information that is available so that decisions can be made on the relationship the individual has with the issue. This is a standard public relations device known as knowledge gap reduction: if journalists have plenty of good information about an issue or event, they cannot help but engage positively with it. In the case of the individual, information and intelligence is something we crave in our everyday existence: if we know a bit about our opponent's habits and behavior in general, we can use that on the golf course; we are more comfortable with our capacity to beat her.

The United States as a Global Institution

An institution, according to scholar Thomas Zweifel, is constituted internationally when it has three nations as contracting parties (Zweifel 2006: 60). So the United States of America, while it is the world's most powerful nation, is also its most powerful institution as it has built alliances with a large number of other nations, most recently the group known as the "Coalition of the Willing" that was formed in 2003 to wage war on Iraq.

The United States, as the world's most powerful nation, is reported in the news media uniquely. No nation has the hegemony of the United States in global terms, so no other nation is reported as the Western news media investigates and reports the United States.

In writing about the United States and its dominance of the 20th century, scholar Thomas Reeves argues that the news media, more than any other *institution*, has the power to "define truth, beauty and virtue, to determine the very confines of reality. The authority of churches, schools, government and even the family paled in comparison" (Reeves 2000: 296). Reeves names a number of newspapers as being the most powerful in America—the *New York Times*, the *Wall Street Journal*, the *Washington Post*, the *Chicago Tribune* and the *Los Angeles Times*—and having the power to influence and persuade even the most cynical and jaundiced citizen. But the influence of the news media was not sufficient to investigate and deduce that the terrorist attacks on New York and Washington would occur, nor to stop the Coalition of the Willing two years later when it ignored a United Nations directive and began a war with Iraq. And, as I have argued elsewhere, the news media is an *agent* rather than an *institution* of democracy.

The United States news media report the institution of the United States as if it were a big friendly relative. The rest of the Western news media, Canada, Australia, Britain, Germany, Spain, Italy, the Netherlands, Belgium (maybe not France), report the United States as if it were a big friendly neighbor, one who might come around and help you lay a few bricks on a Sunday morning if you provided a barbeque and some beers. The ownership of the news media in Britain and Australia by a U.S. citizen, Rupert Murdoch, partly reflects this position. But it is also the long-term nature of the relationship between the United States and its Western allies since World War II that stabilizes the media image. No matter how bad people are, (America as a nuclear power, for example) it is hard to be angry with them when they have saved your life.

The United States as an institution uses communication strategies and tactics that are undifferentiated from other institutional goals and objectives. As a brand, it has reputation and trust that it links to its communication strategies in exactly the same way that popular culture brands such as Coca-Cola and Starbucks have generated reputations around the world.

Mayhew argues that a transfer of product marketing techniques into the sociopolitical sphere has transformed the way we think about civil society and that we now imagine it as one homogenized product; we are unable to differentiate between a government policy and a brand of cola. Mayhew calls us a "New Public," a citizenry existing in a place where our opinions are shaped by marketers and public relations spin doctors so that we are unable to differentiate, even if we wanted to. Mayhew looks to journalism as the institution that can save the New Public from being sucked into a product vortex, but journalism has as much trouble differentiating product marketing from policy formulation as we do. For the *Chicago Tribune* journalist, the idea that the institution of the United States might make some poor global decision is still better than the alternative: the possibility that the French might make an even worse decision. Far better to report the poor French decision (cheese-eating surrender monkeys) and leave aside the not-so-poor U.S. decision. After all, evaluation of news worthiness is a matter of comparative degrees.

For the *Economist* and other élite news media, there is another important issue that must be weighed up when reporting the United States as a global institution. It is that, unlike the media of the Habermasian Enlightenment, the United States is now the preeminent institution of liberal democracy in the world, and as such must be considered respectfully by other agents and institutions (the Western news media included) that also value highly the principles of liberal democracy. For the *Economist* and other liberal free-market supporters, there is the added incentive that the United States is the father of free trade. It is always difficult to argue against one's father.

The European Union

Economic prosperity and free trade are arguably the most important elements for continued peaceful existence between nations, and it is no coincidence that the European Union began its life as an economic entity. Yet national governments within the Union experience economic tensions that are often reported by news media out of context with the overall objectives of union.

The EU is imagined by global news media as either a poorly organized, badly run aggregation of states with no common purpose other than trade, or as the answer to all of Europe's historical problems of conflict, poverty, and unemployment. For news media within the Union—EU national country media in Britain, the Netherlands, France, Germany and Spain, for example, as well as foreign correspondents—there are two possible conflicting images: how the Union is imagined from the outside and how it is imagined from inside. The European (including British) news media, when investigating the Union from their own countries, produce material that is mostly parochial. When imagining how the rest of the Western world, or indeed any other quadrant of the world sees them, they tend to report in a less parochial manner, with the appearance of cohesive tensions betweens states. The *Economist* reports the Union from the perspective of one who sees it as an important and powerful trading area.

While I do not consider Britain's *Daily Mail* to be an élite newspaper, the position it took in early 2003 on the issue of a European constitution is worth recording. Columnist Simon Heffer argued that "steadily, slyly, Eurocrats have devised a constitution which—and we do not exaggerate—could soon destroy Britain's nationhood. More far-reaching than Maastricht, it lets Brussels control everything for our borders to our banks" (*Daily Mail*, May 8, 2003, p. 12). The élite right-of-center *Daily Telegraph* followed with a leader saying "this is it, the moment we have repeatedly been told would never come about. The EU is about to transform itself, *de jure* and *de facto*, into a single state" (*Daily Telegraph* May 12, 2003, p. 21). What the British press were getting hot and heavy about was the idea that they were to become members of a European Union that had a constitution, a position which they thought undemocratic given that the British public had not been invited to vote on the issue at either a general election or a referendum. But they had not given the idea much thought in the whole of the previous year: it had been on the European parliamentary agenda since February 28, 2002. And, as we now know, neither the French nor the Dutch were keen for a constitution to be drawn up (citing fear of globalization as a major factor in their decisions); both countries voted against the proposal in May and June 2005.

For the *Economist*, the idea that both country's leaders supported the proposal, and planned to ask their electors again at general elections in 2007, was against the principles of democracy. In May 2007 it argued that "there is something undemocratic about asking electorates to endorse a text and, when they deliver a resounding no, asking them again" (*Economist* June 27, 2006, p. 22).

The most important element—and the most difficult—for the British news media in imagining a united Europe is the existence in Britain of a Westminster parliamentary democracy with a two-party preferred system. Parliament is alive to the challenges and tensions of one party constantly struggling to defeat the other on the floor of the Commons as if they were bitter enemies locked in mortal combat. In truth, the old division of Whigs and Tories along capitalist and socialist lines has vanished. During the past three hundred years the Tories have shifted to the old position occupied by the Whigs. The Labor Party, originally a worker's party with socialist policies, has shifted with them. So we have two parties which are barely distinguishable from each other competing desperately to persuade constituents that

112

the policies they present are different, while in reality they both favor market economies and conservative government. But for the British news media, the old divisions remain, at least in their imaginations, and individual journalists and other editorial staff align themselves bitterly with one or the other party. Struggles play out between both sides until the Europeans start messing about in the game. For the British, who have had three hundred years of parliamentary conflict to report (real and imagined) the idea that the Europeans will devise a union that strips their British citizens of their culture is the most appalling thing imaginable. So they get hot and heavy. Until it is time to focus on the domestic game, then they forget about globalization for a while.

One of the most interesting news media narratives on the EU appeared in the *Economist* in mid–June 2006. The newspaper publishes weekly "columns" (one-page opinion pieces) in which unidentified journalist commentators get to offer their opinion of issues and events that might also be appearing as regular news. For the June 17 edition, the newspaper adopted the long-dead style of one of its predecessors, Richard Steele's *Tatler*, by offering a witty summation of the "state of play" within the "clubhouse" of the EU. Drawing on former UK foreign secretary Jack Straw's witticism (relating to the proposed plans for an EU constitution)—when he said that even local golf clubs have one—the *Economist* drew on the analogy to mercilessly attack (good-naturedly) the EU club, its defeat in the "Lisbon Cup" against the "American Capitalist Association"; its comprehensive beating by the "Mandarin Club"; the desire of some members to revoke the membership of "Polish plumbers"; an improved security system for the "clubhouse" and most importantly, better service contracts for cooks, waiters and cleaners!

The use of parody to discuss the important issues and events confronting the EU is not a new device for the Western news media. What is interesting is that it still thinks it is worth trotting out, three hundred years after the whistle blew on the first game.

A number of academic studies have identified particular characteristics of EU reporting. Most acknowledge that the EU has difficulty in representing an image that might bring its complex operations and processes to the attention of citizens. In television news particularly the EU is represented in a negative fashion which American media scholar Pippa Norris identifies as being a contributing factor in poor relations between European leaders and their constituent publics (Norris 2000).

The African Union

Like the European Union, the African Union is an acknowledgment of the need for socioeconomic coherency and cohesion in a globalized trading world. According to the *Economist*, it is interested in owning most of Africa's problems, and "desperately trying to keep the peace in the war ravaged western region of Darfur" (*Economist* December 3, 2005, p. 9). But the Western news media imagine the African Union as an organization which, if it does not take care, might trip over its shoelaces. They imagine the African Union as a fledgling organization with no real impact in African affairs; they imagine it as a child who is yet to understand the real world of adults.

Zweifler (2006) outlines the origins of the AU in the politically and socially bereft Organization of African Unity (OAU), which emerged from the hardship of colonization in 1963 to become, by 2002, the democratically focused African Union. I suggest, however, that there is some hangover from the OAU in the way the Western news media imagine the AU, and that the AU is thought of differently because it is not based in democracy as the Western news media have come to accept Western institutions and supranational organizations.

The AU emerged from the OAU and was framed against the image of the EU. But while its mandate is the spread of democracy—actively sought—it created institutions which allowed some retention of national sovereignty rather than allowing them to become supranational. This has lead to some better outcomes than equivalent issues and events in the EU, but to worse outcomes in such activities as peacekeeping.

Because of the difficulties associated with keeping correspondents on the ground in Africa, most Western news media use the resources of the organizations they are reporting to draw deductive arguments. Web sites for organizations such as the African Union provide names, places and the details of the actions that occurred around issues, for the specific purpose of informing the news media. The communiqué, for example, that detailed the meeting between the AU Commissioner for Peace and Security, Mr. Said Djinnit and Special Representative of the AU for Sudan, Mr. Baba Gana Kingibe, set out details of the declaration of commitment to the Darfur Peace Agreement. The information in the communiqué was adapted to support reporting of the issue by the Western news media.

The important thing for the Western news media is to interpret the rhetoric so that issues of policy that are hiding behind it can be dislodged and debated in the public sphere, rather than *in camera*. Policy can hinge on the result of a word change, but news media get hooked up in the magic of attachment—the image of contestants as they are seen by their labels—*janjaweed* in Sudan is a strong example. As is *genocide*. Both words reveal emotional images that are supported strongly by Western news media. *Janjaweed* are a Sudanese government-backed Arab militia believed to have committed war crimes.[2]

The first use of the word *genocide* to describe the actions of *janjaweed* came from then U.S. Secretary of State Colin Powell in 2004. Since that time the Bush administration has labeled the actions of the *janjaweed* as "genocidal" and "ethnic cleansing" against the Darfurian black African population. But the United Nations resisted the label. The UN called the actions an "inexcusable tragedy" and described the Sudan as being in a "state of anarchy," but stopped short of calling it genocide because of its policy implications. If the UN referred to the actions as genocidal, it created the opportunity—under international law—for other nations to intervene. There is, however, no such pause for reflection by the Western news media. *Time* magazine headlined a May 8, 2006, story, "The Front Lines of Genocide," across a two-page picture of Sudanese Liberation Army rebel fighters standing to attention during a meeting with UN representative Jan Pronk.[3] The difficulty for the UN, and its promises to deploy twenty thousand peacekeepers in Darfur to stop the killing and dislocation of millions of people, lay in the fact that *janjaweed* was doing most of the killing. It was also related to the issue of UN peacekeepers being spread across more zones of conflict than at any time in their history.

For the Western news media, the whole "problem" in Sudan could be distilled to satisfy a number of possible angles. If it was not about the interests of China and India in securing the bountiful reserves of oil within the Sudanese border (in which they had financial and capital investment interests), it was about conflict between Christian African rebels and the Arab Islamic government. But it might also have been about conflict between black African Islamists and Arab Islamists. Whatever the angle, the issue's narrative was generally one that had its basis in human rights, war crimes, genocide and the global crisis in peacekeeping deployment.

For the African Union, the Western news media reporting on

issues and events in Sudan was less critical. They were more interested in the failures of the UN to respond rapidly than in the failure
of the African Union troops to act effectively. There was a general
image among the Western news media that the African Union was trying its little heart out, and that it should therefore have been given
points for trying. Much easier to attack the UN or the United States,
which the *Economist* did in December 2005 in a special report suggesting the complexity of the relationships made reporting fact more
difficulty. It noted that the Central Intelligence Agency (CIA) was
working with the Arab Islamic government on antiterrorism, while
the same country was on the State Department's list of countries that
sponsor terrorism (*Economist* December 3, 2005).

Throughout early 2006, Western news media élites, the *Economist,* the *New York Times*, the BBC, the *Times*, were universal in their
call for the Sudanese government to allow UN forward troops into
Darfur to assist AU peacekeeping troops. Most news media ran
straight editorials and op-ed pieces in an attempt to persuade Sudanese
president Omar Hassan al-Bashir of the virtue in diplomacy. The *New
York Times* of April 2 ran a long essay by journalist Elizabeth Rubin
(almost eight thousand words) which began with a peaceful image of
afternoon among trees and art galleries in The Hague, an image the
writer claimed was not in keeping with how war-torn places such as
Sarajevo and Sudan imagined it, given it was also home to the International Criminal Court.

The fact that the news media generally patronized the African
Union's peacekeeping capabilities, along with their general feeling that
the UN was incapable of quick action, led to a number of calls for
NATO to become involved in a more interventionist way, especially
in Darfur.

North Atlantic Treaty Organization

The Western news media has had an interesting and at times fractured relationship with the North Atlantic Treaty Organization
(NATO). There is a widespread belief in power, and NATO, as the
world's premier military alliance, has plenty. But the image of NATO
as a military alliance whose power and capacity to alter the balance
in global conflict is at the point that it was for the UN a generation
ago. In other words, the Western news media imagine NATO to be
the powerful organization that the UN was imagined to be in the

1970s. The important difference is that the UN was established as a global organization while NATO was a regional one.

For the élite Western news media and others, the idea that NATO could become a global institution began with its intervention in the Balkans conflict in the early 1990s. While it began as an alliance of twelve nations after World War II, NATO has expanded as other countries have desired to come under its protective umbrella. By 2003 the organization had moved outside its Euro-American boundaries to become involved in Afghanistan, and by 2004 in Iraq. Its original role as a military mutual defense organization against the Warsaw Pact has expanded into peacekeeping, regional security, control of weapons trade and disarmament (Zweifel 2006).

The difficulty in reporting NATO, for the Western news media, lies in their relationship to their primary stakeholders: citizens of Western countries. Humans imagine links between known information and unknown information prescribed as news. Ambiguity in the delivery of news is not a common objective for journalism, but it exists in so many other forms of media that it crosses over into news as it is imagined by individual citizens. Names of movies (*The World's Fastest Indian*, for example) invoke images not associated with the actual. Language plays a distinct role in the imagining of issues and events so that something like "turbo vet" is not imagined as a very fast animal doctor, but rather a powerful Corvette motor car. For the average citizen, the image of an organization such as NATO, which might be headquartered in Brussels, but requires collective government decisions to be made on policy, is so complex that the news media prefer to set it aside rather than attempt to localize it. This is part of the problem of localization as it relates to the outdated model of journalism which the Western news media adhere to. Here we need to contemplate the idea that organizations such as NATO are so complex and intangible (except for easily digestible events such as aircraft bombing chosen targets) that the model of journalism that has existed historically for the past three hundred years was never capable of interpreting them. For Lippmann (1922), the idea that truth is observable provides an explanation for how the news media interpret NATO. Events such as aircraft bombings or naval fleet maneuvers are observable and, thus, truthful. What are less amenable to interpretation are the issues that led to the events, given the lack of a supranational governance.

The level at which NATO operates allows it to exert influence that is not available to other similar organizations, most notably the UN, as it is constantly "on the radar" of the Western news media. NATO is also on the radar, but I would argue that it is allowed to fly pretty much unimpeded because the model of journalism used by the Western news media is not effective in framing the issues and events that proscribe NATO. This sentiment applies to some other organizations with similar shape, but with the additional dimension applied by Zweifel (2006): that institutions such as the World Trade Organization, North American Free Trade Agreement, Association of South East Asian Nations and the Organization for Economic Co-operation and Development are not accountable to civil society as they are unrepresentative. (For a discussion of the influence of the World Trade Organization and its relationship to Western news media, see chapter 8).

The World Bank and the International Monetary Fund

For most of its life, up until twenty years ago, the World Bank—a product of Keynesian economic policy—was in the business of lending money to countries so they could build things: bridges, roads and other infrastructure that would assist them to compete in the global trading market. Things changed in mid–1985, when the United States under President Ronald Reagan suggested that economic growth should be the goal of all developing countries and that lending should be therefore based on economic growth rather than domestic cost cutting. The incremental change in the Bank's lending policies since then has shifted to societal investment in health, education and other intangible instruments, making life more difficult for the Western news media to report on the Bank in a straightforward, observable way.

In the past, a newspaper or television broadcast depicted images of a bridge as if it were a conclusive piece of evidence that a developing country was making its way towards free-market status. Now, investigations and reporting are a little more difficult; the observation of truths such as bridges and power stations is harder, given educational and health outcomes are not as evident in the short term.

Western news media rely on institutions such as the World Bank for statistics to reinforce their stories. In a special report of February 2, 2002, the *Economist* cited information supplied by the World Bank four times, the UN three times and the World Trade Organization once to support its argument in its three-page report.

Like the World Bank, the International Monetary Fund (IMF) began life at Bretton Woods in 1944. Its terms of reference include the promotion of international monetary cooperation, the promotion of foreign-exchange stability, the creation of multilateral systems of payments between members and, most importantly for our purposes, assisting the expansion and balanced growth of international trade. So the World Bank and the IMF have direct links to other vital global institutions, the World Trade Organization and the UN.

Stakeholder participation in the activities of the World Bank and IMF are limited to their members, making them interesting global institutions in how they are imagined by the Western news media.

While the IMF and World Bank are important sources for Western news media, they are also institutions (or agents, depending upon your viewpoint) that receive a large amount of criticism from the news media. This is partly a reaction to the media's opinion of the institutions as complex organizations unable to be interpreted at a local level, and partly as a response to the news media framing the institutions as oppressors of developing nations rather than support structures.

The collapse of the Doha Round of trade negotiations in July 2006 provoked a number of responses from Western news media. New Zealand's *Dominion Post* of August 2, 2006, saw the IMF and World Bank as providing old-world advice that included a "one size fits all" perspective on world trade, where the message "trade liberalization is good for you" was all that mattered. *Agence France Presse* reported on August 1 a warning from the head of the IMF, Rodrigo Rato, that national and regional trade deals would be a patchwork that would not substantially improve the lot of poor countries as could the more ambitious idea of multilateral global trade.

The *Wall Street Journal* of July 31 made a comparison between the voting regime in the IMF with that of the WTO, arguing the WTO was far less capable of making a decision given its consensual model. In the same edition, the *Journal* reported on the repayment of half its debt to the IMF by Uruguay which, unlike its South American neighbors Argentina and Brazil, sees itself in a friendly relationship with the institution. (Argentina celebrated the full payment of its debt as a mark of independence from the institution in early 2006.) Leading British newspaper the *Observer* suggested the breakdown in trade talks rested with America and that austere economic policies imposed on developing countries by the IMF and World Bank were the work of America. Meanwhile Singapore's *Straits Times*, an interesting non–Western newspaper, preferred to imagine the September 2006 IMF World Bank meeting in Singapore in terms of the number of cooks and the amount of food it would take to sustain the meeting. The *Straits Times*, not well-known for its objective or factual reporting, appeared to be more interested in localizing the event as one that would occupy a team of three hundred cooks making five hundred different appetizers, five hundred main courses and three hundred different types of pastries. On a more serious note, the *International Herald Tribune* wrote of the same September meeting that it was likely to be dominated by the issue of voting rights or quotas within the organization. In this it drew upon a standard journalistic technique—the undefined number whose opinion carry enormous weight—to suggest that "few doubt that the system needs to be changed to better reflect the new dynamism of the East Asian economies" (*International Herald Tribune* July 29, 2006). With an alternative argument, the *Hindu* of July 29, 2006, made an ironic attack on the IMF and World Bank as partners in a global movement to alleviate the burden of poverty within developing countries. The *Hindu* argued that poverty is not a static condition that people can be raised out of and that its existence is more complex than institutions such as the IMF make out. The position of the Western news media, and others as we can see, is one of misunderstanding, cynicism, or both, towards these global institutions.

Organization for Economic Cooperation and Development

The OECD claims to be an organization of thirty member countries "sharing a commitment to democratic government and the market economy" (OECD Web site). It claims active relationships with seventy additional countries and NGOs and civil society. Its role is to assist governments and corporations with good governance through the dissemination of statistical and analytical data in which dialogue, consensus and peer review play a major role.

The OECD refers to itself as an intergovernmental organization with a mandate to communicate transparently with stakeholders that include governments, business, academia, organized labor, civil society organizations, the news media and the general public. It maintains a staff of around two thousand in Paris to carry out its functions and to support the activities of its various committees. The committees work in specific policy areas such as economics, science, employment, education, financial markets and, most important to us, trade. There are around two hundred committees. Like most intergovernmental or supranational institutions, the OECD maintains a steady flow of information through its Web site and through hard copy of media material to media and other stakeholders. How this information is interpreted is of most interest, as it is the interpretation of OECD information by the Western news media that assists in the maintenance of the organization itself.

Country economic surveys, for example, are followed by news coverage interpreted in the way the particular medium imagines the issue. In Australia in July, following publication of a 2006 survey, news media covered the issue in interesting ways. An OECD report is like a report that a good friend gives you as a job reference. But it has to pass the scrutiny of the person who does not want you in the job.

The report from the OECD made a number of pronouncements on Australia:

- A commodities price boom had boosted terms of trade by 30 per cent over the past three years.
- In terms of per capita GDP, it had surpassed all G7 countries except the United States.
- Public sector efficiency could be improved by clarifying government roles and responsibilities.
- The establishment of a national competition policy that had national access was seen as highly effective.
- Strong attempts had been made to create a more flexible industrial relations system.
- It had a high ranking internationally in terms of low wage traps for single parents and one earner households.
- It was better placed than most countries to cope with the effects of an aging workforce and population.

There are, of course, a number of ways to interpret the information in the OECD report. Journalist Malcolm Maiden in Melbourne's main metropolitan daily, the *Age,* used OECD data to discuss interest rate rises where it claimed Australian households were "bearing a debt services burden that puts them close to the top of the OECD league table" (*Age* August 3, 2006, p. 12). Journalist Chris Russell, in the Adelaide broadsheet, the *Advertiser*, said the country must make economic changes or risk squandering gains it had made in commodities, citing the OECD report. It referred to the OECD statement on financial autonomy for the states as "ambitious" (*Advertiser* August 2, 2006, p. 35). In the national business daily, the *Australian Financial Review*, economics editor Alan Mitchell suggested the government would not take the OECD advice that "increases in commodity-price-driven tax revenues should be saved rather than spent on permanent tax cuts." Its comment on the matter was "fat chance" (*Australian Financial Review* August 2, 2006). In the same newspaper a day earlier political correspondent Mark Davis had interpreted the OECD report as prescribing "an aggressive and contentious reform agenda for Australia, including an overhaul of the federal system of government" and warned that "productivity growth is down and the economy is now vulnerable to a downturn in world commodity prices" (*Australian Financial Review* August 1, 2006, p. 1).

If the Australian news media were keen to imagine the OECD report as a negative prescription, they got some strong support from their overseas colleagues, most notably from Raphael Minder in London's *Financial Times* newspaper, who suggested the Australian government was likely to face a "pressing challenge" with the "end of the commodities boom that has underpinned the country's recent economic progress" (*Financial Times* August 1, 2006, p. 5). But the question that needs to be raised here is how the *Financial Times* knew the commodities boom had ended, as it did not appear at the time to be abating in the country in question. The *Financial Times* went even further, interpreting the OECD report as warning Australia about health-care costs and tax. It added that the report questioned Australia's energy policy and water management.

World Health Organization

The global institution known as the World Health Organization (WHO) is represented by the Western news media using a number of competing frames. On one hand it is imagined as an overarching institution capable of alleviating human suffering through the eradication of disease and hunger, and on the other as an immovable object incapable of action at times of crisis or stress.

For the *Economist*, most reporting of the WHO is placed in its Science and Technology Section, and the WHO itself is most often reported as an object of a particular issue rather than as a source.

Throughout 2005, the Western news media took relatively seriously the threat of an avian influenza pandemic, and in their reporting noted the policies and processes the WHO had put in place to deal with such an eventuality.[4] The fact that a pandemic did not occur during the time frame imposed by the media[5] meant that by early 2006 it had almost disappeared from the news, especially television news, despite the earlier enormity of its threat. It remained visible for a number of specific leftover reasons, one being China's admission that a human had died from avian flu as early as 2003, but it had not reported the case to the WHO. The WHO, however, did not lose sight of avian flu's global potential. The organization was mentioned in more than twenty thousand newspaper and agency reports in 2006.

The WHO is a specialized agency under the umbrella of the United Nations. It refers to itself as an agency rather than an institution, but its presence in the global sphere requires us to include it here not for its institutional status, but for its relevance to the Western news media as both source and agent. It was established in 1948 and its objective is the attainment of the highest possible levels of health by all peoples. The WHO defines *health* as a state of complete physical, mental and social well-being and not merely the absence of disease or infirmity. It is governed by one hundred and ninety-two member states through the World Health Assembly (WHA). The WHA itself is composed of representatives of WHO's member states. The main tasks of the World Health Assembly are to approve the WHO program, budget and major policy decisions. The WHA meets in Geneva in May each year to determine policy.

The WHO provides a media service on its Web site where information is accessible by journalists and citizens. Media news statements, such as that on fuel shortages in Lebanon creating a grave threat to human health during the mid–2006 Israel-Hezbollah war, get picked up by Western news media and run as news. This particular piece was run by the *Toronto Star* on August 8, one of the few newspapers to pick up on the importance of the issue.

The WHO press release began by warning that, if fuel deliveries were not made to Lebanon in the week of August 7, 60 percent of all hospitals in Lebanon, in addition to other health facilities, would cease to function. It said due to the damage to infrastructure in the conflict-affected areas of Lebanon, hospitals and other health centers were relying on fuel to run generators, and that power was essential to run operating theaters, life-saving equipment including incubators for newborns, refrigeration for vaccines and treatments including insulin. It argued fuel for power generation was also vital to the provision of safe water and hygiene. It claimed that Lebanon had twelve thousand hospital beds and that, in order to function, each hospital bed needed eighty liters of fuel per week for electric power. Ongoing military operations had hampered fuel delivery and the WHO called for safe passage of fuel supplies to hospitals. The tone of the news release was emotional, with an overriding rationalist perspective in its plea for sanity to prevail, at least when it came to the sick, the injured and the wounded.

For journalist Andrew Mills of the *Toronto Star*, the issue was localized, a tactic we have come to understand, and led with an image of "two bloodied feet stuck out of a CAT scanner at Rafik Hariri University Hospital last night as physicians assessed one of about thirty people injured when an Israeli air strike toppled an apartment building" (*Toronto Star* August 8, 2006, p. 7). Three paragraphs later the newspaper stated that "soon, the Hariri hospital and many others across Lebanon will struggle to keep the lights on, the equipment running and the patients alive." In the following paragraph it quoted from the WHO Web site news release warning that "60 per cent of the country's hospitals will have to shut down if fuel is not delivered to Lebanon this week." It then moved in the next paragraph to cite the UN, reporting that it said the dwindling fuel supply "sits at the crux of a humanitarian disaster ... spiraling out of control" (*Toronto Star* August 8, 2006, p. 7).

The *Toronto Star* news report interpreted and imagined the information supplied by WHO and interspersed it with other imaginings of its own. It reported in the next few paragraphs of the story that "captains" of Beirut-bound fuel tankers were waiting off the coast "not yet satisfied Israel won't attack as they head for shore" (*Toronto Star* August 8, 2006, p. 7).

The newspaper merged the image of a closed airport with the bombing of all major roads so that a more dramatic picture of the issue could be framed. Whether this news report on the issue represented by the WHO had the desired effect is arguable. What is more interesting is that the *Toronto Star* thought it necessary to narrow the focus of the issue to the point of introducing readers to the feet of victims of an Israeli air strike and then expanding it to embrace a range of potentially impossible-to-achieve goals, rather than focusing on the important image framed so well by the WHO news release. The WHO, like the UN and WTO, provides an enormous amount of information about the issues and events that it is involved with, more so than a lot of other institutions and agencies, such as the Association of South East Asian Nations (ASEAN), as we will see below, who imagine the news media in an entirely different way, and who are in turn imagined differently by the news media.

WHO includes in its Web site a comprehensive alphabetical listing of topics, providing background information—known as fact sheets—on every global and local issue in which it is involved. Topics range from abortion and air pollution to waste from health-care activities and yellow fever.

For the Western news media, the WHO is an important source of information on global health issues and events, but it is also the subject of critical investigation, as we would expect, when it is perceived to be lacking in policy direction or action. It can be a source of vital information on issues such as avian flu, in which news media acknowledge its assistance when reporting human deaths from bird flu in China, after China failed to disclose such events for three years. The *New York Times* reported in August 2006 that tests performed by the WHO had led to the discovery that a Chinese man had in fact died of bird flu rather than SARS, as reported three years earlier by the Chinese government.

The issue for the WHO is not so much that the Western news media investigate and report critical findings when the WHO is perceived to be creating bad policy, it is more that other agents, such as Médecins sans Frontières and Oxfam, are operating more widely than ever in the global sphere, and occupying the news media space that WHO believes is its own. This is an issue for all institutions and agents operating in the global public sphere: the finite media space available for them to frame their issue and event strategically.

When reporting on issues and events, Western news media will look to these alternative organizations as important sources because they can contextualize the actions of the more localized organizations such as Oxfam. The *Economist* for example, is far more likely to quote Oxfam than any other agency when reporting on any number of people-related issues including health, poverty and human rights. This is as much a result of these organizations occupying space in the global public sphere and framing their issues so that they resonate with the news media as it is a result of global organizations such as the WHO being perceived as too complex and cumbersome to understand or get to know more fully. But this problem also exists for smaller organizations such as the Association of South East Asian Nations, as we will see.

Association of South East Asian Nations

According to UN secretary-general Kofi Annan, the Association of South East Asian Nations (ASEAN) is "not only a well functioning indispensable reality in the region, it is a real force to be reckoned with far beyond the region ... and a trusted partner of the United Nations in the field of development" (ASEAN Web site). Mr. Annan made these remarks in February 2000 to the Indonesian Council of World Affairs. Indonesia is a leading member of ASEAN and one of five founding members that established the organization in Bangkok in 1967. ASEAN now has ten members—Indonesia, Malaysia, the Philippines, Singapore, Thailand, Brunei Darussalam, Vietnam, Laos, Myanmar and Cambodia. Most of its member countries are considered to be developing, particularly Vietnam, Cambodia, Myanmar and Laos. The aims and purposes of ASEAN are to accelerate economic growth, social progress and cultural development in the region through joint endeavors and to promote regional peace and stability through justice and the rule of law.

But ASEAN is not an organization that inspires much interest in the Western news media beyond the Western countries of New Zealand and Australia that have had an ambivalent relationship with a historical interest in joining it, or in seeing it founder. Journalist Victor Mallett of the *Financial Times* referred to it as "an organization in danger of becoming a diplomatic irrelevance as it approaches the 40th anniversary of its founding" (*Financial Times* August 3, 2006, p. 13).

ASEAN is not reported widely in the West nor does it go out of its way to provide news and information of its activities on a wide scale compared to the media activities of the WHO, the UN or WTO. In July 2006 for example, it posted two news items on its Web site, one a joint media statement of the 24th ASEAN ministers on all energy meeting, and the other on its preferred and endorsed candidate for

UN secretary-general. Britain's the *Independent* and Australia's the *Canberra Times* ran the same story on the issue, with diplomatic editor Anne Penketh reporting that "the United Nations Security council will hold a straw poll next week on the four Asian candidates who are bidding to replace Kofi Annan, in the first decisive step towards picking the UN's next secretary-general" (*Independent* July 21, 2006, p. 29). The stories were word for word,[6] with the seventh paragraph introducing the Thai deputy prime minister, Surakiart Sathirathi, as a candidate who had the strong support of ASEAN.

In May of the same year ASEAN posted nine releases on its Web site, most of which were heralding joint meetings and releasing joint ministerial statements, the contexts of which were generally well-spun. It was a little more prolific in June with ten releases, most of which again were joint statements and a keynote address at the opening ceremony of a workshop on human rights. Rarely does ASEAN make strong pronouncements that might be picked up by the Western news media. In this it has a cultural problem. It does not keep up a strong news presence on its Web site partly because the news media in the region—South East Asian news media including Singapore's *Straits Times*—is locked into reporting government processes and adherents of the region's government's policies rather than acting as objective investigators. ASEAN is more widely reported in Australia than in any other Western country. Australia has a wavering interest in joining the organization, but has historically been excluded because of its Western image and its deep relationships with the United Kingdom and the United States.

ASEAN received a lot more coverage than usual after the collapse of the Doha Round of trade talks in July 2006. The Doha collapse spirited the Western news media into imagining that regional trade deals would increase and that organizations such as ASEAN, the EU, the AU, and South America's Mercosur would benefit from the WTO global trade collapse. Of the nonregional news media, the *Toronto Star* was the most imaginative in reporting that, with the collapse of the Doha Round, organizations such as ASEAN, the African Union and the Gulf Cooperation Council "followed NATO's lead in developing cooperative approaches to security and defence" (*Toronto Star* August 1, 2006, p. 13). While it is uncertain what the *Star* was actually reporting in this, it might provide context to add its comments about another global organization a few paragraphs earlier in the story, when it reported that "that year [2012] saw the UN descend into an existential crisis" (*Toronto Star* August 1, 2006, p. 13). We can see then that the lengthy story, by *Star* reporter Jennifer Welsh, is a satirical look at the future after the collapse of the Doha Round, and one which might have some prescience in its imagining.

In terms of real reporting after the Doha crisis in July 2006, the Australian news media imagined ASEAN as being in a strong position to form a regional trading bloc beyond its historical goals. The *Australian Financial Review* journalist Morgan Mellish saw the issue as one in which ASEAN, as an organization with a total population of 500 million, a combined gross domestic product of US$737 billion and total trade worth US$720 billion, is in a prime position to drive any future ideas about global trade. In typical antipodean fashion however, it added a caveat that "such an idea was certainly a long way off" (*Australian Financial Review* July 31, 2006, p. 12). One might imagine the *Australian Financial Review* was presenting a fictional account, in the same spirit as the *Toronto Star*.

In New Zealand, a similar sentiment prevailed, with the *New Zealand Herald* reporting the desire of that country's trade minister for closer bilateral talks with ASEAN and China, rather than attempting to continue to revive the Doha Round.

The difficulty for ASEAN, as an organization with conflicting cultural economic and political beliefs and ideologies, can be imagined in the same way as those of the WTO: the Western news media are not enthusiastic about the organization's goals and objectives and therefore fails to investigate and report them in a serious fashion. For the Western news media, the complexity of trade and its links to other important issues such as poverty, security and health, are too difficult to report at a global level. They are consequently distilled into localized manageable commodities that can be easily digested by media stakeholders. But in making them digestible, the Western news media reshapes and reimagines global institutions and agencies in ways that does not assist their global goals and objectives.

7

Global News Institutions: The United Nations

This chapter analyzes the role of the United Nations from the perspective of its Department of Public Information (DPI), both as a generator of news about the UN and as a disseminator of news on behalf of its two disparate stakeholder groups as members of the organization: donor countries and recipient countries (effectively developed and developing countries respectively). It will show how the UN's Department of Public Information has attempted to redefine and reaffirm itself at a crucial time of internal division and chaos. It will also demonstrate that the UN, while making positive public statements about the future of globalization, is less keen in practice, given its adoption of a regional system of information and news dissemination to replace its broader country-based system.

A year after the terrorist attacks on the World Trade Center and Pentagon, the United Nations, one of the world's best-known brands by reputation and trust, began a comprehensive review of the work of the organization, titled *Strengthening of the United Nations: An Agenda for Further Change*. The review emerged from the Millennium Summit two years earlier, which itself was part of wider reforms begun in 1997. The review included an investigation into what had already been achieved

— The alignment of activities with priorities
— The strengthening of human rights
— Streamlining reporting procedures
— Clarification of roles and responsibilities within the organization, and
— An investigation into how it could enhance its dissemination of public information by repositioning the strategically important DPI within the organization and in how it was imagined by stakeholders.

The review proposed a new model for the DPI in New York, a new operating concept for UN information centers in the field, and an impact assessment for each of the Department's major product and service lines.

The new model proposed the addition of a Division of Strategic Communications to devise, disseminate and evaluate UN messages around priority themes; an Outreach Division in which services to delegations, liaison with civil society and activities for the general public were grouped together; and a strengthened News and Media Division, which incorporated the Web site. Overall, the restructuring was a contributing factor in the reduction of authority of the UN as a global institution as it sought to engage with the contracting of trade into regional blocs.

The United Nations is both a news medium and news. It disseminates huge volumes of news material everyday through its Department of Public Information—issues and events that it is engaged with on behalf of its 191 stakeholder members—but it is also one of the world's most important topics of media news. The UN is the world's peacekeeper at a time of enormous global conflict, so it is the natural focus of global news media. In this chapter we are interested in both the way the UN generates and disseminates news—how it functions as a news medium—but equally importantly, how the organization itself becomes global news.

The idea that a large organization can be both subject and object of news is not new: governments, corporations and indeed individuals, as we have seen in earlier chapters, are more than capable of generating news and being the topic of news. What is vitally important about the United Nations is its capacity to generate news simply by being what it is: the largest international nongovernmental organization (INGO) in the world, with as much potential power as any organization, nation, or corporation has ever had in the history of modernity.

The way in which the Western news media investigate and report the United Nations defines how it is imagined in the West. While it is an accessible organization—it holds daily tours of its New York headquarters that are always bulging with interested tourists—the UN is also an inaccessible organization. The evident contradiction in this statement will be revealed shortly.

The UN argues that a regional system follows the principles of globalization, yet regionalization is in fact a response by peripheral actors to the challenge of globalization imposed by Western corporations, governments and nongovernment organizations (NGOs). As we have seen in earlier chapters, the regionalization occurring in Asia as it attempts to distance itself from the threats of global terrorism is itself a threat to globalization. Far from being a well-organized, well-resourced department, DPI runs on the smell of an oily rag, using the deep expertise of a few well-trained people to represent an image of professionalism and polish.

In the 1960s, the United Nations set itself up as an international news agency. Forty years later, it has shifted its focus from one in which it is the main supplier of news to developing countries to use the World wide web as a vehicle for dissemination of its issues and activities as they affect its diffuse stakeholder base. The UN has moved from agency advocacy in the 1960s to regionalization of information today. Part of the reason lies in the utility of the Internet and global broadband access, its capacity to transfer large volumes of information between recipients and creators.

The United Nations is an interesting organization. From the outside it appears to generate news and information seamlessly. It is imagined within the public sphere as being competent, with a well-developed hierarchy because it is involved directly in thousands of issues and events and appears to work efficiently with the largest board of directors imaginable: one hundred and ninety-one member countries. Part of its news and information campaign strategy is to provide an image of seamlessness when all is not seamless behind the scenes.

Public Relations and Diplomacy: The Department of Public Information

According to UN undersecretary-general Shashi Tharoor, the head of the Department of Public Information (DPI), the UN works to gain the support of people around the world by reaching out through the news media, NGOs and other organizations within civil society such as educational institutions (Tharoor 2003). In fact what Tharoor says of the UN generally is that it is quite capable of decisive action—in terms of its use of public diplomacy and public relations—but that it is not a good formulator of theory.

For Tharoor and the DPI, the issue is not one of being able to construct one particular message each day that might create global news "worthiness," it is the simultaneousness of putting out several dozen messages everywhere, everyday and dealing with a global audience that is vast, fragmented and whose interests diverge across national and global borders.[1] The balance that the DPI faces each day is to respond to the demands of the sophisticated Western news media while not overlooking or alienating the news media of developing country members.

The DPI is meant to provide news and information to a wide variety of stakeholders, but it is under resourced, fragmented, and disdainful of theoretical models, preferring to rely on outdated practical skills to "spin" the image of an organization in desperate need of renewal. It is so underresourced, despite a mandate from the member states for it to evaluate its communication campaigns around a results-based model, that it has established a link to a well-organized, well-funded international communication organization in an attempt to fund some mid-level evaluation research into UN issues and events.

So that we have some perspective on the issue of funding that the Department is obliged to live with, the U.S. government invested around $1 billion a day in the early years of the Iraq war. For the UN, $1.5 billion is its total yearly budget allocation. Of this, the DPI receives a relatively small amount: $1 million. But what it achieves with its limited resources is remarkable because it is imagined by news media as a well-run, well-resourced department due to its diffuse dissemination of media news material and its construction of classic public relations campaigns.

The UN relies on practical experience to evaluate its future strategic decisions and to frame its news generation. The feeling is that there are a lot of wild theories that can be justified by research and statistics, but the UN is interested in changing the world in certain ways to meet certain ends, so communication strategies are based on very clear messages.

The DPI is unlikely to seek advice from agencies because it believes they are geared towards marketing, a profit motive and selling "product." But the UN itself is trying to sell an idea that will create a behavioral change. Rather than changing behavior so that an individual will buy a product, the UN is in the business of long-term social change. It must also be sensitive to cultural and language differences. Even creating a slogan is difficult because language in one country may be different from another, so a campaign on a particular issue such as the Millennium Development Goals covers a range of social needs that require encapsulating.

There is a lot of overlap in the seven MDG communication campaign objectives. All the agencies are looking at them from different perspectives while the UN is looking from a central focus.

Within DPI there are communication task forces that meet to discuss the effectiveness of campaigns and discuss whether all the agencies should create and manage joint or individual campaigns. All agencies need to raise funds to run their campaigns whereas DPI is funded. A world food program, for example, might be run by the organization outside the UN.

Communication strategy development and issues management is relatively new to the UN. It first saw light in 1995 when the UN undertook an analysis of its communications to see which, if any, of its messages had been carried by the news media and if not why not. It had never been done before. An information strategy or program had never been written before that time. Prior to this, member states felt that anything that was done that was similar to what might be done by "Madison Avenue" public relations agencies was propaganda, and that it was not in the business of public relations nor in the business of interfering with member states and what they did. It was difficult for DPI to do anything that was proactive. Campaigns were not thought about. In the mid–1980s a new head of department tried to bring in the idea of doing a campaign on a thematic issue, but she was ahead of her time. She did not understand the culture of the organization. Since then it has been a slow evolving process until DPI was restructured. Strategic communications were not understood or accepted and the idea of the DPI having "clients" was fought against internally.

Part of the new strategy is to get the right attendance at events at the right level—heads of state—and is considered a success in evaluative terms. At a conference on racism, fourteen folders of media material were collected but they were never analyzed. There was no evaluation of the material. There was an intuitive idea that it was positive coverage because of daily reading by DPI officers, but nothing more. At the time it needed daily monitoring in the media to be able to counter negative publicity.

Conferences are big global events that the UN uses to gain wide media coverage of an event or issue that otherwise would be ignored. Other than at conferences, where it is obvious what is to be done with information, there is a less clear idea about what happens to information or what should happen to it for it to affect stakeholders. To capture media attention about issues and events that do not involve war or peace, the UN might create an event around the launch of a report of some description. A global conference was historically the best tactic to attract news coverage of an issue or event, but they are no longer as effective.

The focus changed to develop other ways to have issues recognized, but they were not well understood because the organization was looking for an all embracing "hook" on which to hang every one of its coats and hats. The only one it had was the secretary-general, but DPI considered that he needed to be used judiciously.

The clients of DPI are the departments of the UN; the UN itself is a client of the DPI. Member states establish priorities, but the DPI has twenty-four additional internal clients within the UN. The secretary-general is also a client, so his "layers of priorities" are critical. The difficulty for DPI is that it is not yet included in policy meetings at the highest level, so communication on issues and events, while it is said to be crucial to the goals of the organization, is not yet taken seriously enough to be included when policy is being formulated, even though policy decisions and their dissemination as news are crucial to the future well-being of the organization itself.

Prior to its structural changes, UN staff were not allowed to talk to the media. Now at all levels of responsibility staff are able to talk. Specialists are encouraged to talk to the media in depth and they are guided by internal procedures put in place by DPI so they know the issue and the answers. This type of internal spin is no different from the way a corporation or government uses experts to frame an issue or event in media terms.

There is, however, an argument that the organization is not in the business of media manipulation and that it is not very good at spin. Part of the reason it wants to be transparent is the fact the UN knows it is not always completely known outside or inside the media; the oil-for-food issue, for example, is a very complicated story that needed to be interpreted clearly.

A number of questions arise at this point. Was there a real interest in the way DPI was restructured? Did it have an impact on the way the organization does business? Did it have an impact with the Western news media? With other stakeholders? As a prolocutor the secretary-general is in a prime position. But is he effective and how is the effectiveness evaluated?

As well as using the secretary-general there is now a strategy to get other messages out by using other people within the organization. This began as part of the restructure. But priorities for strategic campaigns for issues and events still "trickle down" from the priorities of the secretary-general.

The importance of being strategic is not lost on the secretary-general, but it has yet to develop within the culture of the organization at lower levels. The organization's stakeholders should be differentiated from clients. Stakeholders are the news media, and any number of INGOs, but there is no sure understanding of what a stakeholder relationship really is. Because of the political nature of the organization, communication strategies are subject to enormous change during their lifetime. Long-term campaigns are especially vulnerable. This means the organization must be very receptive to the possibility of change in a campaign structure. The UN has not been as effective in strategy development as it could have been because its strategy development is fragmented between departments, all of whom are not conscious of what is happening at all times. An example of a poor strategic campaign occurred in the late 1980s. The UN attempted to create a public opinion polling program in various member states. In four years it polled thirty-eight members. Before the polling was anywhere near complete, the campaign ran out of funding. This is not an unusual situation in the 21st century, given its moderate level of funding.

DPI News Dissemination

News of the issues and activities that occupy the UN comes from three sources within the organization:

— The Department of Public Information
— The office of the secretary-general
— The representatives of member countries.

All three sources play different roles in news generation. The secretary-general provides news of issues and activities, while the under-secretary-general runs and manages the Department.

A media relations strategy is not developed by one person. It is a collection from the secretary-general's office down, and goes through various drafts that are read and commented on. This sometimes damp down the strategy. Usually the deputy secretary-general is involved in major issues and events on behalf of the secretary-general. Global messages are crafted at UN headquarters in New York and redrafted at national level. Desk officers are responsible for crafting central messages for the local level, but there is some concern that they are not adapted in developing countries well enough to be understood. Op-ed pieces are written for specific news media that are international. The DPI writes op-ed pieces that cross boundaries, which is the criterion used by the UN to determine that a global media exists. But news media are boundary spanners in a local sense already because they cross social, cultural and economic internal boundaries of nations and countries. The most direct way a message is disseminated by way of op-ed pieces, public service announcements or broadcast by the organization's own radio programs.

Public service announcements (PSAs) are constructed jointly with nongovernment organizations (NGOs) and others who believe in the same cause—celebrity use is one successful strategy—and in some countries distribution is easy while in others it is less so because there is no regulation governing PSAs in media. There is very little evaluation of PSAs due to a lack of resources. Anecdotal feedback is the most important form of evaluation. There has been no measurement or analysis of the long-term effect of PSAs, nor has there been an evaluation of any pattern that may have developed in PSAs during the life of the UN. PSAs are traditionally within the UN support strategy for major events, so it could be argued that the pattern of PSA coverage will follow any potential pattern of events and issues.

In the past twenty years the issue of the treatment of women has been a major focus of UN conferences and PSAs, but there has been no evaluation of the success of the PSAs as they relate to the conferences. Environment and development are other areas. Sometimes there is a pragmatic response when a celebrity wants to be involved in an issue, so the UN aligns itself with the PSA, but it bears no relationship to any continuing strategy for issues and events.

There are a large number of issues that the UN tries to deal with, but its communication resources are unable to cope with them. Most of the issues and events are long-term rather than short-term. In television it provides raw footage uncaptioned. It provides access to the news media and disseminates its own news material as raw footage. It is not big in television because it has not got the facilities or resources. In radio it no longer provides shortwave; its material is broadcast by partner radio stations. Its print products are fewer than they were, based on resource use and funding. Member states want less emphasis on hard-copy products and more on Internet, but Internet reaches fewer member state stakeholders in developing countries.

Written into all communication strategies is the context of the divide between developed and developing countries and assistance to developing countries, because that drives all issues and events undertaken by the UN. It is now becoming conscious that there is a strong need to produce different messages for different parts of the world; peacekeeping is a good example. Different messages are presented to troop-contributing countries.[2] Additionally, many Western countries are reducing their troop numbers. There are different messages to disseminate to them. But is the UN sure of how to deliver these messages and, indeed, is it sure of what the messages are?

The DPI draws on strong relationships with the news media from three areas: the secretary-general as prolocutor, the creation of media relations campaigns, and the dissemination of press material directly from the News and Media Division. The location of a corp of news media within UN headquarters in New York City provides additional leverage for the Department. Staff frequently make time to have drinks with the press corp, especially news media who cover the Security Council and the General Assembly, but this does not mean the news media are persuaded to cover complex development issues or peacekeeping.

Within the headquarters of the UN, there is a news media gallery for both chambers, the Security Council and the General Assembly, and accredited media have access to open meetings of both bodies. Much of the discussion, however, in the Security Council, and to a lesser extent in the General Assembly, is undertaken in what is called "consultations." These consultations are closed to the media and to the public. It is not uncommon, however, for open Security Council meetings, where decisions on critical issues are being made, to last five minutes, comprised of an introduction and a gaveled vote. The normal process in the Security Council (although not legislated) is for there to be an open meeting on an issue, at which Security Council members, and any other relevant member states, make their public statements. They then retire to consulting rooms for closed consultations where the details of the decision (a resolution or a statement) are ironed out and where the serious negotiations are undertaken. Once there is agreement (which take hours, days or weeks), there is an open meeting at which the predigested text is adopted. Sometimes there might be one or two printed drafts—called blues—

from a state or group of states which might be circulated semi-publicly.

The news media investigation of the decision-making processes takes place initially through an examination of speeches made in public meetings and the statements that ambassadors often make in unofficial explanations to the news media at "stakeouts" outside the Security Council chamber. These are followed up through informal approaches to, or briefings with, the permanent representatives or the member state missions.

In truth, the Security Council leaks like a sieve. Every stakeholder member uses selective leaks to advance its interests. For the news media the fact that they know what the subject under discussion is, and that the respective parties are gathered in one place at one time, is the real advantage. The media can doorstop ambassadors, or use informal contacts in missions to uncover each side's position and bounce that information off the other side to clarify the issues. But there is constant frustration among the news media that a great deal of the factual information cannot be sourced (and is therefore hard to publish). This creates an inevitable and enormous bias in favor of those who are able or prepared to press their positions on the record, at the stakeout, for example.

The process, however, also provides a heavy degree of deniability to Security Council members. France, for example, was able to state that it was not providing many troops to the upgrading of the United Nations' Interim Force in Lebanon (UNIFIL) because the rules of engagement were unclear. In truth, everyone at the UN, including the news media, knew France played a key role in drafting those rules of engagement (as well as the mandating resolution). But this was done "behind closed doors," unofficially, in circumstances where no one could easily take them to task over their public pronouncement.

Meanwhile, individual journalists, from the *Wall Street Journal*, for example, are sympathetic to the issues and events being disseminated by the UN as news, but they are not the main focus because they alone are not sufficient to achieve the news media goals and objectives of the organization.

One of the biggest problems for the DPI is the ability to coordinate outreach to the news media. On World Aids Day, for example, all agencies were trying to pitch separately to newspaper opinion editors because they all wanted the head of their own department in the media. The News and Media Division and the Communications Strategy Division sometimes work together towards this goal. If it is the secretary-general who is making the running, then everyone else moves back. But the secretary-general usually only gets involved when there is a priority. There is an internal coordinating mechanism on when how and in what capacity he should be used.

What then is the value in placement of a three-page piece by the secretary-general in the *Economist*? Support for the UN is low at élite levels and the *Economist* is not a newspaper pitched at mass reader-ship. So the value must lie elsewhere.

Oil for Food as a Media News Story

Media thrive on crisis, emergency and disaster. Even the most innocuous, mediocre weekly suburban newspaper gets hot and heavy when disaster strikes. A tree falling on a car in a storm will generate hundreds of column centimeters attacking the local authority for not being vigilant and pruning the trees before they have a chance to squash someone's property.[3] And five times out of ten, there will be someone who deserves to take blame. The other 50 percent of the time the news media frame material as if there is implied blame: someone is accountable but is opaque in the overall investigation of the crisis. For the media, the individual who is attempting to frame the crisis— the source—is not always viewed as objective.

According to U.S. scholar Kathleen Fearn-Banks (2002), a crisis has a five-stage life cycle:

Detection	Recovery
Preparation	Evaluation
Containment	

Early detection or warning offers an opportunity to divert a cri-sis and halt its life cycle at Stage One. I am referring here to the turn-ing point of an unnatural issue or event as crisis. It is the unnatural issue or event that occupies the news media because it has a direct impact on reputation and image.

Action films have been around for a long time and provide an example of a turning point. The first of the genre was set in the Amer-ican West where cowboys herded cattle. The action always included a cattle stampede. Rustlers would fire pistols into the air and the steers would run away, frightened by the noise. Cowboys guarding the herd would take off after it and at some point would "turn" it from a dangerous path and calm it to a walk before rounding it up. The turning point was always the most interesting part. The *detection* of the potential crisis was hearing the gunshots. The *preparation* for dealing with the crisis was staying in the saddle. *Containment* became the turning point and *recovery* was when the herd slowed to a walk. *Evaluation* happened after the dust settled. The range boss would count the number of dead cowboys and the number of missing steers, and decide how much damage the crisis, or event, had caused.

News media will engage in attack journalism if they perceive a crisis is not being played out in accordance with certain rules and actions related to reputation restoration. The orthodox taxonomies of reputation restoration are:

Denial	Correction
Evasion	Rapprochement
Irritation reduction	

Denial is obvious and to be avoided, yet it is most often the first thing an organization or individual uses. "I didn't do it" is a common phrase employed by individuals even when they are caught in the act and by organizations that believe blame can be redirected away from them at all times. Individuals within organizations will deny responsibility for all types of actions, happily shifting blame to colleagues or other stakeholders.

Publicly, organizations that deny blame create an enormous risk of continued media attack. In some cases the objective of denying blame or responsibility is strategic: it provides an organization with additional time in which to frame an alternative strategy.

In what became known as the oil-for-food *crisis*, the United Nations caused itself to become immersed in a crisis that should never have existed, then presented tactics that it knew had to eventually be exposed by global news media. It was a crisis that damaged severely the image of an organization that had built its reputation on exemplary conduct.

The Oil for Food Program devised by the UN was an ethical and well-thought-out strategy that allowed Iraq to use a portion of its large petroleum export revenue to purchase humanitarian relief in that country. The program began in 1996 as the West imposed economic sanctions against Iraq over its human rights atrocities. In the first five years of operation, the program generated US$127 billion in humanitarian supplies (UN News Center). The UN found itself in crisis over the program when it was revealed in the media that high-level UN staff had provided sensitive tendering information to rival bidders in the aid program and that the secretary-general's son may had been working for a company with direct involvement in the program.

The UN publishes all of its news releases on its Web site. An investigation of the news releases reveals that the organization, despite its preeminence and highly valued reputation, used each one of the available taxonomies in a vain attempt to restore its reputation after the revelations of its activities in the *New York Times*.

Denial. We can see from a release dated April 28, 2004, that Secretary-General Kofi Annan did not deny the allegations outright, but attempted to reduce the heat in the crisis by saying some of the allegations were "outrageous."

Evasion. While there is no evidence that the UN attempted to evade the crisis, news releases issued on December 1 and December 8, 2004, show that there was an attempt to divert attention from the issue with tactics such as a vote of confidence in the secretary-general from UN staff and the General Assembly, respectively. A day later on December 9, a further diversion came from an endorsement of the secretary-general by the U.S. government.

Irritation reduction. In May 2004 the secretary-general announced publicly his support for the establishment of an independent inquiry into the allegations. In so doing, the UN sought to reduce the irritation that was becoming constant through media investigation of all those associated directly and indirectly with the program. A further irritation reduction occurred on October 13 when the UN announced it would fund the independent inquiry from money remaining within the program after it ceased operating. Irritation reduction increased in the new year. In January 2005 the UN preempted the independent inquiry's finding with an announcement of a full management review of the organization. Such an announcement could lead nowhere other than to correction and rapprochement.

Correction. To begin the correction process in retrieving its reputation, on February 3, 2005, the secretary-general announced disciplinary action would be taken against officials involved in the program. To correct the action, the UN announced five days later on February 7 that it would take disciplinary action against two highly placed staff members, the head of the program, Benon Sevan, and the deputy director of the Security Council Affairs Division, Joseph Stephanides. Both were given two weeks to respond to allegations of misconduct. On June 1, 2005, the secretary-general announced that he had terminated the employment of Joseph Stephanides from the UN. Benon Sevan had already retired.

Rapprochement. In August 2005 the UN began embracing the rapprochement stage of the crisis by announcing a review of its procurement procedures. Later, at the World Information Summit in September 2005 in New York, and in press material in December 2005, it agreed to establish an ethics office so that crises such as Oil for Food would never again emerge. To demonstrate that it was serious about its ethics in the future, and that it had completed its rapprochement, the proposed ethics office was to have independent oversight and auditing function.

Fallout from the Oil for Food Program

The oil-for-food crisis did not end with the establishment of the ethics office. It had wider ramifications that were pursued by the news media in other parts of the world where there had been alleged collusion in defrauding the program. The Australian news media was an example of the chase that ensued to assist in the media's campaign to dislodge the conservative government of Prime Minister John Howard. Since his government's decision to join the Coalition of the Willing and to become involved in a war against Iraq, the Australian news media, which had been mostly against the war, had investigated all available avenues that might bring the government into disrepute with citizens.

The oil-for-food crisis provided the lever by implicating the Australian government. Australia had provided millions of dollars worth of wheat (one of Australia's leading export commodities) to Iraq and a government instrumentality, the Australian Wheat Board (AWB), had allegedly known about the deals that Saddam Hussein had enacted.

The Australian news media, particularly the *Sydney Morning Herald* and its sister newspaper, the *Age* (Melbourne-based), along with the left-leaning public broadcaster, the ABC, pursued the government, influencing the prime minister to set up a commission of inquiry into AWB involvement in the crisis.

The UN as News

As the world's most important INGO, the UN is well-placed to be newsworthy and to have news value. But, like other institutions of globalization, the Western news media are ambivalent about its existence. Like governments and corporations, the UN is perceived to be "fair game" by some, while others treat it with too much reverence. (Imagine for a moment the struggle between supporters and detractors in the newsroom of the *New York Times* on discovering it had evidence of mismanagement and fraud in the humanitarian aid program, Oil for Food.)

The UN is a complex organization that is beyond the immediate comprehension of most citizens and many journalists. For many citizens, particularly in developing countries, it has taken the place of authority traditionally imposed by the church or the state. It is imagined as savior as its blue-bereted peacekeeping troops are established around the world. In this, Western news media are obligated to investigate it as they would church or state, examining the micro-issues so that citizens can know exactly what this hallowed institution is providing. The difficulty with this position lies in the argument that citizens do not always want to know what their church or state is doing other than providing them with relief and hope. For the Western news media, journalistic investigation is designed to unpick all the stitches and seams and to lay bare the bones of an organization so that citizens can make informed judgments about its policies. There is, however, rarely enough detail in news to provide an informed opinion. As I have mentioned elsewhere, the angle imposed on a news story by the Western news media will reflect the political or socioeconomic position of the medium itself, thus they will report the UN from opposing points of view.

The Western news media reports the UN as any number of instruments depending upon the story angle and the newsworthiness of its connection. At a women's conference in Beijing which included an adjoining NGO conference, the *New York Times* bureau chief at UN headquarters attended because she knew the background to the conference issues. But she did not report the NGO conference, nor investigate why the Chinese government located the NGO conference miles from the official conference because it was not of interest to her, even though it was important to the UN. The NGO conference was located in a remote place, where the roads were almost impassable because of mud, which stopped a number of delegates, news media and other stakeholders from getting there.

The UN Web site in early 2006 provided a large amount of information about the proposed July presidential and parliamentary elections in the central African nation of the Republic of Congo (to which Congolese diplomats working in developed countries were shipped months in advance to assist with the election processes). But Western news media reported the processes and lead up to the elections framed by established liberal democratic standards. The *Economist* of April 15 found an angle that included the UN and secretary-general Kofi Annan, by highlighting riots in the capital, Kinshasa, which, prior to Mr. Annan's visit had been quelled by police using tear gas and beatings. When Mr. Annan visited the capital in March, the *Economist* said, the police let the demonstrations take place without the beatings and tear gas that had accompanied them the previous week. The newspaper concluded that the investment of financial and human resources by the UN in the Congo elections—seventeen thousand peacekeepers and $400 million—were such that the elections would run smoothly, but the denouement of the story reflected that "it will be a tough mandate to fill." The injection of the UN secretary-general into the last few paragraphs of the story, and the implication that the UN itself had invested $400 million in the political process, was a standard device in Western news reporting: the addition of a quote from an expert or an image of a highly placed individual provides objectivity. The editorial conclusion was not. It was used by élite media such as the *Economist* to demonstrate the importance of its own position and importance in the framing of news.

Since 2003, when the UN directive to not start a war in Iraq was ignored by U.S. president George W. Bush, the Western news media has reevaluated its reverence for the world's leading humanitarian organization. In some ways, the UN has become a sidebar to the main story (as reflected above in the Congo example) and treated by the Western news media as if it will never again be a powerful global institution. But this is not a reflection of the reality of the UN, simply a reflection of the image of it that occupies the Western news media. As I have mentioned elsewhere, the media require conflict and cleavage for news to have value, for it to be seen in terms of winners and losers. After 2003, the UN was imagined to be a loser, so it has been relegated to a lower competition—it can no longer be seen to be playing in the same league as the most powerful player, the United States.

The relegation to a lesser position allows the Western news media to frame the UN in accordance with how they want the organization to be perceived. The Western news media have adopted a position on the UN similar to that taken by other élites such as academics, government officials and politicians. The position is best enunciated by Zweifler (2006), who argues that the difficulty for the UN lies in the opaqueness of its decision-making processes. Zweifler suggests that most of the decisions made by the UN happen in quiet consultation and negotiation, particularly the Security Council, away from the public spaces that the organization claims to occupy. Both the Security Council and the General Assembly obscure their work, unintentionally, a situation that leads the news media to dig deeper and investigate all decisions more thoroughly than they might if they had the perception of being more transparent. Unlike other government instrumentalities, where public space is available for observation of proceedings and voting on issues, like transnational corporate board meetings, the UN restricts access to delegates representing the interests of their citizen constituents. Here the news media play the role defined by Macauley: they interpret meaning in the procedures and votes, find story angles and file copy or tape. But the first access that the news media has to the procedures and votes is either the written media statement provided by the DPI or a media conference. Access to the UN—public space for observation of proceedings—is not practical as it is in national and provincial parliaments, thus there is a reliance on mediated news of UN activity on a daily basis. Even when national parliaments provide public space, the accessibility is ignored by a majority of citizens who have neither the inclination nor the financial capacity to undertake travel to national parliamentary sites. The expectation that Iowa farmers will travel to Washington, Polish plumbers to Krakow, or Brazilian sales assistants to Brasilia, are irrational: they have an expectation that their parliamentary representatives and the news media will supply them with distilled versions of what they need to know.

But for the UN, the dissemination of information as news through member state representatives gets lost among the other layers of information that filter back to countries of origin. This is where the news media have the opportunity to fill the gap for global citizens about their most important global institution. Unfortunately, the news media, particularly the Western news media, have a jaundiced view of the organization, reporting it as a sidebar to the main story: the hegemonic position of the United States and its competitive position in geopolitics.

As Zweifel (2006) points out, within the six main bodies of the UN, the General Assembly, the Security Council, the Economic and Social Council, the Trusteeship Council, the International Court of Justice and the Secretariat, there are dozens of agencies and autonomous bodies (forty alone within the Economic and Social Council), some of which receive enormous media attention, while others languish. The agencies and instruments that receive the most news media attention in the West are those that have the imprimatur of the UN—through dissemination by the DPI—and that reflect the issues and events that the UN itself most wishes to promote. In this the news media focus, naturally, is on the success or failure (the competitive position) of the Millennium Development Goals.

The Millennium Development Goals: Competitive News Frames for Western Media

One of the aims of the Millennium Development Goals (MDGs) was to get the news media to understand the term "sustainable development." The UN believes it was successful in this although it has not evaluated it rigorously. Its coverage in *Time* magazine suggests it has been successful because the DPI thinks of *Time* as being a mainstream and important news medium. Evaluation is very new to the DPI. In the past it thought it had done well if it got media coverage and it was positive. The member states created a mandate for DPI to evaluate all activities for cost-effectiveness. But it cannot do it because it is underresourced. The office of oversight also has an evaluation role.

United Nations reliance on news media to disseminate its various complex messages is enormous. It must therefore create images of issues and events that resonate strongly and can sustain angles so that journalists can frame them as news.

The original mandate of protecting states against aggression and of assisting in the prevention of large-scale wars has been surpassed by the late 20th-century changes to its charter that allow any country to join and embrace the additional concepts of good interstate relations, better intra- and extrastate human rights, and a focus on global economic, cultural and social issues.

Because it is a global organization, the UN must adhere to a policy of globalization, but this is frequently in conflict with member states who see globalization as a tool of the West for enhancement of the West's well-being. For the UN to overcome this problem and to be seen to be working for the benefit of all member states, it framed its 21st-century goals so that they would resonate with a large number of stakeholders, particularly donor member states (the developed world), citizens of donor states and the Western news media. As we know, news media require a sharp hook on which to attach their own stakeholder bait.[4] The result of UN deliberations on its future as a global organization with a globalized mandate became known as the Millennium Declaration. The eight goals of the Millennium Declaration, with their accompanying eighteen targets, have been the subject of wide-ranging Western news media attention.

The Western news media take their lead from a number of sources, not least from country delegates to whom they are aligned. Country delegates, therefore, offer a particular and powerful perspective on issues and events that are adopted by the news media.

In mid–2004 I sat in the UN Security Council waiting, along with a packed delegation, to hear UN special advisor on MDGs and director of the Millennium Project, Jeffrey Sachs, speak about the progress made with the MDGs. Sachs kept the Security Council waiting for twenty-five minutes, as he had been held up at another meeting and crosstown traffic in New York City that day had been particularly bad. On arriving, he apologized briefly for his lateness, then proceeded to attack UN country member delegates for their poor response to the MDGs, particularly the target #1 goal, to halve by 2015 the proportion of people whose income is less than $1 a day. Most delegates listened attentively, and, at the end of Sachs's vicious verbal attack, got up and left the Security Council to go to lunch. The conversation on the way out was mostly about the impossibility of the goal despite its obvious value to a great number of the world's people (the people the delegates represent).[5]

For the Western news media, the frame adopted by their delegate countries is both a news issue itself and a reason to focus on countries with large numbers of their population living in poverty. Tangible progress towards the #1 goal would be expected to attract positive news coverage. The likelihood, however, is that it would be framed as insufficient evidence that the goal will be reached by the prescribed time.

For the *Economist*, and other élite Western news media, the

MDGs are newsworthy and have news value as stand-alone issues, but also they provide valuable continuity links to developing country narratives that can be framed as news. In June 2002 the *Economist* framed such a story around the World Food Summit in Rome, convened by the Food and Agriculture Organization (FAO), an agent of the UN, in which it stated in its opening paragraph that "a gathering at which President Robert Mugabe of Zimbabwe is able to lecture world leaders on 'fast track land acquisition' as a route to rural reform was always going to be something of a circus" (*Economist* June 15, 2002, p. 73). It is clear from this statement that the newspaper has a specific viewpoint about the issue of hunger, a viewpoint it made clear in its introductory paragraph, stating that good governance in poor countries would end hunger faster than rich world aid. The newspaper's cynical view of the issue is revealed throughout the story. It questions the FAO figures that halving hunger by 2015 would yield $120 billion in gains each year from longer, more productive lives. It suggests what is needed is clearer strategies and better estimates from accurate measurements of the number of chronically hungry and where they live. In this it quotes FAO figures from the MDGs. As a counterbalance it suggests a privately funded agency, The International Food Policy Research Institute, in Washington, has completed research into household surveys and how food reaches families, a better marker. The newspaper suggested new farming practices in developing countries was an important initiative, citing World Bank strategies that originated with African leaders—known as New Partnership for Africa's Development—that include farming practices as being important in economic growth. It then added its editorial comment: "little money or manpower has yet materialized" (*Economist* June 15, 2002, p. 73). The story concluded that good governance was the key to reducing hunger, a well-known formula that was not mastered by many countries.[6]

War and Peace: The Two Big News Stories

The original mandate for the UN might be the avoidance of war and the establishment of peace, for which it has achieved remarkable successes around the world, but for the Western news media the issue is not so black and white.

News media require conflict to give news stories some shock

value. When the news media receive most of their statistical and usable information that can be turned into news from a small number of regular sources, it is inevitable that they will eventually question the value of those sources. Global information comes from global sources and agents and the most relevant and able to deliver are those institutions and agents that invest in information resources. So it is only a question of time before a newspaper such as the *Economist* starts investigating the value of the information supplied by the institutions and agencies. This will happen in its general news. In other departments, such as Science and Technology, the newspaper will access information from a variety of UN agencies to support its stories. A piece on global nutrition in July 2004, for example, quoted the World Food Program (WFP), the World Health Organization (WHO), Food and Agricultural Organization (FAO), the UN Standing Committee on Nutrition, the International Food Policy Research Institute, the United Nations University, and the Academy for Educational Development in supporting its local angle—a daily bowl of porridge for school children in Malawi, southern Africa, that acts as a teaching aid. Six of the seven agencies used in the story are UN-based. The story angle was positive towards the institutions but it was not a general news story. A few months later, in November 2004, the *Economist* published a three-page special report titled *Fighting for Survival*, stating at the outset that the United Nations and the rule of law were in crisis. At first blush the article hinted that it was an investigation into the failures and downward spiral of the world's most important organization. The report began and continued its attack from its position as an élite global news medium without resorting to the naming of sources ("many wondered," "many believed") to underpin claims such as "the criticism [of the UN] reached such a pitch after last year's Iraq war that many wondered whether a body increasingly seen as ineffective and anachronistic could, or indeed should, survive" (*Economist* November 20, 2004, p. 23). Most of the three pages, however, was devoted to an investigation of the UN as it was imagined by the *Economist*—as an anachronistic institution that was not really effectively assisting in the process of globalized liberalization of trade: the overarching ideology of the newspaper itself.

The following month, the *Economist* invited UN secretary-general Kofi Annan to contribute a guest piece—an irregular act: in June 2002 it invited Jagdish Bhagwati to discuss trade barriers—that might be seen to balance the November attack.

According to DPI, the secretary-general regularly talks to media editorial boards, so it was not difficult to persuade the board of the *Economist* to provide a right of reply.[7]

Mr. Annan's essay rebutted the November attack, adding his own interpretation on the future of the organization as it was being seen by the panel of experts who reviewed the UN's security arrangements. Mr. Annan outlined clearly his own interpretation of the future for the UN and what he thought might occur in 2005 at the summit of world leaders reviewing progress on the Millennium Declaration.

The following week the newspaper ran a leader in which it supported the right of the secretary-general to "get on with his job" until such time as he was found guilty of being party to the oil-for-food crisis. It suggested, despite its own earlier attempts to provoke an image of guilt by association, that Mr. Annan was not "the boss of a firm or the president of a country at whose desk the buck must stop automatically," but the "servant of his political masters" and as such was innocent until proven guilty (*Economist* December 11, 2004, p. 11).

We now know that the results of the inquiry into the oil-for-food crisis, coordinated by former U.S. Federal Reserve secretary Paul Volcker, found Mr. Annan guilty of nothing. But waiting for nothing is not what the Western news media are all about. War always makes better news copy than peace.

8

Trade and Participation: Conflicts and Effects of Global Capital and the World Trade Organization

This chapter outlines and develops reasons why participation in global trade is important to the maintenance of the image of global media. Global trade is seen to be both a savior of developed and developing countries, depending upon whom we talk to. For developed nations, free trade will assist developing countries to work their way out of poverty. World Bank statistics are presented to argue such a case. For developing countries, the idea that reducing their tariff and other trade barriers will assist them to become like the developed countries appears to be a rhetorical device being used by the developed countries for their own purposes. Advocating for and against the developed and developing countries are stakeholders with interests in the advancement of globalization and with the retreat of globalization. Among them are the Western news media, who have differing opinions and views about the realities of liberalized trade, its economic, political and social values, and worth.

For the powerful developed trading nations and trading blocs, the most important issue in world trade liberalization is manufactured goods and services. Agricultural products make up only small percentages of economic activity, whereas for developing countries agriculture, both for domestic consumption and export, makes up large percentages. In the United States, agriculture accounts for 1 percent of economic activity, and in the EU it accounts for 2.2 percent. Yet the importance of agriculture in the overall frame of trade liberalization and globalization has placed agriculture at the front of the minds of citizens of developed countries, through overbalanced coverage of the issue by the Western news media. But it is not for farmers in devel-

151

oped countries, or the governments that support them, that the Western news media are keen to exaggerate the issue. It is to demonstrate the inequality, at least within the image framed by the news media, of a developing world that will be overcome by the freeing of agricultural trade markets.

How the media frame their arguments against trade liberalization, while attempting to keep the image of support for the organizations that underpin their own existence, is the subject of this chapter.

The World Trade Organization

When the Western news media decide to exercise their power by attacking institutions that they feel are not doing what they should, one might expect that the attacks, whether employing an informational or conversational model of journalism, would be accurate and uniform in their reporting. This is not always the case, however, as we can see from the *Wall Street Journal* report of the Doha Round of trade talks of May 2006. In localizing the story angle the *Wall Street Journal* reporter Scott Miller made the statement that "France's passion for food culture and its policy of coddling farmers lies at the heart of the current deadlock in the World Trade Organization's global trade talks" (*Wall Street Journal* May 16, 2006, p. 1). Miller went on to argue that, while the talks were designed to boost developing nations, the French are so keen to maintain their existing trade barrier on agriculture that they were prepared to "veto" policy that did not protect agriculture.

While the main functions of the WTO are to provide a forum for trade negotiations and the administration of trade agreements, its membership operates by consensus rather than voting quotas that exist at the World Bank and IMF, or the veto power that exists in the UN Security Council for the five permanent members. So while France does not have the right of power to prevent a legislative action within the WTO, it does have the capacity to block any proposed trade deal for a period of time. Whatever the case, the idea that one powerful country could block trade talks that are designed specifically to benefit developing countries appears to be against the spirit of the existence of the WTO.

This is the image of French nationalism taken up by the *Washington Post* in a leader editorial at the end of April 2006, the day the Doha Round talks stalled in Geneva. The *Post* did not mince words.

It blamed the failure of the latest talks on the European Union and its protection of small farmers in Ireland, Poland, and France. It argued that "a successful Doha Round would contribute to the struggle against poverty" (*Washington Post* April 30, 2006, p. 6), saying that proposed farm subsidy reductions by the Bush administration could have been met equally by the EU but that France, and particularly its president Jacques Chirac, blocked any progress on EU reductions and became more of a problem when Mr. Chirac withdrew a labor law in the face of student protest. The *Post* called Chirac a "non leader" incapable of confronting France's "protest-happy farmers" (*Washington Post* April 30, 2006, p. 6).

In contrast, the *Wall Street Journal* story of May 16 was not so much a direct attack on the WTO as a warm feature article about the joys of country life in France. It portrayed it as being one of the most enjoyable lifestyles in the world, so much so that English and Welsh sheep farmers have relocated to take advantage of the government subsidies and local friendlies. Here the *Journal* was also attacking the UK and its reduction in subsidies to agriculture by providing a visceral image: France has twenty-six thousand farmer's markets in which farmers sell their produce directly to consumers twice a week, while in the UK there are five hundred markets.

A simple textual analysis of the *Wall Street Journal* article shows its leaning towards the idea of warm fuzzy localness, the place that is most likely to resonate with citizens as they are the buyers of the farm produce. The most interesting information that it provides, however, comes from the French trade minister Christine Lagarde, who says that on her return to France from living in the United States, she began searching out local brands in her grocery store aisles because "we French all have a little farmer inside us." Miller's acceptance of the use of *grocery store* rather than *supermarket*, and *little farmer* instead of *producer*, provides evidence of a leaning towards the simple life of the village, a life that Miller and Lagarde imply is threatened by EU tariff reduction and WTO imposition of trade deregulation. This story, however, can also be read as its opposite. As it is placed in one of the world's élite news media, it has the potential to be imagined as a counterbalance: the appalling position of the French, given that EU agriculture accounts for 2.2 percent of economic activity and that U.S. agriculture accounts for 1 percent. For those in the investment business who read the *Wall Street Journal* and invest in manufacturing and services—those industries that make up

the rest of the economic activity in both the United States and the EU—
it could be seen as a call to arms against the French. So the *Wall Street
Journal* and the *Washington Post*, while taking different angles on the
story, are pretty much saying the same thing.

Participation in Global Trade

The World Trade Organization—whose short history we will
examine in a moment—for those who are not inside it could be likened
to how a former Australian prime minister described a fractious parliamentary opponent, like wrestling with a column of smoke. The
WTO, like a column of smoke, appears to shift and sway but contin-
ues ever upwards in a liberalization spiral that is always ungraspable.
And any organization that is not available on a daily basis to provide
media comment, to make statements that "fit" the news frames or the
media agenda, is doomed to receive less than favorable coverage, coverage that has its basis in comments and information obtained from
more available sources, such as antiglobalization advocates. The WTO
has one hundred and forty-nine stakeholders,[1] so it is a formidable
institution with a formidable task.

The WTO is essentially a dispute settlement forum to which members take their disputes rather than imposing sanctions on each other.
In mid–2006, the number of disputes being evaluated by complainant
were highest among the two most powerful groups, the United States
and the EU against each other, with the EU having twenty-nine against
the United States and the United States having sixteen against the EU.[2]

After the deadline for April 30 passed, most Western news media
stated the Doha round was almost dead and moved on to another
topic. It was left to developing country media to continue to discuss
the WTO and its associated issues, particularly those with a major
interest, Vietnam, for example. But others such as the Latvian News
Agency, Kyodo News Agency, Vietnam News Briefs Service, the Dow
Jones Chinese Financial Wire service and the *Asian Wall Street Journal* also pursued the issue of free trade. *Agence France Presse* was the
most prominent Western news agency.

In mid–2006, the WTO imposed an arbitrary deadline on members—aimed mainly at the United States and the EU—to agree on a
reduction in agricultural subsidies. Western news media reported the
issue in a number of ways. Journalist Greg Hitt in the European edition of the *Wall Street Journal* suggested the EU and the United States

were "at odds over a Bush-backed proposal to make deep cuts in trade, distorting farm subsidies" (*Wall Street Journal* June 16, 2006, p. 6), adding that a parallel issue was the EU and the United States joined against developing countries India and Brazil to persuade those countries to make deep cuts to their tariffs on manufactured goods. This would open large markets for the United States and EU. For the *New York Times* edition of the same day the issue was not "the so-called emerging markets like China [added by the *New York Times*], India or Brazil" but rather, journalist Steven Weisman suggested, the problems were caused by "a few wealthy European countries opposed to lowering their barriers on farm imports" (*New York Times* June 16, 2006, p. 1). The *New York Times* story ran across a narrower angle than the *Wall Street Journal*, beginning with a conversational image of the newly appointed U.S. trade representative Susan Schwab. Three days earlier, the *Washington Post* staff writer Paul Blustein wrote a story that began by presenting an image of Schwab as someone very different from that imagined by Washington's "chattering classes" (*WP* June 13, 2006, p. 1).

On June 22, Japan's *Asahi Shimbun* newspaper published a straight story on the brokering of a deal between Japan and the United States for the resumption of beef exports to Japan. What is most interesting about this issue is not the Japanese ban on U.S. beef that had been in place since January 2006 due to concerns over bovine spongiform encephalopathy (BSE) and its association with Creutzfeldt-Jakob disease (CJD), but the fact that the United States was keen to demonstrate how quickly it could comply with a WTO directive. This was not investigated in the wider Western news media so that a connection might be made between the way the United States was imagining its future involvement with its trade partners in the WTO.

The head of the WTO, Pascal Lamy, argues that the organization, as a multilateral trading system, will work efficiently and effectively because it has its basis in efficiency, stability, predictability and equity in international trade. For Lamy, the issue is one of the "efficiency of an international division of labor free from artificial protection, [combined with] ... a set of rules, standards and parameters that are regularly updated and whose effective implementation is guaranteed by a judicial mechanism that is unique in the archipelago of global governance" (Lamy June 5, 2006, WTO website). What this means in less rhetorical language is that trade will flourish when everyone sticks to the rules and when everyone stops acting alone. Lamy's comments were made at the International Economic Forum of the Americas in Montreal. The Western news media pretty much ignored the speech. The *Hindustan Times* ran a piece the day before the speech that provided space for India's minister of commerce and industry Kamal Nath to discredit Lamy's earlier comments on new offers made by the EU and United States. The *Times* was, in fact, reporting an earlier interview Nath had provided to the European tourism magazine *India & You.*

In mid–June 2006 the BBC undertook to broadcast a wide-ranging interview with Mr. Lamy (June 24, 2006). But the interviewer became narrow in focus, questioning the approaching deadline for the Doha Round (July 2006), and asking Mr. Lamy if he, as director-general of the WTO, thought the round had any future. Other equally absurd questions created a comical aspect to the interview when it had the potential to provide broad information to its stakeholders in keeping with its original 1920s statement of objectives that it was set up to "inform, educate and entertain." While the BBC has shifted in competitive terms to more entertainment than information and education, the current affairs interview has the potential to continue the information and education tradition. The interview with Pascal Lamy demonstrated instead that the issue of world trade can be distilled to personality politics and residual bitterness between countries (England and France) that emerge when an interviewer is incapable of developing a significant frame around an issue or event.

Powerful Trading Nations

As we have seen, trade underpins sociopolitical activity and has done so successfully for more than three hundred years. But history shows that it has been one-sided. The circular model of conquest-commerce-conquest demonstrates that those countries with the greatest military capacity can develop trade after they have conquered and overcome their competitors. The trade, of course, was mostly one way, back to the country of origin that had done the conquering. Powerful nations—England, France, the Netherlands and Spain in Europe, and the United States in North America—were the beneficiaries of conquest in Africa, South America and the Asia-Pacific. The conquest-commerce-conquest model has had broad ramifications that are manifest in the image we now have of developed, powerful trading blocs, and the developing countries, located mainly in the three areas where conquest was greatest.

The most powerful trading nations are still those that enjoyed the fruits of conquest during the early period of the Renaissance, the difference is that some have joined together rather than continue to compete separately—England, France, the Netherlands and Spain—while the other main competitor, the United States, has maintained its position as a leading trade entity in regional and global terms.

The influence and persuasion applied by powerful trading nations, both on each other and on less powerful nations, is undeniable. The WTO plays a significant role in dealing with overt influence at a global level. At a local level, the Western news media participate in the communication that influences patterns of trade by investigating and reporting on a variety of trade-related issues and events. They imagine trade as they imagine other issues, things to be distilled to manageable components so that they will have meaning in their interpretation for the widest possible stakeholders. Trade is imagined as if it were a routine event and this is the position that powerful trading nations wish it to be imagined as. By "routinizing the unexpected" (see Tuchman) the Western news media can frame trade issues and events so that they resonate with citizen stakeholders, while at the same time ensuring they do not unbalance the complexity of the way the issues and events play out in the élite world of transnationals, governments and global institutions. This is not to suggest that the Western news media are beholden to their corporate owners (see McChesney [1999], and Sparrow [1999], for example), rather it is to position them so that we can see the model that they apply to their journalistic representations is flawed. As I have discussed elsewhere, the idea that the news media need to localize complex issues and events so that they will resonate with citizen stakeholders leaves languishing the real investigation of issues as news.

Western news media are not unified in their investigation of global trade. While one newspaper reports a deadline for trade talks as the death of the global Doha Round, another argues the problem resides with an intransigent European Union. Yet another presents evidence (as news) that regional trade deals such as ASEAN and NAFTA are undermining the pursuit of successful global negotiations. A unified position, or at least a position which investigates the issue of global trade from a global angle, would assist the process of freeing globalized trade in the same way that a unified global discourse among all world nations would assist in identifying and resolving issues that hamper global advancement.

For the Western news media, abandonment of the localization model would provide a focus for a paradigm shift in reporting world trade. We will discuss this in detail in chapter 10. For now I want to focus on a specific issue—trade-related intellectual property (TRIP)—to get a feel for the hegemony that the leading nations have and why it might be cause for concern among developing nations.

How does trade-related intellectual property differ from other intellectual property?

What is intellectual property?

What is the origin of protection for intellectual property?

Do the news media investigate the issue itself, or tangential issues that it can localize?

How does one specific news medium report on TRIPs?

When news media begin the act of investigating and reporting an issue or event, they must first decide what it is they investigating. The amount of research time spent on an issue is in inverse relationship to the amount of time spent on writing the story. Reporters work to tight deadlines and the idea that they can spend weeks researching a story is a luxury that does not exist in the real world of Western journalism. So reporters need to quickly identify what it is they are investigating. To do this they have to find an angle relatively quickly. Let's take the example of trade-related intellectual property and see how many angles can be identified within the élite news media.

Identifying TRIPs is the first step. What is it? How does it work? What was it set up to achieve? These are standard questions we might ask when we are seeking direct factual information about the issue. When we have this information, we can then investigate the alternative sources and what they have to say about the issue. For the journalist, the alternative sources are often the first source. They are on hand and available so there is less chance a journalist will spend valuable time going to original documentation. The difficulty with this is the notion that the journalist will inevitably pick up a version of the truth that suits the source provider. Transnationals that have a vested interest in the issue have the resources to present their side of the story in a way that appears to offer a balanced, objective account. It becomes the story. For the journalist, the capacity to grasp the real meaning of an issue without succumbing to the unbalanced information provided by alternative sources is the difference between reporting in an information model and reporting in a conversational model.

When reporting different types of issues and events, the grasp of the underlying principles, the understanding of the existence of the issue or event, make the job of reporting somewhat easier. Some issues and events are relatively easy to decode, to understand so that the interpretation of their meaning can be investigated and reported to a wide stakeholder base. Other, more complex issues, are more difficult to decode. A piece of legislation introduced into a domestic parliament that increases the rights of citizens, is straightforward, and can be reported in a straightforward manner. There might be two sides, or even more to the issue, but all sides can be reported with some level of objectivity. For the journalist, the more complex the issue, the more research that needs to be undertaken into its origins, its processes and its objectives, the more difficult it is to interpret its meaning so that it can be widely understood by stakeholder publics.

The example of TRIPs as it has been drawn under the umbrella of the WTO is a good example. Within the Uruguay Round of the General Agreement on Tariffs and Trade (GATT) intellectual property became an issue of substance between developed countries and developing countries, particularly with reference to pharmaceuticals and information technology.

Intellectual property rights are those rights that protect the invention, development, research, testing and design of ideas and knowledge that go towards the making of creative products and services. They are the rights of individuals and organizations to have their inventions, ideas and knowledge protected from the exploitation of others. Different levels of enforcement and protection exist throughout the world, not only for copyright of performance-type material, but for trademarks, geographical indications, industrial designs, patents, layout designs of integrated circuits and trade secrets. Intellectual property rights include the right to prevent others from using inventions, designs or other creations and to use that right to negotiate payment in return for others using them. Books, paintings and film might be copyrighted, while inventions can be patented. Brand names and logos can be registered as trademarks. In the mid–1990s developing countries saw the inclusion of intellectual property in trade rules as a way to introduce more order and predictability into the global issue of intellectual property rights. Consequently the WTO TRIPs Agreement was seen as a way to narrow the gaps in the way various rights were protected around the world, and to bring them under a common international rule. The action was seen as striking a balance between the long-term benefits and short-term costs to global society. The WTO claims that society benefits in the long term when intellectual property protection encourages creation and invention, especially when the period of protection expires and the creations and inventions enter the public sphere (WTO Web site).

For the news media, the most logical sources for all of these different types of intellectual property are lawyers who specialize in them. Governments and transnational corporations are also sources, but they will provide subjective information leaning towards their own image of the issue.

When the news media, like individual citizens, obtain information directly from a source, the material will always reflect the desired position of the source. The WTO Web site, for example, refers to the issue of patent protection for pharmaceutical products. Patent protection, it remarks, is important for its ability to provide pharmaceutical companies with the incentives to do research and development into new medicines while at the same time not preventing "people in poor countries" from having access to medicines. The WTO says this issue was partly settled in 2001 at the November Doha Ministerial Conference, where it was agreed that TRIPs does not and should not prevent members from taking measures to protect public health.

This statement reflects the position of the WTO, but the alternative "angle" as Zweifel (2006) shows, was that large pharmaceutical companies were protected by twenty-year patents, and that they showed no interest in letting cheaper generic medicines into countries such as Brazil and India, where governments were struggling to come to terms with pandemics such as AIDS and malaria. When South Africa attempted to import generic drugs to fight AIDS, at a fraction of the price of the patented drugs, thirty-nine pharmaceutical companies took legal action against the South African government's proposal. Global public opinion, however, was in favor of the South African proposal, and the drug companies were forced to drop the case in April 2001 (Zweifel 2006: 124). Brazil made use of the South African case by taking its own case to the UN Human Rights Commission, before which it argued that its citizens had a right to affordable medicines and that it intended to continue to distribute cheap generic AIDS drugs. The United States threatened trade retaliation against Brazil, and voted against the action and its UN proposal. But public opinion was again overpowering, and in June 2001 the United States shifted its position. In September 2001, the United States used an anthrax scare to make legislative changes in drug patents in the name of national security, and in November 2001 Brazil and India used the example to win concessions in the WTO that led to developing nations being able to apply a fifteen-year grace period for implementing TRIPs. While the WTO as a source provides information as it is seen by its members, it can also be seen in a different way by those taking information from alternative sources. In this case the Brazilian and Indian governments would have provided information in a very different form from that provided by the pharmaceutical companies in the developed world.

It would be hard to believe that news media space for the issue would have been available immediately after 9/11. Between September and November 2001, it is unimaginable that a health issue in the developing world would have competed for space with the attacks on the World Trade Center and Pentagon.

In April 2001, British newspaper the *Guardian* reported on the South African AIDS issue by saying that its [the newspaper's] "industry sources" referred to it as a "public relations disaster." But in fact it was a public relations triumph because the "global" public had access to information that allowed opinion to be informed and to influence governments and, in turn, transnational pharmaceutical companies to reverse the strategy. The *Guardian* journalist, Charlotte Denny, quoted one source, the NGO Oxfam, as arguing that the plan put to the WTO by the EU on behalf of South Africa "was a step forward but did not go far enough" (*Guardian* April 7, 2001, p. 2). (For a detailed discussion of the use of NGOs as sources, see chapter 11.)

For the *Independent* economics editor Diane Coyle, the issue was one to be localized. It began a news story a few days later by revealing that then UK secretary of state for international development, Clare Short, had "set up an expert commission to recommend changes to the international rules on intellectual property" (*Independent* April 16, 2001, p. 13), and that it followed the "recent controversy" over the high cost of AIDS drugs in developing countries. The story highlighted Oxfam by saying the pharmaceutical concessions had been made because of the success of a campaign by Oxfam and another NGO, Médecins sans Frontières.

For *Financial Times* reporter Adrian Michaels, the issue was not one of triumph for the developing countries, but a cautionary warning with its basis in German folklore. Its story angle was that large pharmaceutical companies charge a lot for their drugs but they use the money to fund new research. Giving the drugs away would "kill the golden goose" according to the newspaper's source, Pfizer chief executive Hank McKinnell. Mr. McKinnell used the space to divert the attack on his company, the largest pharmaceutical group in the world, by blaming India for "making billions of dollars stealing our technology and selling it, not only in India but any place around the world that they can get away with it" (*Financial Times* April 26, 2001, p. 18).

For the *Guardian*, implied direct involvement and self-praise led its story on June 16 in which it claimed "since *The Guardian*'s award-winning series began, prices have been slashed, but the fight goes on" (*Guardian* June 16, 2001, p. 14). The language of the story, written by Sarah Boseley and James Astill, reflected the newspaper's combative position within the issue as it suggested the United States and EU would come under "unprecedented pressure" and that "international outrage" greeted the pharmaceutical court case against South Africa. The story quoted Oxfam and the idea that it hoped the United States would soften its line and "concede some ground because of the sheer weight of public opinion" (*Guardian* June 16, 2001, p. 14).

The use of one particular source invades most of the reporting of this issue at that particular moment in history. All the élite British news media at the time used Oxfam as their source. We will discuss this further in the following chapter.

Developing Trading Nations

The idea of developing nations participating in global trade is dichotomous. It is simple because the developed countries make a simple case for developing country inclusion. It is complicated because the rules governing inclusion seem skewed in favor of the developed nations.

Before embarking on an investigation into news media images of developing trading nations (an immediate image suggests poor farmers in Madagascar growing bananas and coffee), we need to ponder the idea of global trade and how developing countries fit its image.

For most Western nations, the idea of global trade is a good thing rather than a bad thing. It allows the free transfer of goods and services at prices that are affordable for enough of the population to continue to support it. With the invention of global institutions such as the WTO and UN, in which all nations have theoretically the same capacity for involvement,[3] Western strategies frame the institutions as

Western nations influence the shape of the institutions. Within this frame was built the concept of aid and assistance to developing countries so that they could begin to build their own socioeconomic institutions in the image of the West. As we now know, the idea of the Western model of aid and assistance applied to culturally diverse nations proved wholly inadequate. Fukuyama (2006) suggests that as a result of three decades of aid between the 1970s and 1990s some countries such as Somalia and Liberia not only reduced their per capita income (the opposite of the proposed effect of aid) but made it disappear completely. For Fukuyama, the idea of aid as a positive mechanism for equality in competitive trade can now be seen to be equivalent to the "natural resources curse" that afflicted many African states where, given the abundance of resources, good governance was nonexistent (Fukuyama 2006a: 122).

For developing nations, universal designs for the application of institutions such as banking and finance can be more easily adapted from Western institutional examples than other, less universal concepts such as education and health. For developing nations, powerful influence is exerted from a number of quarters to persuade them of their obligations if they are to act responsibly and maintain their membership in the global trading network.[4] Politically, influence is applied at global organizational level (WTO), regional level (EU) and national level (U.S.). Economically influence is exerted by transnational corporations and morally it is exerted by media.

Developing countries are under enormous pressure to play by Western rules. Developing nation governments are driven to compete in global trade markets while at the same time they are vilified or patronized in the media for ignoring the plight of their citizens who are underfed, undereducated and underpaid. From a different direction comes the developed world's approbation when environmental issues arise that are seen by the West to be unacceptable. Yet at the same time the unacceptable environmental action in developing countries is being undertaken in Western countries within flawed environmental protection legislation.

The complexity of the issue of global trade by developing nations needs to be subdivided so that we do not consider China and Brazil as developing countries in the same image as we think of Liberia, Sierra Leone or other war-torn African nations.

For transnational corporations the strategy is straightforward: persuade developing countries of the benefits of allowing access to labor and land for manufacturing plants. For Western governments, the strategy is linked to that of the transnationals, but includes the issue of balancing competition for goods and services produced within their domestic markets. For global institutions, influencing developing nations to compete in a global trading market is more complex because it involves additional factors of environment, social equity and human rights.[5]

For the Western news media, the issue is even more complicated. They must be seen to investigate and report in a balanced fashion that provides for all stakeholders. The Western news media must cover all the angles from the interests of the corporations, the national governments, the global organizations, the citizens of developed countries, and citizens of developing countries if they are truly to be seen as global themselves. But this is an impossible task, so they localize all issues and events and frame developing countries within their own business and reporting models that have little relevance.

The most obvious tactic for the news media is to attack the institutions that have assisted in persuading the developing countries of their obligation to membership. As I have mentioned elsewhere, the idea of attacking large, unseen organizations is the first rule of Western journalism. Like governments, they are easy targets because they are too big to fight back quickly. By the time they have realized they are under attack, the attackers have moved on. At the next level news media can attack specific countries and their governments, depending upon the level of activity that they imagine is occurring to reach goals and objectives within the orthodox frame. A wonderful example appeared in the *Economist* in mid–2005. It began by stating that Madagascar "must try to reap more of a benefit from its plentiful gemstones" (*Economist* July 30, 2005, p. 42). And there is no coincidence that Hollywood produced a cartoon movie called *Madagascar* at the same time as that country was being discussed at global institutional level.

The difficulty for the news media lies in how to interpret the word *developing* (or *emerging*, depending upon which medium you are investigating). For the *Economist* to lump China, India and Brazil into the same group as Uganda, Sudan and Ethiopia is nothing short of ridiculous. Yet, the lumping occurs so that stakeholders can imagine the divide between developed and developing countries more easily. And recent reporting by Western news media appears to be similarly framed as it was twenty years ago.

The issue for the media is twofold. It is the idea of the global being good, while as individuals—journalists as individual citizens—we are tied historically and therefore inexorably to the idea of a sense of place, an identity that is historically grounded in who we are as individuals, who we are related to, what has occurred to us as individuals, and what we did, and are yet to do, in the places we live, the places we call home. This idea of a sense of place has been well documented by U.S. scholar Joshua Meyrowitz (1985), among others, arguing that media itself is responsible for our dislocation, our sense of not having a place, and it is this as much as anything else that creates the circumstances in which the individual journalist findings him- or herself needing to locate or localize a story so that it too has a sense of place. Globalization provides no real sense of place other than the notion of global citizenship, but it is not easy to reconcile global citizenship with who we are and where we come from as individuals. We are so closely connected to our sense of history—family, home, school, work—that we think we can unattach and become global because it exists in theory. Very few of us, however, are able to make any sort of transition from local citizen to the world stage. In the West, the fabrication of models of exchange—trade, transport, well-being that allows us to travel if we choose—is not part of the culture of the developing world. Sense of place is just as important there, and, indeed, has not been overcome by the fabricated models that create a global imagination among Westerners. Add this to the belief in self and the importance of self-identity and the complexity for the Western journalist is almost insurmountable. Because we in the West have given up on history and a sense of place, we expect the same to happen in the developing world and are perplexed by a resistance to its adoption.

As human beings we are less interested in being able to form a harmonious world citizenship in which we can have access to global goods and services than in settling in one place and staying put.

The Western news media impose their own sense of place on how they imagine developing country issues and events. Let's look at two examples from the *Economist*. In the Madagascar example published on July 30, 2005, mentioned above, the story revolves around the discovery in 1998 of the world's largest reserves of blue sapphires that inspired a rush to build towns that attracted "tens of thousands of miners, prospectors and dealers" (*Economist* July 30, 2005, p. 42). The angle of the story invoked in the Western imagination childhood stories of the discovery of King Solomon's mines, also in Africa, and the lure of discovery, conquest and wealth. The real angle on the story, however, was that the Malgaches were a corrupt lot with no qualms about smuggling the sapphires to Thailand: the newspaper suggests 90 percent of those in the mining sector were involved in some illegal trade, but if the trade in sapphires and other precious gems were properly managed, it might yield $400m a year in "benefits to ordinary people" (*Economist* July 30, 2005, p. 42). For the *Economist*, the issue of the discovery of such wealth required an orderly and controlled environment that had the potential to benefit all. The same as what? The orderly and well-managed gold rushes in the United States, Canada and Australia in the 19th century? The orderly and well-managed plunder of South America and Africa by Europeans in the 16th and 17th centuries? Or possibly the orderly and well-managed transfer of oil from the Middle East to the West.

In late June 2006, under a leader banner, the *Economist* published a story about U.S. tax rates and how it was distorted for those who work abroad. The story angle was the increase in the number of people working abroad, especially from the emerging economies of China, India and Brazil, following their American, European and Japanese competitors. The newspaper argued for an abolition of double taxing for American expatriate workers, now that more "companies" were sending workers away from home base. But it was the introduction to the opinion piece that was most interesting, reinforcing as it did my argument about sense of place. The story began by saying that globalization was impersonal when discussed as trade flows, foreign direct investment and financial markets because it was really people who buy, sell and make the goods and services that flow around the world. It then represented an image of people "flitting" around the world finding new customers for the goods and services, keeping "distant assembly lines running" (*Economist* June 24, 2006, p. 10). So while the leader writer and, therefore, the newspaper would like to imagine the world as being full of global citizens and benevolent governments all contributing to the well-being of their fellow humans, the real issue was that instruments such as taxation effectively keep individuals within their small domestic sphere, rather than allowing them to parade on the global stage. If we follow the *Economist's* deductive reasoning, we can argue that governments, too, are made up of individuals and the tax system that stops the flow of workers might be what they want in place, to provide a sense of place.

While the news media are attempting to imagine all possible angles within an imposed model, they must also look to provide space for coverage of another stakeholder group with an interest in how the developing world is portrayed in the West: the forces of antiglobalization.

The Rhetoric of Antiglobalization

Capitalism relies for its function on a market in which there is little or no intervention from governments or other variables. As early as the 18th century, Adam Smith, in his book *The Wealth of Nations*, argued for self-correcting markets and small government.

The wider distribution of capitalism and its relative defeats of fascism and communism in the global economy have occurred because capitalism, for its continuity and life, needs constantly bigger markets and cheaper inputs, such as raw materials and labor. This has led to integration, both vertical and horizontal, in which businesses organize across political and geographic boundaries.

This "policy" of integration, while it is not something that can be easily defined as being "arranged" by any specific group, has the imprimatur of the United Nations. If we accept that the economies of the world have become integrated, for whatever reason, then we can argue that there will be strict limits on what can and cannot be done and whose interests will be supported.

Capitalism and, thus, global capital is characterized by tensions between competing interests. These interests include the military, bureaucracies, religious groups, political parties, and lobby groups. In the example of the United States after September 11, 2001, the interests of the corporations were put to one side by the government of George W. Bush through pressure from a number of areas, which meant it could no longer continue to be a government that was set up simply to serve capitalism and the corporation. The political momentum forced the government and its allies to pursue policies that were not necessarily in the interest of capital and the corporation. In other words, the government was split in two and has since been trying to present an image of "America as Business" alongside an image of "America as Superpower."

But this is not a significant enough shift for those opposed to the idea of global trade. Antiglobalizers—organizations and individuals with an interest in localizing everything from goods and services, to culture and society—have a powerful voice in the Western news media. The rhetoric of the antiglobalizers, as I have shown elsewhere (see Stanton 2006) is no different from that of the globalizers. The same strategies and tactics are pursued by both in a zero-sum game. Both sides, in other words, believe they are right and that right will out, with one clear winner and one clear loser.

Antiglobalization rhetoric has some powerful allies. As we have seen briefly above and will see in more detail in chapter 9, nongovernment organizations have a powerful voice in the media. Oxfam, for example, a British-based charitable organization, provides aid throughout the developing world. It also invests heavily in research that shows why globalization is not as good as the globalizers make it out to be. And it is given space within a large number of news media to show that their stories are balanced.

For the antiglobalizers, the objective is to have the capacity to reduce the knowledge gap between their ideology and that of the media they wish to attract. This is not as difficult as it may sound, simply because the citizen as journalist is usually far more attracted to the underdog, the one imagined as having a big heart and being ready for a fight despite being outweighed and outperformed. The very term *grassroots* as it is applied to some antiglobalization groups inspires in the media an image of democracy springing from the soil, replacing the socialist virtues that were lost in the struggle against capitalism. Such rhetoric has a powerful subliminal effect. It allows some antiglobal material that would not normally see the light of day to be published in élite Western news media. This occurs because the news media frequently fail to differentiate between categories of antiglobalizers.

Globalization is an emotional word because it is poorly understood. It can mean different things to different stakeholders, but it is the idea of an economic and political hegemony from within the existing developed countries that appears to raise the most alarm.

Antiglobalizers use rhetorical devices to enhance this alarm. Bhagwati argues that there are two distinct groups opposed to globalization, and particularly to what he refers to as economic globalization. He suggests one group has deep-seated ideological opposition to corporations and, thus, to capitalism. However much globalization increases the well-being of citizens in developing countries through the alleviation of poverty and hunger, this group, Bhagwati says, will remain opposed because they imagine globalization to be the cause of the problem (Bhagwati 2004: 4). A second group he argues, have genuine, though poorly formed, views of globalization. This group imagines it to have an effect on socioeconomic and environmental conditions in developing countries, but are willing to engage with reasoned argument on the issue.

The Western news media presents an image of globalization that has the potential to resonate with the second group. For the first, the media are a weapon in the hegemonic armory of the West, but for the second group there is the potential for the news media to play a decisive role in the struggle against globalization. The adoption of public relations strategies and tactics by the stakeholders within this group—NGOs, etc.—allows them to be seen by their constituencies to be engaging with the issue with the potential to shift its direction within the public sphere.

Some news media, the *Economist*, the *New York Times* and the *Wall Street Journal*, for example, provide space for hardcore antiglobalizers when a political issue or event threatens or becomes violent. The BBC, on the other hand, has been accused of showing alarming consideration for one side of an issue over another (see, for example, the 2004 case of alleged bias against Israel in favor of Palestine).

9

Citizens and Participation: The Role of NGOs

This chapter presents an image of citizen as consumer, but as one who is capable of understanding the dimensions of news disseminated through the *imagine* model. Citizens as individuals are not part of the imaginative process for Western news journalism. Nor are they engaged with the democratic process other than as voters every three or four years.

News is a commodity that is traded at élite levels between producers and consumers. There is no space for the public to engage in the trade other than as observers. Observation status is accorded to the public to validate news as a tradable yet scarce commodity. Receipt of the commodity by a buyer provides no validation on its own; there must be a third party that is unable to purchase or use the commodity for it to have value. The public, for example, as I have mentioned above, is unable to purchase coal directly from the producer because the public has observer status in the production and generation of energy from coal. The whole process of extraction, production and generation of electricity from coal bypasses the citizen in a complicated relationship between producers and generators, much the same as the complicated process of news production and generation bypasses the citizen whose only recourse is to engage with the process as an end user. There is no coincidence in the fact that producer and generator act in the same way for coal as they do for news. Reporters and journalists, when acting as producers on behalf of generators set aside the act of being citizen—end use—and move into a position of power with a direct relationship to commodity owners. By removing themselves from the act of citizen, reporters and journalist are able to act as producers on behalf of generators much the same way as theater actors take on a stage role different to their normal lives. Reporters and journalists must work with a degree of separation from normalcy to act as producers. Otherwise the vagaries, the dross of everyday existence, would come into play as part of the process of

170

news production. It is difficult enough for reporters and journalists to imagine news in terms other than those proscribed by wealth and power in the West without the addition of the burden of citizenship.

As good citizens, we actively seek information for a variety of reasons, but it is rarely information that has a bearing on our behavior and attitude. We cannot always act on the information in relation to our own selves or to others. News of local weather may help us decide what to wear each day, but news of global weather has no bearing on our behavior. If we are traveling it may help, but we will need additional information by the time of our arrival.

As individuals, humans are not very good at looking after themselves. They require constant care from others to enable their lives to take some sort of shape. This is axiomatic for all human beings throughout the world.

In his journey of self-discovery, Henry David Thoreau lived for two years and two months in the mid–19th century in a house he built himself beside a lake in Concord, Massachusetts. Thoreau, a Harvard graduate, attempted to show that man could live a happy and complete life without interference from others. In this he was acknowledging what had been known and practiced by a great number of societies for some time. The importance of Thoreau's experiment lies in the ability of those with resources to act out some form of existence. For the billion or so individuals living in poverty, on less than $1 a day, the idea of looking after one's self is ludicrous. The opportunities to act out some form of existence other than living in poverty are nonexistent. It is a difficult concept for well-off citizens in developed countries to imagine. And few get to see the real poverty that exists in Africa, India and South America. It is hard enough for well-off citizens of developed countries to drive through poor suburbs in the world's leading cities—New York, London, Paris—let alone engage with the idea that hundreds of millions of people are unable to change their circumstances, no matter how hard they try.

Reporting Citizens in the Developed World

In Europe, North America, Australia and parts of Asia, citizens generally have a high standard of living. They have access to education, medication and occupation. They feel fulfilled and gratified because they live with the knowledge that consumption of goods and services sustains them. They act out their lives through involvement or engagement with others, against whom they measure their success and fulfillment. They rarely take to the woods for a couple of years to grow their own food and build their own shelter. If they do, it is through the lens of the popular media, so that it can be broadcast into the lives of all those who have no inclination to do so, but wish to see how others might do it.

As a society of voyeurs, citizens in developed countries build relationships that they wish to be seen by others as being of value. As part of the evaluative process of their actions, they look to institutionalize their legitimacy. Thus, citizens have conceived the establishment of two of the most important institutions in the legitimization process: democracy and the news media. By setting up and imaging these institutions, citizens proscribe all actions as either legitimate or illegitimate, depending upon whether or not they fall within either frame.

In order to be part of the legitimating, the news media must frame their product—news—against this backdrop. They frequently make a choice. And as I have argued above, they do so as agents rather than institutionally. When reporting upon the institutions and the state in which they are educated, medicated and occupied, they are not always gentle. They taxonomize citizens according to their affiliations. Taxonomies can be political, economic, social, technological, environmental, cultural or legal. They can be ethical or moral. And they can have internal layers: a social taxonomy can have subdivisions of family, religion or hobbies. A news medium might be less interested in a citizen who is a good Catholic family man with seven children and weekends devoted to golf, until it is revealed he spends his evenings downloading child pornography from the Internet.

The Western news media attempt to draw distinctions around how they might investigate and report citizens in the developed world, but they rarely achieve much success. Their taxonomies fail when citizens become more than one imagined element, or display elements that are discordant with orthodox images. A United States president will be applauded if he bears an image that displays erudition, statesmanship and grooming (the televisual image of President Bartlett of *West Wing* fame). If, on the other hand, he swaggers, wears cowboy boots and big buckles, he might be in for a rough time.[1] Bill Gates is another example. While he was the head of Microsoft, he was framed as a computer geek with a lot of money. As the head of the Gates Foundation he is imagined as one who is "free of the vicissitudes of votes and public opinion, philanthropists can take on causes that are unpopular or neglected. They can innovate by promoting remedies that are otherwise unfeasible or remote" (*Economist* June 24, 2006, p. 10). But this definition also applies to the same Bill Gates who was head of Microsoft: he could have done the same stuff a long time ago.

When the news media report on issues and events in the developed world such as the construction of a new bridge, road or building, they provide images of the human links that support the activity, not the citizens themselves. Stories will mention ports, terminals and ships, but not the individuals who contribute to the loading and unloading, transport and security. As we would expect, the issue will be reported to reflect the image of the action. Individuals have a place in the story at two points: firstly as a local angle and secondly when something goes awry. As we will see below, news media report issues and events of citizens in developing countries in a slightly different way. There is a shift towards reporting the most important developing countries—China, India and Brazil, those countries that are imagined as being most important by the news media—as part of a new model: no local angle for the first paragraph to set the story in a nice friendly style. But more of this later.

Citizens in the developed world act as a support cast for the main story. In the developing world, the image of citizen as poverty-stricken and uneducated, is the story.

Western news media frame developed world stories around the institutions, governments and transnational corporations that form the basis of Western liberal democratic society. The individuals and citizens who are the elements of those societies are imagined as local angles so that the story will resonate with stakeholder publics. For the élite media the stakeholder publics of most interest are the individuals and citizens who control the institutions, governments and transnational corporations. So it is normative for a newspaper of the standing of the *Economist* to begin stories with "Romano Prodi's new center left government probably owes something of its recent electoral success to a sense that his predecessor as prime minister, Silvio Berlusconi, had been a little too keen to please the Bush administration" (*Economist* June 24, 2006, p. 61). A lead paragraph of this nature allows the newspaper to pitch to its élite market, while at the same time presenting a conversational image to the casual reader. Such a device allows the newspaper to represent itself so that it appears to be leading the reader in a friendly, familiar direction—conversational—when in fact it is setting up a complex story about the Italian-U.S. political relationship and the legal question of an Italian intelligence officer's death in Iraq. The localization of the angle, for at least the first paragraph, provides an entry to the story that is not sustained. To rework the angle, however, and begin where it should, with the death of the officer and the accompanying legalities, would demonstrate the global nature of the story and that is not always something readers begin looking for.

A second piece, in the same edition, began, "when Dominique de Villepin posed for the cameras in February, flanked by two energy bosses who had agreed to merge their companies, France's prime minister must have felt he had pulled off a spectacular conjuring trick" (*Economist* June 24, 2006, p. 60). The real story, one that takes a few paragraphs to discover, is the mandate the French prime minister thought he had to accept a merger of two French companies to stymie an Italian company in its proposed takeover of one of them did not exist and that the issue was to be investigated by the European Commission. The story adds another important angle a few paragraphs from the end. It reveals what it claims is a "widespread feeling of popular disgust over a close-knit political-industrial élite, which appears to organize affairs to suit itself and to embrace the rewards of capitalism without accepting the risks" (*Economist* June 24, 2006, p. 60). Surely, this is the real angle on the story? And what about revealing the names of these political-industrial élite, the members of a club the newspaper adds, "come from the same sort of élite postgraduate schools" (*Economist* June 24, 2006, p. 60)? Surely there is room in one of the world's leading weekly newspapers for additional material about something as interesting as this? The problem in revealing who the members of the club are is that it might risk revealing their relationships to the élite news media that are avoiding reporting them.

A more evocative lead paragraph in a third story in the same edition pronounced: "Gordon Brown and David Cameron rarely get to attack each other directly. Their sole arm-wrestle so far was during the budget in March, when the leader of the opposition traditionally gets to reply to the chancellor in the House of Commons" (*Economist* June 24, 2006, p. 67). Not a bad bit of imagery. Leaders of governments arm-wrestling? Goes down well with readers in the Dry Bean

Saloon outside Ogallala, Nebraska. Makes them feel at one with their own elected representatives. It might have had a little more punch if it had been described as their "sole nude mud wrestle." But a global newspaper can't be too careful.

Reporting Citizens in the Developing World

As we can see, citizens as individuals in the developed world rarely get a mention in the élite news media unless they are themselves élite, or the cause of a problem, or both. Otherwise, space is reserved for élites: politicians, business leaders, institutional governors. In the developing world, the citizen has a slightly different role to play.

We have spent some time contemplating the Habermasian ideal of the public sphere in which rational discourse plays out for the benefit of the chosen few (see chapter 5). What we are interested in here is how the Western news media imagine the role of citizens in the developing world and their participation in issues and events that will lead their countries to establish themselves as embodiments of the developed country model.

Habermas examined the English model of the early years of the Enlightenment to support his argument for the existence of a public sphere. Mansbridge provided a similar analysis in the United States (see Schudson 1999). But there is no evidence, other than that undertaken by anthropologists (see for example, Walker 1972) who frame their work around issues of anthropological importance rather than sociological ones, that a similar type of communicative space exists in the developing world. Public spheres exist and have done so for far longer than those imagined within developed countries, but they exist at a different level than that imagined by Habermas. They are less spaces for public discourse, more spaces for public theater. They are not venues for the development of social institutions but they have the potential to become so.

The Western news media report issues and events in the developing world as if they have a direct attachment to citizenship and the role of the individual. But citizens and individuals have no attachment to anything. In most developing countries they do not even have the franchise. For the vast majority, there is no connection with any aspect of trade in goods and services other than the supply of labor. They have no connection to education, health benefits, organized unionism, or general well-being as do citizens of the Western world. They have no connection to the news media nor to any of the other institutions that comprise the sovereignty of their country of origin. They have limited access to mobility in the form of travel or transport and limited access to technology in the form of media, telecommunications or information technology. In other words, they are as effective as if they did not exist. Their disenfranchised poverty-stricken state makes them prime images for the Western news media. But even then, when the news media report struggles between stakeholder groups in developing countries, the vast majority are grouped under banners such as poverty, war-torn regions or human rights. The powerful, those who form groups designed to overpower the vast majority in the same way as the vast majority in developed countries are overpowered by the powerful—the *janjaweed*, Hamas, the Taliban, or Hezbollah—all of them tag themselves with names that will strike the right image with the Western news media. And the Western news media accept the tags, investigate the groups, but fail to pay attention to the stories of the vast disenfranchised majority.

When the *Economist* runs a story of the first one hundred days of the Chilean government under Michelle Bachelet, it does so by invoking images of her promises of social stability and fiscal management, and to give voters a say, then reports of a strike by schoolchildren who are not happy about financial investment in education. But the newspaper says only that an opinion poll shows "Chileans" think there should be a ministerial reshuffle, while one who voted for her is quoted as saying, "she's just the same as all the other politicians," but fails to name the woman, calling her instead "one working class mother" (*Economist* June 24, 2006, p. 51). Such devices make a mockery of the model of localization of the news angle that the Western media pride themselves on. Is the name of the voter not as important in this scenario as that of the president? Clearly not. Are all Chileans lumped together for the purposes of an opinion poll? Who voted in the poll? Who polled the constituents? How were they selected as participants in the poll?

Citizens in developing countries are lumped together because they are imagined the same way that news is commodified and homogenized: they fit the image that is required for the week's publishing and broadcast deadlines.

In the developed world, citizens have certain expectations, no matter what their financial circumstances. If they own an automobile, they expect to be able to drive it to a garage so that a qualified mechanic can make a roadworthiness inspection of the vehicle. They then expect to be able to effect any necessary repairs, download the details to a motor vehicle authority and collect a new registration warranty, all within the space of an hour or two. It is a task that fits into an allotted space. It is a task that is signaled some weeks before the due date so that the citizen has time to organize and manage the process. Even if it is forgotten about until 2 a.m. the morning of the day it expires, it can be done. There is an expectation that has been built into the citizen's imagination (subconsciously) that the flow of issues and events that form their personal lives will not be obstructed by political or economic barriers. The citizen manages her personal life and her small business, her four children, her daily workout at the gym, her devotion to her church and her SUV without thinking too much about what goes on outside her district. In fact, she has rarely been outside her district because she has never applied for or gained a travel passport; in forty-five years she has never been outside the borders of the country in which she was born. She has difficulty remembering the name of her national government representative. Her husband has been promising to take her somewhere different for dinner—to an Indian restaurant—but it has not transpired. Our citizen is typical of citizens across the developed world. She is of no interest to the news media because she is not engaged with issues and events outside her personal life.

But citizens in developing countries are of interest to the news media because they have fewer expectations than our suburban house-wife/mother/businesswoman.

Leaving aside for a moment the three countries which are the biggest focus for the news media—India, China and Brazil—a citizen in a developing country in Africa or Asia has certain expectations that relate directly to her financial circumstances. She expects that she will be attacked by rebel insurgents, that she or her children will go to bed that night without having eaten, or that her village will be washed away by a tsunami. Our developing world citizen manages her personal life without thinking too much about what goes on outside her district. In fact, she has never been outside her district, except for a year when she was dislocated to another part of the country (to which she had to walk). She has difficulty remembering the name of her country's president. Her husband died of AIDS four years ago.

Our citizen is typical of citizens across the developing world. She is of great interest to the news media because she is living within the frame of the issues and events that interest the news media.

The question that arises here is what will happen to her when the news media move on to other events, when the developing world begins to show that it is moving towards the developed world? For the time being, a story broadcast by the BBC in June 2006 emphasizes the point. It is a story of a terrifying ordeal by a man, Ochola John, twenty-five, captured in Uganda by rebels under the direction of Joseph Kony. His ears, lips, nose and hands were cut off during a torturous few days in which his fellow female captors were repeatedly raped before being mutilated and killed. In April 2006 the *Toronto Star* found a Honduran illegal immigrant, but named him simply Roberto, thirty-five, who had been working in Canada for five years laying bricks for $18 an hour (*Toronto Star* April 22, 2006, p. 1). Roberto localized, or underpinned, the story on illegal workers generally in Canada and the image of the illegal worker from developing countries desperate to become like their counterparts in the developed world. From the developed world perspective this news story demonstrated conclusively that the developed world system works so badly that more than two hundred thousand people work illegally in Canada because they want to be there rather than in their homeland.

Meanwhile, we can see what is already occurring if we examine news material on our three important developers: India, China and Brazil. The individuals within these countries—the more than two billion people—are both too vast in numbers for the media to single out individuals, but, more importantly, the policies of the institutions and governments that run the countries are becoming the focus because they are beginning to act more like Western nations.

A story on China's intention to build a third industrial zone to support Shenzen and Shanghai is framed positively in the *Economist* as if it were a competing developed industrial country. Binhai, as it is known, is imagined as the "darling" of China's President Hu Jintao, just as the previous zones were dear to previous presidents.

For the *Irish Times*, the issue of foreign workers from developing Eastern European countries is framed positively against the amount of money expatriated by them—although they remain unnamed—and how it contributes significantly to a reduction in poverty and boosts spending on health and education (*Irish Times* May 22, 2006).[2]

The evidence points to the news media shifting their focus from individuals suffering hardship in developing countries to the countries themselves, and those of most interest as they undertake economic reform, the élites. The question is, what will be the shape of the model of reporting when the Western news media have no more hungry, sick, dislocated citizens in developing countries to imagine? The truth is, like their counterparts in developed countries, they will still be there, but they will be of no great interest because they will have shifted in the imagination of the news media. They will be, like our good middle-class working mom, part of the uninteresting, unnewsworthy mass of middle class.

Nongovernment Organizations

Developing countries receive aid and support from developed countries through a number of channels. If they are members of the UN, they are referred to as recipient countries and they receive aid from donor countries, the World Bank and the IMF. If they are members of the WTO, they receive support and aid from developed countries. They also receive immeasurable support and assistance from a wide range of international and national nongovernment organizations.

Nongovernment organizations are defined by their name: they are free of government authority and usually separated from corporations as organizations because of their nonprofit nature. They can be well-financed organizations such as the International Red Cross or Amnesty International, or they can receive limited funding and act on behalf of members where issues and events are local—to oppose a housing development in a sensitive coastal environment, for example. By definition the latter are more likely to be referred to as special interest groups or community groups rather than NGOs, and for the purposes of this work, we will set them aside.

According to Bhagwati, the number of NGOs in the world could be more than two million (Bhagwati 2004: 36). He estimates that only a small percentage of these are focused on the sociopolitical and economic issues of globalization and trade. If this is the case, then we are very interested in the balance of coverage achieved by them in the Western news media. If, as Bhagwati claims, thousands of NGOs are focused on other issues that are not trade-related but local in their intent—geographic, environmental, population, health, education and war among them—how is it that the Western news media imagine

NGOs to have a valid and newsworthy presence within the global trade discourse? Is it that the NGOs have positioned themselves beyond their level—at what I call mezzanine level—so that they appear to have greater importance and credibility in the discourse? Is it that they are better strategists, capable of occupying space in the discourse because they understand the competition, understand how the game is played and play by the rules? I think there are elements of both that support the position of the NGOs in the coverage of trade issues in the Western news media.

The Concept of Mezzanine Status

Nongovernment organizations use different strategies to attempt to gain funding for support of their issues and events, and their influence can be anywhere between enormously successful and dispiriting, depending upon how they choose to frame their argument and how investing bodies and individuals choose to respond. In a post-materialist world, economic incentives frequently outweigh social incentives, so an issue can be complex in its process of achievement, yet simple in its presentation. NGOs actively use news media to assist them in shaping their persuasive intent by selecting appropriate competing news frames (Andsager 2001). If interest groups and community groups can present a persuasive argument to funding bodies that is supported by news media, they have a better chance of success given the role of news media in shaping public opinion.

Investment in NGOs resonates dually with the dilution of accountability theory (Funnell 2001: 1) and the argument that the rise of neo-liberalism has occurred as a reaction to the increasing influence of interest groups and social movements (Marsh 2001: 178).

Sociocultural interest groups play an important role in defining the political process (Kingdon 1995), but they are viewed combatively and perceived to exist to overthrow authority and disrupt the democratic process. On the other hand, interest groups and organizations that present an argument in alignment with an institutionalized policy of economic development are more likely to receive favorable treatment. Bhagwati identifies two groups of NGOs in the trade sphere: those who support globalization and those who oppose it. Some of these achieve alignment, while others fail. Achieving alignment requires an NGO to create what I term a public relations "mezzanine" strategy. A mezzanine strategy is one where an NGO presents its credentials in such a way that it will be perceived to be aligned with the high-level power and influence of entities such as governments, transnational corporations, and global media corporations, while in reality it is bumping along with other interest and community groups at a much lower level. A mezzanine strategy can assist an NGO to be perceived in such a way.

For a mezzanine strategy to exist, we must imagine NGOs in a hierarchical sense occupying differing strata. If governments, corporations and media occupy the highest level—to which we assume all other organizations aspire—at the base level lie community "grassroots" groups, which by their very nature are usually resourcefully and financially the poorest of those seeking to influence those at the highest levels. In-between lie NGOs, lobby groups, special interest groups and community groups.

Mezzanine status allows NGOs to capture the unidentified space somewhere between grassroots groups and the high levels of government and transnationals. They lie outside acknowledged frames that require high-level institutions and governments to act confrontationally when dealing with low-level special interest groups opposed to their policies. Thus, they are capable of presenting simple persuasive strategies while requiring little in the way of supporting governance and transparency that is the ethical province of higher-level institutions, governments and transnationals, and frequently the moral province of grassroots groups.

Mezzanine groups are thus capable of influence and persuasion at a high level, outside established conventions of confrontation that occur between governments and grassroots groups, without allowing their various publics, as it has been argued by Mayhew (1997) to redeem rhetorical tokens. Grassroots groups, community groups and special interest groups are viewed as confrontational by institutionalized power, provoking cleavage rather than consensus. Mezzanine status, because it lies outside this framework and is difficult to label, works by using a degree of consensus, removing cleavage and confrontation and allowing an organization to present harmonious proposals and strategies.

A clue to mezzanine success lies in the capacity of an organization to present a strategy to news media and to governments in such a way that it will appear to emulate the institutions it is attempting to persuade and influence. Grassroots and community groups frequently fail in their campaigns to persuade and influence because they have a limited understanding of the complexity of the relationship between governments, transnational corporations and news media.

Intergovernmental Organizational Status for NGOs

The acceptance of NGOs into the policymaking and governance sphere of intergovernmental organizations such as the UN, the WTO and the AU is an indication of their increased influence in the past thirty years. Beginning with the International Conference on Environment and Development in Rio de Janeiro in 1992, Bruhl and Rittberger argue that "NGOs have been more actively involved in world conferences than ever before" (Bruhl & Rittberger 2001: 34).[3]

In 1996 the UN resolved to narrow the participation gap by allowing NGOs to be accredited to its Economic and Social Council. By 2004, this arrangement had been extended to the point where organizations such as the International Communication Association (ICA) were acknowledged as being an NGO for the purposes of supporting research within the UN's Department of Public Information.

NGOs from developed and developing countries are civil society actors in the globalized trade play. In this, developed country NGOs frequently position themselves as prolocutors for the developing countries which, the NGOs argue, are unable to represent themselves adequately. NGOs originating in developed countries have been instrumental in providing humanitarian relief, debt relief and a reduction in human-rights abuses in both developing and developed countries. When combined with their mezzanine status, the image of the NGO is elevated dramatically for the Western news media.

NGOs and Their Relationship to News Media

If, as I have argued, NGOs can set up a strategy that positions them so they appear, without the need to draw on rhetorical tokens to support their reputation, to be part of the issue of globalization, (looking out from the room rather than being outside looking in), then they will always get the same amount of coverage as other players in the game.[4] They will always be seen as the counterbalance to an objective story. Thus, we have the situation in which Oxfam, a global charity based in Britain, was quoted in any number of stories on globalizations, especially on the Doha Round and WTO talks, because Oxfam invests heavily in research that provides it with its position in opposition to the issue. In other words, it creates a legitimacy for itself based in its research and its self-positioning as a global institution. This raises a number of interesting questions.

How do the media decide which of the NGOs involved in the issue of the globalization of trade fall into which camp? How do they differentiate between NGOs in developing countries opposed to global trade, and supporting global trade? How do they differentiate between NGOs in developed countries, set up specifically to provide research that supports globalization and those set up to produce research to oppose it? Are NGOs in developing countries opposed to global trade more activist than those located in developed countries?

NGOs and the Western news media have much in common. The most basic commonality is their observer status at the policy creation table. Neither NGOs nor the news media have seats at the table, a position that they find irritating and which some believe is indefensible. Like news media, NGOs need a focus for their imagining so they channel it towards the sphere of influence they think is most vulnerable. They interpret the policies of intergovernmental organizations such as the WTO as being what Tussie and Riggirozzi call "the nerve center of globalization" (Tussie & Riggirozzi 2001: 172). By imagining the WTO and other high-level organizations as powerful brokers for Western interests, NGOs provide the news media with a persuasive argument that fits their binary model of conflict and consensus. Thus, they build a relationship with the news media that is symbiotic. It is a relationship that requires allies and the availability of the NGOs who position themselves at a mezzanine level are the most obvious. Occasionally, however, the news media will turn and attack the NGOs if they think things are getting too cozy. Or when they believe that NGOs are not playing by the rules.[5]

The majority of the Western news media are likely to use civil society organizations to support their stories whereas others, the *Economist*, for example, are just as likely to avoid NGOs in favor of supporting investigations with material from intergovernmental organizations such as the World Bank, IMF or UN. The *Economist* is just as likely to question the role of NGOs in lengthy investigative pieces as it did in 2004 under the headline "a rigged dialogue with society" (*Economist* October 23, 2004, p. 64). Earlier, in September 2003, it had already increased the stakes suggesting that "pompous" charities calling themselves NGOs ought to be audited the same way that other businesses are. Cries of pain and anguish were heard across the planet. After all, are NGOs not set up to do good?

The news media attempt to differentiate between large aid agencies such as the International Committee of the Red Cross, Oxfam, CARE and Médecins sans Frontières and to hold them up as the leaders among civil society organizations. This is more often the result of good media management by the agencies than any other single factor.

In the 2004 story in the *Economist*, five NGOs that were being funded by the European Commission were exposed for agreeing that they were the natural conduits between the EC and citizens. The Young European Federalists, the Federalist Voice, the Active Citizenship Network, the European Network Against Racism and the Polish NGO Office were all guilty of supporting the intergovernmental organization that funded them.

Investigations into the activities of NGOs however, are infrequent. The *Economist* examples occurred once a year. Others, the *New York Times*, the *Washington Post*, the *Times*, the BBC, and CNN are equally tardy. News media find more cleavage in governments, transnationals and intergovernmental agencies than they look for in NGOs.

In an editorial leader of May 13, 2006, the *Economist* presented an interesting angle on the relationship between the news media and NGOs. In highlighting a trade fair for humanitarianism being held in the materialist state of Dubai—the irony of which became the story— the newspaper highlighted the idea that low-cost housing for aid workers in the emirate, along with its tax-free status, might make a good place where "they [aid workers] and foreign correspondents can hunker down on their way to emergencies." It added an additional ironic touch by suggesting Dubai is a relatively good place for such activity because it is "close to disaster prone bits of Africa and Asia" (*Economist* May 13, 2006, p. 14). The idea that aid workers and journalists travel together, share accommodation and airline flights is not new. What the story in the *Economist* presented was the image of journalists and aid workers in proximity for long periods of time. Such proximity is conducive to professional and personal relationship building and for journalists to rely on the relationships for information that becomes news copy.

An instructive piece in a leading Australia newspaper, the *Aus-*

tralian Financial Review in May 2006 provided a revealing glimpse into the world of the journalist. The reporter, Julie Macken, writing about a group of Australian businessmen who had decided to bypass governments in their quest for a cleaner environment, said it was much easier in the "old days" to pick who the good guys and bad guys were when confronted with corporate and environmental problems. "The bad guys wore suits, talked share prices and raped and pillaged as they raked in squillions. The good guys wore primary colors, talked *Gaia* principles and got arrested for blocking log trucks" (*Australian Financial Review* May 6, 2006, p. 25). Macken lamented the loss of the distinction while applauding the advancement of business where "suits are just as likely to talk sustainability and triple bottom line [and] environmentalists sit in the boardroom talking stakeholder value and synergies between corporate and conservation ambitions" (*Australian Financial Review* May 6, 2006, p. 25).

I am not sure the *Australian Financial Review's* reporter's image was an accurate reflection of reality, or simply a wish that it might have been close to the truth. If we extend the metaphor a little further, we can see why news media have difficulty in distinguishing good guy actors from bad guy actors on the issue of globalized trade. In the binary model of conversational journalism, if the good guys are the NGOs, then the bad guys must be the intergovernmental institutions such as the WTO that the NGOs attack. For the news media, this is a simple calculus.

Let's go back to the *Australian Financial Review* story for a moment to see how it might fit this argument. It took some time to get to the point. After the initial introduction—the idea of good guys and bad guys—the story drifted into what appeared to be a side issue, the size and scope of a U.S.-based conservation NGO called The Nature Conservancy (TNC). But it was not a side issue. It was the point of the story that the NGO, with membership of nine hundred thousand, revenues of $784 million and assets of $2.8 billion, was the subject of news media reporting in the United States after a lengthy research investigation by the *Washington Post*. According to the *Australian Financial Review*, "with that kind of roll call and that much money involved, it was probably only *a matter of time before the media began testing the integrity of the organization*" (my italics) (*Australian Financial Review* May 6, 2006, p. 25). Again, this was pure speculation on the part of the newspaper and a wish that news media might be imagined as being the journals of record they are meant to be. But that was not the end of the story. Its substance concerned the arrival of a reinvented TNC in Australia, an NGO that had changed its governance and was something that interested Australian conservation groups, Greening Australia and Australian Bush Heritage, along with a handful of businesspeople with an interest in conservation. It was, in other words, nothing more than a puff piece for an NGO that had built a relationship with a handful of mid-level business people. It was a standard story about NGOs in developed countries in a national newspaper with a business focus.

From another perspective, the idea of NGOs working towards the elevation of developing countries from poverty, disease and war, is laudable. But it brings with it the thought that NGOs in developing countries might build an image of themselves as being more important to the future success of a country than that country's elected or authoritarian government. This is not a topic taken up frequently by the Western news media. It might get space in the developing world news media, as a story on civil society groups in Congo receiving death threats did in the newspaper *All Africa* in May 2006. The newspaper story highlighted threats made against an organization known as the Natural Resources Network, an organization that emerged from a joint workshop between African news media and NGOs concerned with exploitation of natural resources in the Democratic Republic of Congo. While the death threats were the focus of the story, the issue of the news media and NGOs collaborating over a national issue such as resource use is something that would not occur transparently in the developed world. It is this collaboration that reveals the extent of NGO involvement in politics in developing and developed countries rather than simply acting as aid agencies.

The same issue was the subject of an *Agence France Presse* report, but in this story a Dutch NGO, Netherlands Institute for Southern Africa, was quoted as having produced an eighty-page research report that demonstrated conclusively that the Congolese government, in collaboration with the World Bank and other aid donors, had "plundered the country's rich natural resources for personal gain while leaving their people mired in extreme poverty" (*Agence France Presse* April 26, 2006). The possibility of the African news media reporting in such an aggressive manner is limited by its lack of freedom from government control.

Media and NGO Participation in Local and Global Politics

The Western news media and nongovernment organizations are active participants as agents and as entities in local and global politics. NGOs, whether they are community, not-for-profit, or special interest groups have different ideologies and, therefore, different reasons for existence. Ideologies come in all shapes and sizes. Among the most common and most easily identified are:

— Liberalism and Conservatism, both vying for dominance in the Western world
— Socialism, with its path towards liberty and choice
— Feminism and its positive recasting of political language
— Green ideology as a buttress against all others

Ideology is the shaping of ideas to form a coherent argument that will justify actions. Possession of an ideology is a call to action to affect change, or counteraction to retain the status quo. NGOs adopt ideologies, frame and present issues around those ideologies, and attempt to persuade and exert influence on governments or corporations, or on other organizations and agents such as the news media.

An attempt has been made to taxonomize all organizations that fall outside government and corporate spheres (Demetrious & Hughes 2004). But the convenience of this typology fails to acknowledge the paradox of both the special characteristics of such NGOs and their contemporary adherence to professional public relations strategies and tactics. Of more importance is the acknowledgment that the NGOs themselves need not be categorized in any meaningful way. If taxonomies are required, they should be measured against the frequency and use of strategies and tactics applied by individual organizations. Research of this nature will provide similar evidence of their intentions to that of corporations and governments when their policies are measured against strategy selection. An understanding of the nature of the organization and its ideology through an analysis of its strategies and tactics leads to an understanding of its policies and its strategic direction.

An NGO ideology is usually shaped by the objective of support and assistance. It would be fair to say that most NGOs adopt liberal or conservative ideologies. Their status as not-for-profit organizations means they generally work closely with governments to achieve their goals and objectives. Governments in the Western world are either liberal or conservative. Not-for-profit organizations operate within a systems and structural environment. Many large NGOs have a bureaucratic structure similar to governments. Smaller, less bureaucratic not-for-profits rely for their continued existence on the support of unpaid volunteers. The boards of directors of NGOs are comprised of volunteers, as are the thousands of individual citizens who contribute time and energy to their global and local activities. The ideology of the NGO is thus grounded in support and maintenance of others over self.

It is this image of selflessness that assists the NGO in its pursuit of news media space. Médecins sans Frontières (MSF) is a good example of an NGO that has a strong appeal for journalists in the West. The organization defines itself as an independent humanitarian medical aid agency committed to two objectives; providing medical aid wherever needed, regardless of race, religion, politics or sex, and raising awareness of the plight of the people they help. The second objective is pitched at a variety of stakeholders, most notable among them the Western news media. It operates in more than seventy countries providing emergency medical assistance to human populations in danger. In carrying out this role it seeks to raise awareness of crisis situations, a frame that is one of the most conspicuous in the news media's imagination. MSF claims, accurately, that only a small percentage of the populations that find themselves in a situation of danger gain the attention of the media. The organization therefore claims to be unique in that it is staffed by volunteers who frequently travel to places that people have never heard of to assist those who have fallen victim to man-made and natural disasters. Of equal importance for the organization is that its volunteers then return from these places, armed with first-hand accounts that become valuable sources for the news media. We might even argue that the volunteers within MSF have replaced the reporters and foreign news correspondents who were once the first eyewitnesses of the events now being seen by MSF volunteers. The importance of this is not lost in the reduction of the number of journalists being employed by large Western news media. Thus, the news media have a natural affiliation for this type of NGO both socially, as it is élite individuals (medical practitioners) who are volunteering for these tours and who are thus able to enunciate their narratives in a form that is highly recognizable and desirable in the news. In other words, they know the importance of a good sound bite as much as they know the importance of a sterile dressing. As an organization that obtains funding from noncorporate sources, it also has the capacity to investigate and report on activities it sees as being unethical in medical practice. In June 2006 MSF published a press release on its Web site headed, "Abbott picks and chooses which patients get crucial new version of AIDS drug in developing countries" (MSF Web site). The story related to an American pharmaceutical company that Médecins sans Frontières accused of the action it spelt out in its headline. It went on to accuse Abbott Laboratories of Chicago of refusing to sell or partially fulfilling orders for a new drug—*lopinavir/ritonavir*, a second-line HIV drug that did not require refrigeration—despite its recommendation by the WHO as having critically important advantages over the older version. MSF accused Abbott, the sole global manufacturer of the drug, of limiting its price to $500 for sale in the poorest of developing countries. MSF argued it excluded others such as Thailand and Guatemala—less poor—but places where AIDS patients were equally in need of treatment.

Western news media did not provide space for the MSF pronouncement. A hugely complex eight-thousand-word feature in the *New York Times* of August 6, may have had some basis in information supplied by MSF, but otherwise the Western news media were deathly quiet on the issue. Three of the world's leading news agencies, Agence France Presse, Dow Jones and Reuters ran short five- to fifteen-paragraph pieces in July, two acclaiming the arrival of the drug, know as Kaletra, in Nigeria and Lagos and the third announcing the same drug becoming available in Europe. The Agence France Presse piece went as far as referring to the MSF call for Abbott to register the drug in nine countries, including Thailand and Guatemala, but stopped short of reporting the NGO's problems with the drug manufacturer distributing in those countries. So much for NGOs having a good relationship with the Western news media.

10

Conclusions: Rethinking Global News Media

This concluding chapter argues for a rethink about how issues and events can be imagined in terms other than global or local. It presents the case for change in how the news media should be imagining global news in the first half of the 20th century and how it should engage with global news generators in effective terms if they are to rebuild a position of objectivity within a future framework. It offers the possibility that a new model for journalism can be created and sustained by investigating and reporting truth, rather than imagined truths.

In August 2006, the newspaper that has been the primary target of this book's investigation, the *Economist*, published a vitally important three-page special report on the global newspaper industry, in which it made a number of statements that have been the consistent theme of this book. Most importantly, it stated that newspapers need to be more "imaginative." It was referring specifically to the relationship of the traditional newspaper to the Internet and how the *Wall Street Journal* in the 1990s had been imaginative by posting a five hundred and seventy-two-page backstory on its Web site. But this misses the real point of how journalism can be transformed through the use of imagination. As we have seen, there is more to imagining than using new technology to act out traditional methods.

Next, it stated that research into the "tastes of mainstream newspaper readers has long shown that people like short stories and news that is relevant to them: local reporting, sports, entertainment, weather and traffic," and that "long pieces about foreign affairs are low on reader's priorities—the more so now that the Internet enables people to scan international news headlines in moments" (*Economist* August 26, 2006). It stated further that the idea of national and international news being imagined as a commodity made one newspaper almost indistinguishable from another.

If we follow this line of argument, we arrive at a point where we are unable to imagine a future in which the newspaper, or any other global news medium, is capable of delivering global issues and events as news. Global issues and events will cease to be interpreted and reported by news media: they will instead be reported on their corporate Web sites by the institutions and agents that are attached to them—the WTO, the UN, the World Bank—and they will seek to attract attention without the full value of interpretation and mediation. Stakeholder publics will be left to make their own interpretations, to form opinions, and to act on those opinions, based solely on information from the source. They will continue, as the *Economist* stated further in its report, to "want their paper to tell them how to get richer, and what they might do in the evening" (*Economist* August 26, 2006) rather than inform them of issues and events outside their immediate sphere of influence. Such a scenario would have dire consequences for the developing world. News of issues and events in the developing world provides critical links between the developed and the developing worlds beyond the occasional natural disaster report. Without news media reports of the issues and events that underpin the problems of the developing world—poverty, famine, disease—citizens in the developed world would be persuaded less that there is a need to apply themselves to these problems. They would, in other words, be denied any contact other than direct contact from institutions and agencies, those with a direct interest in developing world problems. This itself would be cause for alarm because, as we know, we as citizens in the developed world place great store in the efficacy of the messages received from the news media. We are far less likely to believe messages coming directly from what we perceive to be self-interested institutions and agencies as sources. To the unimaginable detriment of citizens in the developing world, such a scenario would allow citizens in the Western world to dig deeper into their own self-importance and well-being.

The difficulty for the *Economist*, as for other global newspapers and broadcasters of record, lies in their inability to recognize the end of the economic cycle that sustained them for three hundred years. But more importantly, the real problem is their inability to see that an alternative is not beyond imagination. While ever they strive to compete with entertainment, lifestyle and get-rich-quick media, their days are always going to be numbered. They have, in effect, already died as they have been absorbed into new media. As the *Economist* stated so obviously: "still more changes to the content and form of newspapers are likely as business people gain power at newspaper firms" (*Economist* August 26, 2006). The last lament for the *Economist* was when the *Philadelphia Inquirer* took control of that newspaper's design away from the editorial department and handed it ceremonially to the advertising department. But this is not new. Newspaper advertising departments have always had implicit control over newspaper design through the sale of space. Editorial departments have never been in control of space ratios, and the shocking claim that a global newspaper of importance such as the *Wall Street Journal* should stoop to placing advertisements on its front page is simply a reversion to an activity that occurred widely in the West less than fifty years ago.

So what does this mean for the future of global news reporting?

When the *Jim Lehrer News Hour* on American public broadcasting allows a news anchor to ask what "global citizens" think of the Israel-Lebanon conflict, Western newsworthiness comes into question. When the same broadcaster provides airtime for a Lebanese-born American citizen to say, "Israel is indiscriminately bombing civilian targets in Lebanon," then news as we know it is in serious trouble. Both these mediated broadcasts took place in August 2006 while the Israel-Lebanon conflict was at its peak. But neither the images nor the message should have been allowed to be broadcast without at least equal time for an Israeli citizen to make similar uninformed comments. This is not journalism. And it is not where the global news media or the Western news media should be heading. Truth in journalism has been rejected in favor of processes traditionally imagined as being the province of spin doctors. But even the best spin doctor would have difficulty with the ethics of this particular PBS broadcast.

So what is it that allows us to imagine the Western news media can even begin to rethink their position and to reassess the model that they have used to interpret and report issues and events for the past three hundred years? And why would they want to?

Part of the answer lies in the idea of truth in reporting. The image of the Western news media that has been fabricated by the news media themselves, and by their stakeholders (and stakeseekers), is of a highly placed institution that represents the interests of a wide variety and number of stakeholders. In reality they are simply agents of opinion working on behalf of a narrow constituency with narrow secular interests.

I have argued closely in this work for a transformation of the existing model of journalism that is based on an investigation of a number of premises that require deconstruction.

The first, the concept that the Western news media are well-respected institutions, has its basis in the Habermasian notion that the press is the "pre-eminent institution" of the public sphere (Habermas 1989: 181). As I have argued above, the press, or, in its more widely accepted form, the media, are not in fact an institution but agents working on behalf of stakeholders who use them in the Habermasian sense as a "platform for advertising" (Habermas 1989: 181). We must differentiate between institutions and agents in a global sense if we are going to understand how the news media function as local agents rather than as a global institution.

As I pointed out in chapter 4, globalization rests on a platform, the three pillars of which are as strong as one another and represent corporations, governments and the news media. In an uninformed world, all three pillars are elevated to the status of institution while representing the interests of agency. On this imagined platform sit the real institutions of globalization, among them the United Nations, the World Trade Organization, the World Bank, and the International Monetary Fund.

The three pillars of the tau act as agents for each other, and independently, to exchange information that benefits their own stakeholders. For corporations, these stakeholders are shareholders seeking information that can lead to profit. For governments, they are citizens seeking information that can lead to increased well-being. For the news media, they are readers, listeners and viewers seeking information that can increase both profit and well-being. The news media, rather than being imagined as a preeminent institution within the public sphere, are in truth agents for corporate and government stakeholders seeking profit and well-being. Herein lies the difficulty for the news media. Habermas suggests their early transformation from merchants of news to dealers in public opinion set the news media on a particular path. What it did in fact was far more serious. It created the circumstances that have locked the news media into the reporting model that they have been unable to escape from for the past three hundred years.

As agents of public opinion, the news media are reliant on their fellow agent networks—corporations and governments—to source information that can be interpreted as opinion. They must seek source credibility, but they cannot look outside the frame of corporation and government, their interdependent agencies, for their material. This requirement of the news media to be reliant upon predetermined sources forces all interpretation of issues and events into a narrow frame proscribed by the actions or policies of the corporations and governments as the defining pillars within the relationship. It follows then that the news media cannot interpret meaning in the policies of the institutions of globalization outside this proscribed frame. To report on the institution of the UN, for example, is to report as if it were an agent in the same frame as a national government or a transnational corporation. The news media have no available tools to interpret it outside this narrow frame. Unfortunately, they have not developed alternative innovative tools over a period of time, so that they might be able to interpret meaning in institutional policy outside a narrow, secular frame.

Public opinion has altered the shape of the public sphere to the extent that the news media define their capacity for reporting through pragmatism and populist political representation. For national governments a similar position is adopted when delivering popular policy. It is much more difficult to deliver policies that might have long-term benefits, than simple, short-term popular policies. For corporations, the production of goods and services based on consumer opinion and, therefore, demand is an equivalent policy position. When the news media interpret the policies and actions of global institutions they do so within the narrow frame of agency that they have developed through their relationships with national governments and corporations. This is unacceptable. The news media narrow the frame and imagine the institutions of globalization to represent the same interests as corporations and governments.

The first stage in the transformation of the Western news media model lies in the ability of the actors to step away from the tau and to unlock themselves from agency and its traditional representation of governments and corporations. They must begin to distinguish between agency and institution, and to define global institutional issues and events within the context of a different public sphere. It is no longer acceptable for the news media to act in the Habermasian sense of public sphere, as receptacle for interpretation of narrow opinion.

Secondly, they must undertake a paradigm shift from the existing informational model to a model that draws on the worthy elements of the old conversational model while also drawing in new elements that will underpin the shift.

It must be viewed in the Mayhewian sense of a new sphere where publics are competent and able to differentiate opinion and truth and to recognize the value in institutional discourse at a global level. Mayhew provides an important counterpoint to the Habermasian notion of the news media as institution. He argues that the public is overwhelmed by information disseminated by professional communicators who seek "instrumental ends unconstrained by civic virtue or liberal communicative ideals" (Mayhew 1997: 185). For Mayhew the problem for the news media and citizens as publics is the sheer volume of information entering the public sphere that requires mediation and interpretation because it is supplied by ruthless advertising and public relations offering rhetorical tokens without any possibility of redemption of those tokens within the public sphere. Mayhew is attempting to engage with the idea that truth is not part of the information that enters the public sphere from either public relations practitioners or advertisers, and that while both frame their communications around rhetorical devices such as profit and well-being, there is never an opportunity within the public sphere for stakeholders to question these rhetorical devices nor to seek their redemption.

Mayhew argues that the emergence of public relations as an institution of persuasion in the early 20th century shifted the balance of the public sphere away from the Habermasian ideal in which journalism played an important role. But, like its mirror image, journalism, public relations is an agent of governments and corporations rather than an institution of the public sphere. The true public sphere lies in the representation of the global through institutional discourse, rather than through agency discourse on behalf of client stakeholders such as governments and corporations.

The drawback in this is the fact that Mayhew blamed public relations and advertising for citizen disengagement with the public sphere, rather than blaming the media. This, however, is not an accurate reflection of the true position of citizen engagement in the public sphere. Mediated discourse framed within the informational model of journalism forms the opinions of citizens. Publicity is interpreted and mediated so that citizens are not directly exposed to its persuasive motivation. It is the responsibility of the Western news media to interpret and report, thus the discourses of the news media must be an accurate reflection of the truth in issues and events. For Mayhew, the problem is one of the media not having the resources to investigate and interpret accurately all the available information. But the availability of resources has a direct relationship to media ownership and the distribution of resources. So we have a combination of a lack of available resources with an inability to interpret the complexity of global issues and events. This leads to reporting that, in its partial delivery, has the capacity to place inordinate amounts of misinformation in the public sphere.

Thirdly, as citizens, we have ways of communicating our own and collective interests. Where once we spoke of stories, and the telling of stories to identify what it is we were communicating, we now refer to our communication with each other by the more important *narrative*. Or we talk of *conversations* to mean more than the word itself once defined. We talk of a conversation rather than a story to define what it is we are discussing. This implies an innate desire for a return to the conversational model of reporting that occupied the public space prior to the elevation of the information model of reporting as a business process. The difference between conversation and storytelling is that for them to have relevance, conversations require a number of competing opinions. They are the underpinning of political journalism. Ordinary citizens, however, are confronted by a complex web of conversations at élite and ordinary levels that they are expected to understand and engage with in an informed fashion. To be uninformed is to be unfashionable.

The Western news media rely on the idea of citizen engagement with issues and events that embrace both the simplicity of the local and the complexity of the global. Citizens, however, are unable to engage with complex global issues because the Western news media distort them by framing them in the local. Citizens thus come to an issue or event with an uninformed opinion as it relates to them personally. Rather than creating an informed collective, this serves to disengage and fragment opinion along lines that can be imagined in the same way as a local event in a neighborhood street.

But citizens are no longer deeply involved in neighborhood issues and events because they spend too much time worrying about global issues such as war, with which they have no direct engagement. This causes them to be half-aware of the global and half-aware of the local with the consequence that they feel fragmented and not strongly attached to either. This fragmentation and lack of attachment leaves them anxious and concerned that they are inadequate as individuals.

And the opinions that form and shape those feelings are mostly mediated.

Isolation is a factor in the seeking of wider information. The more isolated we are, the more we seek to increase the circumference of the information that we think we need to become informed. Local news is more important to us because we can act upon it. Property prices, traffic delays and gas prices are all pieces of information that might have some local relevance to us. But citizens also need global information for comparative reasons. An Australian reading a story in the *Economist* about a pogrom in central Africa has no use for the information other than a passing interest in the affairs of others from which to make a comparison: how lucky it is not happening to her in Australia. She cannot act on the information in any meaningful way.

Seeking global information as news for interpretation also allows us to make a more odious comparison and to act—if falsely. News of Brazilian rain-forest logging may inflame a Parisian to resist in the future, buying some Brazilian commodity—coffee, for example. But how accurate is the news of rain-forest clearing and what is the unintended consequence of the Parisian boycott—unemployment in Brazil, perhaps?

Global news acts as a trigger for Western citizens to assist the actions and policies of large organizations operating transnationally in developing countries. And much of that information, while presented as news, is in fact constructed by public relations acting on behalf of those who wish to influence and persuade. But the job of the media to investigate and report accurately is not being achieved.

The problem for the Western news media brings us to my fourth point, that they, too, are less informed than they need to be on complex issues and events, and they are thus unable to fulfill the needs of citizens and other stakeholders except élites who already have a high level of knowledge about the issues and events.

To achieve any success, the Western news media must abandon their representation of global institutional news as a local commodity and begin to investigate and interpret complex institutions of globalization as they really are, as complex institutions of globalization. For this fifth and final point to have impact, the Western news media must reconsider their relationships with stakeholders other than governments and corporations. They must see themselves as agents in the global, investigating and reporting issues and events in such a way that they can be interpreted by a wide range of stakeholders within the public sphere, rather than representing only the interests of their fellow élites in the private sphere.

Towards a Transformation

It is no coincidence that my argument is based on the events of 9/11, when journalism was confronted with nothing other than the truth in the terrorist attacks that required them to report the images of airplanes flying into the sides of buildings. The events of 9/11 shocked the Western news media out of their conservative and traditionally value-laden existence for a brief moment, a moment in which they investigated and reported an event as it actually was. The Western news media investigated and reported and left the interpretation and opinion forming to the stakeholder—the viewer or reader—who engaged with the reported information. But the denotative images had to be followed by connotative meaning and interpretation, a function of the news media that is critical for a balanced view to emerge within Western society.

How then do the Western news media reimagine themselves so that they can continue to interpret and report vital global issues and events, so that infotainment and lifestyle reporting fails in its attempt to remove from the minds of Western citizens vital issues such as global trade and developing-world poverty?

The answer, far from being blown in the wind, is relatively simple. It requires global news media organizations to do a number of things. First, they must stop competing for space with lifestyle media. Complex global issues such as world trade will never occupy the same space in the minds of Western citizens as that occupied by buying a new vehicle or deciding where to eat out.

Secondly, they must acknowledge their place as élites and stop pretending they can distill complex issues into ten-paragraph local angle stories for general consumption. Dropping this veil will allow average citizens to comprehend that there are complex issues in the public sphere and that they can't all be distilled into digestible chunks the same as a dog-food advertisement. Poverty in the developing world is not something that can be compared for its tantalizing shape or its mouthwatering taste. By acknowledging their relationship to other élite institutions and agencies, global Western news media will present their credentials more truthfully than they do by attempting to pretend they are acting on behalf of average citizen stakeholders. In this they will free themselves to investigate and report the complex issues surrounding world trade in a different form. This form, as the fourth point in my argument, must take a different shape from that imposed on them by the belief in a global public sphere. From the Habermasian perspective, newspapers as "institutions for the publication of news" were transformed around three hundred years ago to become "carriers and leaders of public opinion" (1989: 182). This reshaping of the medium has continued so that we now have a newspaper such as the *Economist* opining about readers being uninterested in long pieces on foreign affairs, requiring instead "short stories and news that is relevant to them: local reporting, sports, entertainment, weather and traffic" (*Economist* August 16, 2006). As we can see, however, this appalling situation that the global news media find themselves in has been generated internally; they should never have shifted so determinedly from a decidedly political position—one in which they sold news—to an economic position which involved the interpretation of public opinion and the dispensing of their own opinions; the opinions of the newspaper owners to support the sale of advertising space.

In almost three hundred years, very little has changed in the way news has been differentiated. In the 18th century, it was the vital court, wars, taxes, harvests and foreign trade news that was exchanged between élites, while news items of miracle cures, murders, storms and pestilence were allowed to filter downwards to become what Habermas describes as "the residual elements of what was actually available" (1989: 21), a reference that is sustained at the beginning of the 21st century when we think about the popular media. It is at this point that the differentiation must be reestablished so that complex global issues can be interpreted without fear of losing readership and requiring, as the *Economist* states, to attract between twenty and one hundred online readers when a newspaper loses one print reader.

While the Western global news media attempt to compete with popular media for lifestyle readers, they will never be in a position to interpret and report complex global issues. But complex global issues will not go away just because they are not reported adequately in the West. General Western ignorance of the issues, forced by downward competition for media space, will create a divergence that can lead nowhere other than towards disaster. While the élite Western news media attempt to compete for economic position with popular cultural ideas, and remain locked into Western values and norms that present pop culture as an abiding truth, they will continue their downward economic spiral and continue to be politically insignificant.

A new paradigm for global news media will appear when there is a revelation from within that they have diffuse stakeholders, that a business model based on advertising sales is not the only model, that competent reporting does not require all news to be localized and that citizens of developed countries, far from being incapable of interpreting and acting on complex global issues and events, are much closer to reality than the Western news media think they are.

Notes

Chapter 1

1. Apologies to Gay Tuchman, who claims news reporting "routinizes the unexpected"; much the same, I suggest, as a sushi train routinizes the unexpected delight associated with eating raw fish.

2. Throughout the book, when there is a quote from a newspaper, I have cited the name of the journalist or reporter writing the story and included the citation in the bibliography. For the *Economist*, which does not use bylines for its reporters, there are no named citations in the bibliography.

3. I have chosen to support my argument by drawing attention to specific global trade issues and events that underpin the global market economy, and to focus on the role of the United Nations as an organization that attempts to ameliorate the advances of the welfare state within the dynamic of a global market economy.

4. The idea of taking 1976 as a starting point for comparing how Western media imagines news is relevant to the fact that I am writing in the present. To understand the present it is important to consider the past. A generation is sufficient time in which to consider changes in media news reporting so that assumptions can be made about the future of reporting in later chapters.

5. An interesting aside is that human blood temperature works best at around 98.6°F (37°C) so anything up to this point is physically undemanding. If, as a journalist, I imagine 95°F (35°C)

to be an extremely high temperature, then anything above is going to have been caused—in my framing of the issue—by some exogenous influence, global warming, for example.

6. But specialization does not make a journalist an expert.

7. Friedman acknowledges his own evolution as emerging expert when the *New York Times* created a specialty position for him "at the intersection of finance and foreign policy" that enabled him to better understand the nature of global markets (*The Lexis and the Olive Tree*, p. 379).

Chapter 2

1. Even then it might take on a local angle to show that it has some relevance to all stakeholders.

2. For example, the relationship between the Republic of Korea and The People's Republic of North Korea and how it is reported in the United States.

3. See Snooks (1998), for a substantial explanation of the cycle of conquest and commerce as it has existed in the West for the past three hundred years.

4. I am not suggesting they ignore issues and events such as global disasters or crises unless they are localized. An earthquake in Indonesia will receive media attention around the world. It will have a heightened localization when the government and institutions within the country donate relief funding to the victims of the disaster, but it will also be reported generally. The in-

volvement of the local government or institutions will naturally occur after the event, so any attachment should be considered to be feature material rather than news.

5. The only variable is the grain index. Both Japan and Korea are net consumers of rice, rather than wheat.

6. The English-language newspaper the *Korea Times* reported in late May 2006 that the Kaesong project had the support of Guido Westerwelle, chairman of the German Free Democratic Party (FDP), who stated during a visit to Korea that, had Germany had a similar opportunity during the time of its division, it would have done the same thing.

7. The added complexity of this particular issue lies in the argument that Japan is almost as Western in its use of news media as the traditional West and that communities of its own citizens are as outraged by the issue of whaling as are those in the West.

8. A *60 Minutes* reporter, Richard Carlton, died of a heart attack at the scene.

9. Lippmann had been a Washington insider for thirty years before Johnson arrived from Texas.

Chapter 3

1. It is here that the binary is usually invoked by the global news media: we are not given choices other than like or dislike.

2. The history of these publications and their publishers and writers is well documented. What is most interesting though is that they were not newspapers as we know newspapers—as a daily record of issues and events within a town, city or other community. They were a series of commentaries that used the same diurnal form as the newspaper to present issues and events, but they presented them as a continuum, a daily commentary with a particular frame that suited the particular political position of the author. They were, in effect, the precursors of the *Economist*, the *New York Times* and other journals of record.

3. In September 2006, while prime minister Thaksin was visiting the United States, a military coup took place in Thailand. It was imagined by *The Economist* under a heading, "Old Soldiers, Old Habits," as a shift from the land of smiles back to the land of coups (23. 9. 2006, p. 27).

4. Violence would alter the image of the friendly Thai that has been part of a continuous and successful public relations campaign by various national governments as a boost for tourism.

Chapter 4

1. In the drama series *Deadwood* a rich woman, Alma Garrett, is told by an unscrupulous hotel owner, E.B. Farnham, that she might like to sell her claim to one of the richest gold mines because the town is in jeopardy. Her able mining adviser suggests that there is a lot of rhetoric doing the rounds of the 19th-century gold town, but his own keen observations record that the river is still running and the town still seems to be trading profitably.

2. *Transact* means to carry through, implying some type of border or boundary across which business might be conducted.

3. Leaving aside for the moment the idea that corporations and individuals would not pay taxes if no tax law existed.

4. The French policy on immigration is that all immigrants must become French citizens and adopt French culture and French values, but the specter of the "Polish Plumber" looms large in the French imagination.

5. The issue of a European constitution occupies the minds of a large number of national politicians throughout Europe.

6. The two countries that voted in 2005 against constitutional union.

7. An example of the news media distinction between left and right is the French press, specifically *Le Monde* and *Le Figaro*, described adequately as left of center and right of center respectively. This does not mean they are stuffed with Marxists or evangelists.

Chapter 5

1. Setting aside such events as war, which are reported differently from issues and events during peacetime.

2. The *International Herald Tribune* refers to itself as "the world's daily newspaper."

3. Imagine for a moment, you are flying on a commercial jet airliner between Japan and Taiwan, or some other north Asia country, and a North Korean rocket skims past your window, unannounced.

4. The *Economist* speculated the American-Iranian discourse was causing North Korea pain.

Chapter 6

1. The Brussels press corp is similar in nature to the Washington press corp.

2. The idea of a government supporting a rebel group without identifying clearly its involvement is similar to a corporation or other organization in the West creating a front group to counterbalance a legitimate environmental group in its actions against the corporation.

3. Since 2004 the African Union had installed more than seven thousand troops in Darfur with little quantifiable success, according to the Western news media.

4. It was an "eventuality" for the media as most defined the threat as something that would happen no matter how many precautions were taken.

5. A large number of academic commentators joined the rush to imagine a globally uncontrollable threat.

6. The *Canberra Times* story was a direct lift from the *Independent* run the following day without a byline on p. 20.

Chapter 7

1. In this Tharoor is responding to the image of the president of the United States and his media communications team. Since 1992, and the election of Bill Clinton, both President Clinton and President Bush have maintained a communications team that insists on "staying on message" and producing one message each day for the American media and the global media. The idea of one message a day gives the news media only one issue on which to concentrate, a strategy that includes all of the communications team members staying with that specific message, so that there is no room for the news media to get sidetracked.

2. Many developing countries supply troops based on the fact that soldiers are paid more as a UN peacekeeper in a week than they may be paid in a year in their home country.

3. There is a relationship to private property rights in eight out of ten news stories in local weeklies.

4. Readers, viewers and listeners will not stay with a news item if it does not have some meaning.

5. Examples of populations below $1 purchasing power parity per day: Sub Saharan Africa, 49 percent; South Central Asia, 32.6 percent; Eastern Asia and Oceania, 17.8 percent.

6. The International Food Policy Research Institute (IFPRI) is financed by a mix of private and public donors, among them, ironically, the World Bank and the Food and Agriculture Organization (FAO). It has a specific division devoted to the idea of development, strategy and governance, the Web site for

which states that good governance plays an essential role in reaching the goals of overcoming poverty, hunger environmental degradation, unemployment and human diseases. For the Western journalist, the IFPRI Web site is far more accessible than that of the FAO. It is clearly subdivided and clear in its objectives while, in contrast, it is difficult to navigate the FAO site despite the wealth of information that becomes available if one perseveres. The problem for the journalist is one of time: copy deadlines preclude long periods of uninterrupted time to navigate complex sites, so the obvious solution is to take what is being presented. I am assuming here that the journalist might also have been given clear information from making personal contact with the IFPRI, as its Web site reflects the individuals who make up the organization. The same has to be said for the lack of clarity in the FAO site. Incidentally, the UN in 2001 commissioned a book-length work titled *Global Governance and the United Nations System*, edited by Volker Rittberg of the University of Tübingen, Germany.

7. Although it did not specify in its December 4 edition that this was the case, instead running the essay under a strap titled *By Invitation: Kofi Annan.*

Chapter 8

1. Despite difference in counting among the news media [the BBC says 150 (4. 28. 06), the *Observer* 149 (4. 30. 06), the *New York Times* 147 (6. 16. 06)].

2. Plus a number of additional disputes against individual EU members, three for France, three for Belgium, three for Ireland, one the Netherlands, one Sweden, one the UK. Other members had different numbers of disputes seeking settlement but some of the more interesting were: Australia, a total of seven against the European Commission, Hungary, India, Korea, and the United States; Brazil twenty-two against Argentina, Canada, EC, Mexico, Peru, Turkey and the United States; Bangladesh, one against India; Canada, twenty-seven against Australia, Brazil, China, EC, Hungary, India, Japan, Korea and the United States (thirteen alone there); China, two against the United States; the EC, seventy-two against Argentina, Australia, Brazil, Canada, Chile, China, India, Indonesia, Japan, Korea, Mexico, Pakistan, the United States; Hungary, five against Croatia, Czech Republic, Romania, Slovak Republic, Turkey; Korea, thirteen against the EC, Japan, Philippines, the United States. Not all these cases were continuing. Agreement may have been reached but the WTO maintains the information on its Web site for historical purposes.

3. Set aside for a moment the different rules for both organizations that govern member voting.

4. We are less interested here in the strategy of the developed world to gain access to abundant resources in developing countries and more interested in the way developing countries see themselves in the overall play.

5. I am not suggesting corporations are uninterested in human rights or the environment, but as I have shown elsewhere, they are foremost interested in profit.

Chapter 9

1. These elements will be viewed differently at different historical times. Witness the distinction the news media make between George W. Bush and Lyndon B. Johnson. George Bush failed to find his version of Walter Lippmann or Arthur Krock.

2. Eastern Europe fits the same frame as India, China, and Brazil because the countries involved are now part of, or becoming part of, the EU.

3. NGOs, however, have been part of the process since the establishment of the UN, when they were granted observer status and persuaded the UN architects to incorporate human rights in its charter.

4. Rhetorical tokens are those promises defined by Mayhew as representing political offers that are unlikely to be redeemed by citizens in exchange for the value implied in the original offer.

5. Which of course they are at liberty to break because they are outside all guidelines.

Bibliography

Andsager, J. 2001. "How interest groups attempt to shape public opinion with competing news frames." *Journalism and Mass Communication Quarterly*, 77(3): 577–592.

Baerns, B. 1987. "Journalism versus public relations: Determination of latent interaction through analysis of patterns of influence." In D. Paletz, ed., *Political communication research*. New York: Ablex.

Bennett, W., and R. Entman, eds. 2001. *Mediated politics: Communication in the future democracy*. Cambridge, UK: Cambridge University Press.

Benson, R., and E. Neveu, eds. 2005. *Bourdieu and the journalistic field*. Cambridge, UK: Polity.

Bhagwati, J. 2004. *In defense of globalization*. New York: Oxford University Press.

Bloom, E., and L. Bloom. 1980. *Addison and Steele: The critical heritage*. London: Routledge and Keegan Paul.

Blustein, P. 13 June 2006. "Dealt a difficult hand, trade official presses on; Schwab faces skeptics and a deadline." *Washington Post*, p. 1.

Boseley, S., and J. Astill. 16 June 2001. "Battle over cheap drugs goes to WTO." *Guardian*, p. 24.

Botan, C., and V. Hazleton, eds. 2006. *Public relations theory II*. Mahwah, NJ: Lawrence Erlbaum Associates.

Bourdieu, P. 2005. "The political field: The social science field and the journalistic field." In R. Benson and E. Neveu, eds., *Bourdieu and the journalistic field*. Cambridge, UK: Polity.

Bowman, D. 1988. *The captive press*. Melbourne, Victoria, Australia: Penguin.

Boyd-Barrett, O. 2006. "Cyberspace, globalization and empire." *Global Media Communication*, 2(1): 21–41.

Brooker, C., and R. North. 2003 *The great deception: The secret history of the European Union*. London: Continuum.

Bruhl, T., and V. Rittberger. 2001. In V. Rittberger, ed., *Global governance and the United Nations system*. Tokyo: United Nations University Press.

Calhoun, C. Ed. 1992. *Habermas and the public sphere*. Cambridge, MA: MIT Press.

Clausen, L. 2003. *Global news production*. Copenhagen, Denmark: Copenhagen Business School Press.

Cottle, S. 2002. "Television agora and agoraphobia post–September 11." In B. Zelizer and S. Allan, eds., *Journalism after September 11*. London: Routledge.

Bibliography

Coyle, D. 16 April 2001. "UK bids to secure African AIDS drug deal." *Independent*, p. 13.

Croteau, D., and W. Hoynes. 2006. *The business of media: Corporate media and the public interest*. Thousand Oaks, CA: Sage.

Daily Telegraph. 2003. *Europe—the wolf is here*.

Dalton, R. 1996. *Citizen politics: Public opinion and political parties in advanced Western democracies*. New York: Chatham House.

Davis, M. 1 August 2006. "OECD urges states reform." *Australian Financial Review*, p. 1.

de Beer, A., and J. Merrill, eds. 2004. *Global journalism: Topical issues and media systems*. Boston: Pearson.

de Burgh, H. 2000. *Investigative journalism: Context and practice*. London: Routledge.

Demetrious, K., and P. Hughes. 2004. "Publics or stakeholders?: Performing social responsibility through stakeholder software." *Asia Pacific Public Relations Journal* 5(2): 1–12.

Denny, C. 7 April 2001. "Cheap drugs for poor countries." *Guardian*, p. 2.

Emmott, W. 2006. "A long goodbye." *Economist*.

Entman, R. 1993. "Framing: Toward clarification of a fractured paradigm." *Journal of Communication* 43(4): 51–58.

_____. 2003. "Cascading activism: Contesting the White House's frame after 9/11." *Political Communication* 20: 415–432.

Fearn-Banks, K. 2002. *Crisis communications: A casebook approach*. Mahwah, NJ: Lawrence Erlbaum Associates.

Fraser, N. 1992. "Rethinking the public sphere: A contribution to the critique of actually existing democracy." In C. Calhoun, ed., *Habermas and the public sphere*. Cambridge, MA: MIT Press.

Freedan, M. 1996. *Ideologies and political theory: A conceptual approach*. Oxford: Oxford University Press.

Friedman, T. 1999. *The lexus and the olive tree*. London: HarperCollins.

Fritz, B., B. Keefer, and B. Nyhan. 2004. *All the president's spin: George W. Bush, the media and the truth*. New York: Simon and Schuster.

Fukuyama, F. 2006a. *After the neocons: America at the crossroads*. London: Profile Books.

_____. 2006b. "Identity, immigration, and liberal democracy." *Journal of Democracy*, 17(2): 5–20.

Fuller, J. 1996. *News values for an information age*. Chicago: Univ. of Chicago Press.

Funnell, W. 2001. *Government by fiat: The retreat from responsibility*. Sydney, NSW, Australia: University of NSW Press.

Garnham, N. 2000. *Emancipation, the media, and modernity: Arguments about the media and social theory*. New York: Oxford University Press.

Gleissner, M., and C. de Vreese. 2005. "News about the EU constitution: Journalistic challenges and media portrayal of the European Union constitution." *Journalism*, 6(2): 221–242.

Goffman, E. 1974. *Frame analysis*. New York: Harper and Row.

Graber, D. 1988. *Processing the news: How people tame the information tide.* New York: Longman.

Grunig, J., and T. Hunt. 1984. *Managing public relations.* New York: Holt, Rinehart and Winston.

Gunther, R., and A. Maughan, eds. 2000. *Democracy and the media.* New York: Cambridge University Press.

Habermas, J. 1989. *The structural transformation of the public sphere.* Cambridge, MA: MIT Press.

_____. 2006. *Arenas of political communication.* Unpublished plenary paper presented at the International Communication Association conference, Dresden, Germany.

Hackett, R., and Y. Zhao, eds. 2005. *Democratizing global media: One world, many struggles.* Lanham, MD: Rowman and Littlefield.

Hafez, K. 2005. "Globalization, regionalization and democratization: The interaction of three paradigms in the field of mass communication." In R. Hackett and Y. Zhao, eds., *Democratizing global media: One world, many struggles.* Lanham, MD: Rowman and Littlefield.

Hague, D., W. Mackenzie, and A. Barker. 1975. *Public policy and private interests: The institutions of compromise.* London: Macmillan.

Hallin, D., and P. Mancini. 2004. *Comparing media systems: Three models of media and politics.* Cambridge, UK: Cambridge University Press.

Hamilton, J. 2004. *All the news that's fit to sell: How the market transforms information into news.* Princeton, NJ: Princeton University Press.

Hargreaves, I. 2003. *Journalism: truth or dare?* New York: Oxford University Press.

Heffer, S., and E. Amory. 8 May 2003. "Blueprint for tyranny." *The Daily Mail London.*

Herbert, J. 2001. *Practising global journalism: Exploring reporting issues worldwide.* Oxford, UK: Focal Press.

Herman, S., and R. McChesney. 1997. *The global media.* London: Cassell.

Hitt, G. 16 June 2006. "Politics and economics: Bush pushes for trade deal as a deadline looms." *Wall Street Journal,* p. 6.

Janeway, M. 1999. *Republic of denial: Press, politics and public life.* New Haven, CT: Yale University Press.

Keating, M., J. Wanna, and P. Weller, eds. *Institutions on the edge?: Capacity for government.* Sydney, NSW, Australia: Allen and Unwin.

Kingdon, J. W. 1995 *Agendas, Alternatives and Public Policies.* New York: HarperCollins.

Kraus, S., and D. Davis. 1976. *The effects of mass communication on political behavior.* University Park: Pennsylvania State University Press.

Kruckeberg, D., and K. Tsetsura. 2004. "International journalism ethics." In A. de Beer and J. Merrill, eds., *Global journalism: topical issues and media systems.* Boston: Pearson.

Lamy, P. 2006. World Trade Organization. http://www.wto.org.

Leach, R. 1993. *Political ideologies: An Australian introduction.* Brisbane, Queensland, Australia: Queensland University Press.

Lippmann, W. 1922. *Public opinion.* New York: Free Press.

Bibliography

Lipset, S. 1960. *Political man*. London: Heinemann.

Louw, E. 2004. "Journalists reporting from foreign places." In A. de Beer and J. Merrill, eds., 2004 *Global journalism: Topical issues and media systems*. Boston: Pearson.

Macauley, T. 1910. *Reviews, essays and poems*. London: Ward Lock and Co.

Macken, J. 6 May 2006. "Superheroes in suits save the world." *Australian Financial Review*, p. 25.

Maiden, M. 3 August 2006. "It's a good job that we can afford it." *The Age*, p. 12.

Mallett, V. 3 August 2006. "Asia's former tigers are moving towards irrelevance." *Financial Times*, p. 13.

Marsh, I. 2001. "Gaps in policymaking capacities: Interest groups, social movements, think tanks and the media." In M. Keating, J. Wanna, and P. Weller, eds., *Institutions on the edge?: Capacity for government*. Sydney, Allen and Unwin.

Mayhew, L. 1997. *The new public: Professional communication and the means of social influence*. New York: Cambridge University Press.

McChesney, R. 1997. *Corporate media and the threat to democracy*. New York: Seven Stories Press.

_____. 1999. *Rich media, poor democracy*. Chicago: University of Illinois Press.

McNair, B. 2000. *Journalism and democracy: An evaluation of the political public sphere*. London: Routledge.

_____. 2003. *An introduction to political communication*. New York: Routledge.

Mellish, M. 31 July 2006. "Trade off the agenda at summit." *Australian Financial Review*, p. 12.

Meyrowitz, J. 1985. *No sense of place: The impact of electronic media on social behavior*. Oxford: Oxford University Press.

_____. 2004. Unpublished plenary paper presented at International Association for Media and Communication Research, Porto Allegre, Brazil.

Michaels, A. 26 April 2001. "Inside track—big pharma and the golden goose." *Financial Times*, p. 12.

Miller, S. 16 May 2006. "Food fight: French resistance to trade accord has cultural roots—WTO talks promise benefits but farmers retain hold on the nation's stomach—'politicians are frightened.'" *Wall Street Journal*, p. 1.

Mills, A. 8 August 2006. "Without fuel, health crisis looms; Lebanon 'shut off from the world' hospitals facing power shortages." *Toronto Star*, p. 7.

Minder, R. 1 August 2006. "Canberra faces commodities downturn, warns OECD." *Financial Times*, p. 5.

Mitchell, A. 2 August 2006. "Hard decisions for Stevens." *Australian Financial Review*, p. 70.

Moloney, K. 2006. *Rethinking public relations: PR, propaganda and democracy*. London: Routledge.

Navasky, V. 2002. Foreword. In B. Zelizer and S. Allan, eds., *Journalism After September 11*. London: Routledge.

Bibliography

Nimmo, D. D. 1978. *Political communication and public opinion in America.* Santa Monica, CA: Goodyear Publishing.

Norris, P. 2000. *A virtuous circle: Political communications in post-industrial societies.* Cambridge, UK: Cambridge University Press.

Packard, V. 1957. *The hidden persuaders.* London: Penguin.

Padovani, C., and K. Nordenstreng. "From NWICO to WSIS: Another world information and communication order?" *Global Media and Communication* 1(3): 264–272.

Paletz, 1987. *Political communication research: Approaches, studies, assessments.* Norwood, NJ: Ablex.

Pan, Z., and G. Kosicki. 1993. "Framing analysis: An approach to news discourse." *Political Communication* 10: 55–75.

Parker, D. 1991. *The courtesans.* Sydney, NSW, Australia: Allen and Unwin.

Penkith, A. 21 July 2006. "UN to hold 'beauty contest' to pick new secretary general." *The Independent*, p. 29.

Popper, K. 1959. *The logic of scientific discovery.* London: Hutchinson.

Postman, N. 1999. *Building a bridge to the eighteenth century: How the past can improve our future.* New York: Alfred Knopf.

Reeves, T. 2000. *Twentieth-century America: A brief history.* New York: Oxford University Press.

Ricardo, D. 1996. *Principles of political economy and taxation.* New York: Prometheus Books.

Ritchie, D. 2005. *Reporting from Washington: The history of the Washington press corps.* New York: Oxford University Press.

Rittberger, V., ed. 2001. *Global governance and the United Nations system.* Tokyo: United Nations University Press.

Roger, P. 2005. *The American enemy: The history of French anti–Americanism.* Chicago: University of Chicago Press.

Rosen, J. 2002. "September 11 in the mind of American journalism." In B. Zelizer and S. Allan, eds., *Journalism after September 11.* London: Routledge.

_____, and P. Taylor. 1992. *The new news vs. the old news: The press and politics in the 1990s.* New York: Twentieth Century Fund.

Roy, O. 2004. *Globalized Islam: The search for a new ummah.* New York: Columbia University Press.

Schudson, M. 1992. "Was there ever a public sphere? If so, when?: Reflections on the American case." In C. Calhoun, ed., *Habermas and the Public Sphere.* Cambridge, MA: MIT Press.

_____. 1995. *The power of news.* Cambridge, MA: Harvard University Press.

_____. 1999. *The good citizen: A history of American civil life.* Cambridge, MA: Harvard University Press.

_____. 2002. *The sociology of news.* New York: W. W. Norton.

Schumpeter, J. 1976. *Capitalism, socialism and democracy.* London: Allen and Unwin.

Seib, P. 1994. *Campaigns and conscience: The ethics of political journalism.* Westport, CT: Praeger.

Seymour-Ure, C. 1968. *The press, politics and the public.* London: Constable.

Bibliography

_____. 1974. *The political impact of mass media.* London: Constable.

Sherman, S. 1996. *Telling time: Clocks, diaries, and English diurnal form, 1660–1785.* Chicago: University of Chicago Press.

Simms, M., and D. Bolger. 2000. "The Australian print media and partisan bias in the campaign." In M. Simms and J. Warhurst, eds., *Howard's agenda: The 1998 Australian election.* St. Lucia, Queensland, Australia: University of Queensland Press.

Smith, A. 1970. *The wealth of nations.* Middlesex, UK: Penguin. Originally published in 1776.

Snooks, D. 1998. *Longrun dynamics: A general economic and political theory.* Hampshire, UK: Macmillan.

Sparrow, B. 1999. *Uncertain guardians: The news media as a political institution.* Baltimore, MD: Johns Hopkins University Press.

Stanton, R. 2006. *Media relations.* Melbourne, Australia: Oxford University Press.

Tepe, S. 2005. "Turkey's AKP: A model Muslim-democratic party?" *Journal of Democracy* 16(3): 69–82.

Tessler, M. and E. Gao. 2005. "Gauging Arab support for democracy." *Journal of Democracy* 16(3): 83–97.

Tharoor, S. 2003. "Public diplomacy: a United Nations perspective." Unpublished paper presented to the USC Center on Public Diplomacy, Los Angeles.

Tiffen, R. 2000. In H. Tumber, ed., *Media power, professionals and politics.* London: Routledge.

Tuchman, G. 1973. "Making news by doing work: Routinizing the unexpected." *American Journal of Sociology* 79(1): 110–131.

_____. 1978. *Making news: A study in the construction of reality.* New York: Free Press.

Tussie, D., and M. Riggirozzi. 2001. "Pressing ahead with new procedures for old machinery: Global governance and civil society." In V. Rittberger, ed., *Global governance and the United Nations system.* Tokyo: United Nations University Press.

Volkmer, I. 2002. "Journalism and political crisis in the global network world." In B. Zelizer and S. Allan, eds., *Journalism after September 11.* London: Routledge.

Von Mises, L. 1958. *Theory and history.* London: Jonathon Cape.

Walker, M. 1972. *Politics and the power structure: A rural community in the Dominican Republic.* New York: Teacher's College Press.

Weaver, D. H., and W. Wu, eds. 1998. *The global journalist.* Cresskill, NJ: Hampton Press.

Weisman, S. 16 June 2006. "A new trade envoy, with a battle on her hands." *New York Times*, p. 1.

Welsh, J. 1 August 2006. "United Nations in decline; regional bodies more effective in developing co-operative approaches to security and defence." *Toronto Star*, p. 13.

Wolf, M. 2004. *Why globalization works.* New Haven, CT: Yale University Press.

Wright, S., and C. Russell. 2 August 2006. "OECD calls for change as boom recedes." *Advertiser*, p. 35.

Zelizer, B., and S. Allan, eds. 2002. *Journalism after September 11.* London: Routledge.

Zweifel, T. 2006. *International organizations and democracy: Accountability, politics and power.* Boulder, CO: L. Rienner.

Index

Index

Index

Index

Index